Escaping from GOD

THROUGH OKLAHOMA

A MEMOIRE

STAFFORD RAY

Published in Australia by Silverbird Publishing Pty. Ltd.
First published in Australia 2025
This edition published 2025
Copyright © Stafford Ray 2025

Cover design, typesetting: WorkingType (www.workingtype.com.au)

The right of Stafford Ray to be identified as the
Author of the Work has been asserted in accordance with the
Copyright, Designs and Patents Act 1988.

All rights reserved. No part of this publication may be reproduced, stored in a retrieval system, or transmitted, in any form or by any means without the prior written permission of the publisher, nor be otherwise circulated in any form of binding or cover other than that in which it is published and without a similar condition being imposed on the subsequent purchaser.

ISBN: 978-1-7638888-9-0

About the Author

Stafford Ray was born into a the fundamentalist Exclusive (Plymouth) Brethren sect. Of course, radios were banned and TV had not yet been invented, so information was passed along by print and for most of his childhood, that was limited to the Bible and other Holy texts.

His maternal grandmother, Eusebia Turnbull, had the Sydney Morning Herald delivered along with the mail and milk cans six days a week, so when he was dumped on her to be looked after, which was often, he had access to comic strips and the Children's Section. But also at the farm, his resourceful uncle Owen had set up a wireless radio, so the wonders of music, the news and best of all, radio dramas, or serials, were shared.

At about the time his family was 'withdrawn from' he changed schools to Parramatta High School and it was there that was loaned Charles Darwin's 'On the Origin of Species'. Suddenly his observed world made sense and so began a lifelong love of science.

At primary school, his soprano voice was in demand to school musicals, then a few years later a gift of the Complete Works of Shakespeare, being one of the very few non-biblical texts allowed in the house, he read several times, probably out of desperation for something to read. But a love of drama and music was born that would manifest in the writing of many musical plays for classroom use, then later in life, three novels, a collection of short stories and poems, then this memoir.

He also spent many years in Sydney as a TV and recording musician, known and Ford Ray, backing famous entertainers from around the world. His first recording that gained attention was on guitar for

Jimmy Little's Royal Telephone and his favourite, playing bass in the Daly Wilson Big Band with Kerrie Biddell. (Hear on Spotify).

Stafford's plays can be downloaded, free of charge. Help yourself at: **www.staffordray.com** to free downloads of librettos, songs and backings to take you from first rehearsal to final performance.

There you will also find a Model Lesson Plan that not only makes drama teaching easy and fun but ensures that every student is busy all the time, while using all of his or her learning styles, thus multiplying the efficiency of your lesson time. Run a couple of plays and watch your reading ages jump.

This book is dedicated to:
Those who found support and solace in a congregation that really did ask: 'What would Jesus do?' And to those who were not so lucky, but were able to escape from those who demanded their trust as children, then hurt and stunted them in the name of a vindictive and vengeful god of their own creation.

Foreword

All names, except for Loren, my psychiatrist, are of real people. I have tried to be as accurate and honest as memory permitted.

However, if anyone named herein feels that they have been unfairly depicted, please feel free to write your own book.

Session 1

I knock. She opens the door and waves me in. The eyes. She has lovely eyes.

'Hello, I'm Loren. Take a seat. There.'

"Thanks. You're older than your voice... on the phone."

'Would you like tea, coffee?'

"No thanks, I'm okay."

'All right then, let's get started. There's water by your elbow (smiles) talking is thirsty work. So, tell me why you're here.'

"Did you read the referral? Peter said he would brief you. I don't know..."

'Yes, I read your GP's notes, but this is a new start for you. Why did you choose a woman psychologist?'

The voice, deep and sweet. Sarah Vaughn. Lovely smile. Teeth not perfect, clean white teeth. Eyes, clear irises, hazel like Mum's. Sadness too. What is she suffering?

"He did ask, and I said I prefer talking to women. I don't know..."

'Aren't you comfortable opening up to men?'

"No, not usually, unless they're open with me first. Greg was open."

'Who's Greg? A lover?'

We are to get a new fire truck for Wollombi Bush Fire Brigade, which has the home shed in the village. As the fire captain, I am responsible for the readiness of our truck and two trailer pumpers at Bucketty and the Hungry Creek motorcycle track in Murray's Run.

Summer is coming on and I need to check that both units are ready to go.

At Hungry Creek, the pump is on the brook providing water for their swimming pool and at Bucketty, on Jim's poultry farm, the pump is off the trailer and pumping water from a bore to his farm tank.
I call a public meeting at Bucketty and lay it on the line. If the pumpers are not maintained and ready for first response, they will be taken away.

They elect Greg as the new vice-captain, and he is offered an old fire truck if he agrees to build a shed for it.

"(laugh) No, I'm not gay. Greg's a friend. I got to know him through the Rural Fire Brigade when I was a captain and he was vice-captain. Later, he moved to Dooralong and became a close neighbour with our kids going to the same small school. I don't really know why I feel so close."

'In what way is Greg open?'

"He's more like a woman, the way he thinks, the way he expresses feelings, you know."

'Yes, I know, so you're not afraid to be frank with Greg, but you are afraid to be open with other men?'

"Well, yes. But not so much now. I'm more likely to talk about intimate stuff with men now, now that I'm older, and I seem not to worry so much about possible negative reactions, and that surprises me."

'Surprises you?'

"Yes, I'm still surprised when they respond with personal stuff.

Honest stuff. Not like when I was younger, when blokes were all so ready to put anyone down who talked about how they felt. I didn't talk about anything like that."

'So, was it you who was afraid to talk, or they didn't want to know?'

"Both, I guess, but we all pretended we were okay, and that was the rule. We just pretended. I always felt like a bit of an imposter."

'That's pretty common, particularly in some creatives, never being sure of your value.'

"Yes, that's right, so I pretended I knew what I was doing, sort of fake it until you make it. But I guess they were pretending too."

'Why did you think they were pretending?'

"Well, I didn't think they were, not when I was younger. I presumed they were in control of their lives, that they were happy, with no problems. They seemed to not have the sorts of doubts and fears that I felt constantly. I felt I was the only one who was unsure, so I hid it."

'And Greg changed that?'

'Mate, you've had a vasectomy, haven't you?'
How does he know? "Yes, why?"
Sally must have said something.
'I'm thinking about it. Marg's pregnant again and that's enough.'
What's happening here? Why is he asking me this? What's wrong with him? He's talking about stuff I would only think, never say.

"Yes, I was a bit taken aback the first time it happened."

'So, it was unexpected?'

"Yes, it was just so unexpected… like he presumed I wouldn't think it strange."

'So, you had never talked about personal stuff with anyone else? Father, mother, wives?'

"Not since I was really young, so it's hard to remember when I stopped trusting. Maybe I never trusted anyone."

'I doubt that. Children usually trust their adults until something happens to undermine it. What changed for you?'

Running, laughing, looking back at the pup barking. Pup is catching up. Running harder, not looking ahead. Tripping, falling, excruciating pain, then nothing.

"I was seriously scalded when I was about two and a half. I don't remember much about it."

'What can you remember?'

"Running with the dog, then regaining consciousness, sitting on a wet towel covering a wicker chair and Mum staring at me from across the room as if she was afraid to touch me, looking beaten. Then I was unconscious again."

'Where were you scalded? It missed your face.'

With Mum at Fairfield Hospital, in the waiting room. Yellow paint, row of louvred windows, winter warmth behind the glass, smell of disinfectant. Casts on arm and leg, bandages around chest and shoulder.

"Yes, my left arm to above the elbow, left leg almost to the groin and there was a deeper burn on my back that left a scar."

'How did it happen?'

"It was just after we moved to Booralla Road. Dad had rigged up a copper..."

'A copper?'

"A copper boiler. The house frame was up, the roof on, and the kitchen lined but not much else. There was no laundry. Back then, most people boiled clothes in a copper cauldron. Dad was burning out stumps around the house, so he balanced the copper on top of a burning stump, propped up with bits of wood.

"I was playing with my dog, running around the yard and ran into the fire, knocking out a prop, tipping the hot water and clothes over myself. I remember running, and the pup, but not much after that."

'Seems you were lucky to be alive and very lucky not to have suffered more permanent damage.'

"Mum told me I was lucky. It would have been in 1938 and an old Jewish burns specialist who had fled Hitler's Germany just happened to be working at Fairfield Hospital when the ambulance brought me in. He took over and yes, I got first-class treatment. I was lucky."

'Were there any long-term psychological consequences?'

I am frightened. The doctor is there, and he has had a tug at the black scabs on my arm and leg. Dad is holding me so I can't move. Then there is a wad of cottonwool over my nose and mouth, and I dream. I am being chased by American Indians on horseback, wearing magnificent headdresses. The horses are rearing up at me. I wake slowly in bed, terrified.

"I will never forget the smell of ether. I was knocked out before the scabs were removed, and I must have been in bed for quite a while because I remember needing to learn to walk again."

'Did how you see the world change after that? How did you feel?'

Shapes on the wall. Moving in the dark. Something is coming for me. Run to Mum, up the hall into the front room. Try to get into bed with them. Mum holds me away. 'What's the matter?' I can't express what it is and start to cry. Dad pushes me onto the floor. 'Get back to bed and stop being a sook, or you'll get something to cry about!'

"Being scared in my bedroom and being forced to stay there in the dark. Dad never understood my terror."

'What makes you say that?'

"Maybe Mum didn't either. I can't remember ever being cuddled or touched by them. Maybe she felt a lack of permission to touch me, but come to think of it, she was pretty cold when Dad was away too."

'Do you think your father wanted you... when you were conceived?'

Up on the building walking along the top plate. I'm a tightrope walker. He watches from two stories below. Says nothing. He wants me to test my worth. Am I good enough for God to let live? He waits. Maybe he wants me to fall and be done with it. I turn back and he still says nothing until I am down, then says, 'Here, hold the end of this'.

"No, I don't. Like all religious men of his day, sex outside marriage was taboo, and I think he was a virgin when he married. So, like me, I guess, he was keen to be married so he could have sex and like me, I guess he wanted to get established before children began to arrive. "I suspect that he regarded children as an unfortunate by-product of sex."

'So, there were unresolved issues with him when he died?'

"Always. He found fault with almost everything I did until I cut him off, called him on it, when I was fixing the leak in the new house."

'Okay, we'll come back to that. Now, this is important. I want you to try to be in the moment and tell me exactly what your first reaction was when he died. Many men are relieved when their fathers go, so don't be afraid you will be judged on this.'

Numb. Just numb like always when the emotion is too much. Get the lid on it. Too much swirling around. Too many thoughts.

"(pause) Yes, first there was shock, then numbness. I felt elated later. Sort of elated, but not until I saw my brother Bill. When I answered the phone, I just felt numb, and I think I had a premonition of what was to come. Like you saw just now, when the grief broke through. I flew up to Maroochydore and was at Mum's in Bli-Bli the same day.

"Bill drove the thousand kilometres, so he got there next morning, and I met him at the door. His face reflected my feelings. He was smiling, and I understood and smiled back. Or maybe I was already smiling, but that was the moment I realised Bill felt the same.

"That was a surprise, and I was ashamed too. It was only for a second, then we started talking practicalities. But I knew there was part of me that felt I had been set free."

'How do you get on with your brother?'

"We always got on very well, but since Dad died, even better. He's been my best friend for most of my adult life. I may never have been his, but that's okay. There was a short period when there was tension, but that was probably down to his first wife and mine not really getting on. I am very fond of his second wife and their two girls, but there was always a lot of love between me and Bill."

The curtain opens for the Highland all-singing all-dancing Scottish Spectacular at Cooma RSL, four hundred kilometres from home. We are pretty relaxed in the backing band, hidden behind two lines of kilted dancers. Then the opening announcement and the dancers run off to generous applause and there is Fay, smiling, clapping and watching the dancers leave, while I watch her sitting at a front table looking very cosy with a man I don't know.

I know Bill's wife is supposed to be somewhere else and realise right away that she is having a dirty weekend with a lover. The music is second nature, so I continue to watch her until our eyes meet, and her shocked expression assures me she is indeed where she should not be!

Before she has time to react, the dancers are on again. When they clear and I lift my head from the music stand, she is gone. Their marriage lasts two more years during which time she avoids me. Vera says that Fay is being bitchy, causing a rift with her, so Vera is not keen to visit. Nothing is said until after the separation. Bill is the one to ask.

'You knew, didn't you?'

"Yes, I knew two years ago. I saw them at Cooma having a dirty weekend and she knew I knew."

'I know. She asked if you'd blabbed, and I didn't know what she was talking about. Why didn't you say something? Maybe you should have told me.'

"Well, the way it went for me was, she was trying to be discreet so it might have been just a fling and would heal up, but if I told you, you would have either not believed me, or you would have felt you had to do something just because I knew. Sorry, but that's how I felt about it."

'That's okay. I just wondered, that's all.'

'Did your mother ever cuddle you, do you remember?'

We are sitting on Jen's lounge in the Eden house where we are nursing Mum. The doctor has just been. She gets my attention and taps out a message on her 'qwerty' board: 'I just want to die. I'm sick of being like this.' I put my arm around her shoulders and draw her close.

"I know, Mum. You were always so self-sufficient. It must be hard. I would feel the same way."

"(laugh) Yes, she did. She was in her nineties, and I was nursing her after a stroke. She cuddled me then."

'Or were you cuddling her?'

"Mmm. Don't know. Whichever way, it felt good, and she needed it."

'And did your father ever show affection?'

"He showed something. My room was the first bedroom to be completed in the new house, years before Eleanor's room, and he worked out a way of keeping me warm after I was scalded."

'What did he do?'

"He built a wire cage over the bed and secured a small kerosene lamp inside to warm the space."

'You were lucky you weren't gassed or burnt!'

"No. I remember it. My head was outside the frame and the lamp was tied in place and ventilated, so I guess it was safe enough. I couldn't have bedclothes touching my skin, apparently."

'So, he did things and made things for you but didn't show affection?'

"That about sums it up. He showed he cared by doing things for us, but that created problems for us too."

'Can we come back to that? So did the night terrors continue, or did something change eventually?'

Sneak out of bed, tiptoe to the door, turn the knob slowly, pull it carefully inward until it is open. Sneak back into bed, look around.

"(laugh) Yes, it changed when the kerosene refrigerator arrived. That changed everything."

'How so?'

"Dad built it into the wall of the kitchen so that it protruded into the wall of the unlined hallway opposite my bedroom door. If I opened the door, the flame that drove the fridge lit up my room enough for me to see there was nobody there, so I wasn't frightened and was soon asleep.

"If I woke up and needed to pee, I could see."

'Did you need to go to the toilet to pee?'

"(laugh) No, the dunny was fifty yards down the back yard. I had a fruit can under the bed for that."

'Okay, so the threat you felt was self-generated and although it was real for you, it wasn't a real threat. The damage was done by your parents not realising how terrified you were. 'Were there any other events that caused you to lose trust? Some real threat?'

"Breakers at Maroubra beach."

'What happened?'

Thumping noise in the dark that shakes the sand under my feet. Loud, then the hissing. Pulling back against Dad. He drags me toward the noise. Wall of water, lifting, coming at me, curling, then white and thumping down. He holds me there, then we run ahead of the white foam chasing us up the beach like a hissing ghost.

"We were visiting uncle Frank and Auntie Beryl at Maroubra. It was dark. Dad dragged me down the sand towards the breakers. I had never seen the sea before, and I was terrified. "(laugh) Sometimes I think that my love of boats was my way to challenge the fear."

'Did you make a habit of challenging your fears?'

"(smile) Maybe I did. As a child I constantly pushed the limits."

'How?'

"Oh, climbing too high, wading into muddy dams with water up to my nose before I could swim. Too many to tell."

'So, you intentionally put yourself in danger?'

"I guess I did. There were many situations that could have been the end of me, like drowning, falling from heights and later, driving as fast as I was able. Like I say, always pushing the limits."

'All right, we'll explore that later, but let's go back to the scalding. You say you don't remember much of it, and you think you were unconscious. Do you remember any changes apart from fear of the dark? Dreams?'

Black van coming along Edensor Road. A plank mounted fore and aft on the roof. There is writing on the plank, but I can't read. I am trying to get to the house. Trying to run. Terrified. Feet dragging. Heavy feet, dragging through thick mud. Wake crying.

"I had a recurring dream for years. Not every night, but often, where I was trying to run from a black van. It never caught me, but I always woke crying, heart racing in terror."

'Did your parents ever ask you about that?'

"I never told them. I kept that a secret all through my childhood."

'Why, do you think?'

"Not sure. I didn't think it was ever the sort of thing they would want to know about, and I already knew what the reaction would be."

'What would it be?'

"Oh, you know, 'It's only a dream. Don't be silly!'"

'Did you think it was silly?'

"Yes, in a way I did. Somehow, I felt it was my fault. I should have been able to deal with it."

'I hope you don't still believe that.'

"No, I have forgiven my young self for many things and that's one of them."

'Good. Did you ever solve the mystery of the black van?'

"(laugh) Yes, I did. I saw what looked like that very same van in a museum somewhere and it all fell into place."

'Well, what was it?'

"An ambulance. I guess it was built in the late twenties. It was black, with wooden spoked wheels, an external radiator with a brass filler cap. A sign on a plank that ran fore and aft on the roof read 'Ambulance'."

'So did that end the nightmares?'

"(laugh) No. They had stopped by then. The visit to the museum was over twenty years later with my two elder kids."

'Did you tell them about it?'

"No. Kids aren't interested in what bothers their parents. Natural narcissists until after puberty, I reckon."

'(laughs) You could be right. So, let's move on. Do you think the scalding, which certainly was traumatic, and I use the word in its clinical sense, changed the way you saw the world?'

Mum passes me the string bag, a ten-shilling note and a list. I want to go alone to the shop. Down past Mr and Mrs Christian's house, around the corner and along Edensor Road to Rawlings Grocery. Mr Rawlings wraps up the parcels with string. He breaks the string with his fingers and smiles, handing me the bundle. I could never master that string-breaking trick.

"Not that you would notice. I was expected to be responsible for chores when I was very young. Soon after the scalding, before I was four, I went to the corner shop for Mum."

'On your own?'

"(laugh) Yes, but of course, there were very few cars on the roads in those days, and she could watch me most of the way from the kitchen window. I was entrusted with all sorts of missions when I was young. Even more so during the war after Dad was called up, and Mum didn't drive. But by then I was six or seven."

'So how did she get supplies? Did she do all her shopping at... (looks at notes) at Rawlings?'

"We had the ice man come twice a week, 'Old Sol' – I think his name was Solomon – came with ice in a truck under a tarp. He brought a block of ice and put it into the ice chest for Mum.

"He carried it in with a neat pincer device that secured the block, held by a wooden handle. We had bread delivered every second day except on weekends. That arrived by horse-drawn cart. The cart had double doors at the back and the smell! That was something."

"Can I have a half loaf of white with the lump?"

(Baker laughs, breaking a loaf in half along the crease, hands over the half with the convex break) 'There you go, but don't eat any before it gets inside!'

I dawdle, picking at the fresh, flaky bread, to remove and swallow the sticking-out bit before I reach the kitchen door.

"And we had a greengrocer for what we didn't grow in the garden."

'So, you had deliveries. Did you live in the suburbs?'

"No, we were on a seven-acre block at Edensor Park. All around us were seven-acre blocks and many of those were farmed. A few of our neighbours were market gardeners, like Angela's parents."

'Who was Angela?'

"Angela was my age and lived two properties down the hill. They grew tomatoes and cabbages, beans and peas. Most neighbours were Italian, so we didn't play with them."

'Why not?'

"I wonder why not too. I remember feeling an urge to go there, but I knew instinctively that it was not permitted. Maybe they were seen as the enemy. They were officially, during the war, and I remember the prisoners-of-war at Cobbitty."

On the way to Grandma Turnbull's, driving slowly past, staring. Maybe a hundred men in orange boiler suits, walking along the road. 'They're Italian prisoners of war'. Nobody seemed to be minding them. Then, at the back, a man in khaki shorts and shirt, a felt hat and a rifle slung over his shoulder, talking to a couple of Italians beside him. Seemed friendly for an enemy!

"No, we didn't play with them, and I remember with some shame, a lost opportunity to get to know them better."

'Tell me.'

"I was playing cricket with Ron on the road and a boy our age walked up to us. He had a huge grin and expected Ron to acknowledge him, but he didn't. He would have been in the same class as Ron at St Johns Park School. I knew his name as Frankie Scarcella, but we didn't invite him to play, so he left and never came back."

'That's sad.'

"Yes. I think we were given the impression that Italians were dirty and beneath us. There were several Italian families around us, but we never mixed with them, and of course, they were presumed to be Catholic, and we never mixed with Catholics."

Taking the shortcut to the bus through Angela's place. The Alsatian bitch has pups in a kennel beside the path. We stop and play with the pups for a few minutes, then again on the way home. We do this every school day until one day, on the way home, we see that the pups have gone. We knock on the door and ask what happened to them.

Angela's mum rubs her tummy. 'Puppy pie!'

We scream and run home. Angela's mother laughs.

"And I believed for most of my life that Angela's family ate dogs."

'Did they?'

"(laugh) I don't think so. Her Alsatian had pups, and when they were weaned, Angela's mum told us she ate them. Of course, she was joking, but I believed it then."

'What changed your mind?'

"Oh, one day I was thinking about that time and realised that Italians didn't eat dogs. I met many Italians in the music industry and wasn't really surprised to find they were at least as sophisticated as any Anglo, and of course, we ate at Italian restaurants. The pups were probably given away when they were old enough.

"I think Angela's dad worked away from the farm too. Most of the men worked away. My dad did until after he was discharged from the army when he started a sawmilling business with Mum's brother Eric.

"Before the war, his day started with a bike ride to the train station at about five-thirty, then he came home about six, and in those days, he also worked Saturday mornings.

"Shops opened nine to five, and half a day on Saturday. He couldn't shop and few women drove, so there was a demand for deliveries of perishables and of course we are talking of the time before home freezers or even refrigerators."

'What about meat? How did you get fresh meat?'

"There was a meat safe hanging on the southern side veranda, and a Coolgardie safe for butter and the like, but I don't remember Mum keeping meat out there. I think she stored meat in the ice chest in the ice compartment. Most Sundays we had a roast, and I collected that plus our ration book's entitlement of lamb chops from a butcher at Bonnyrigg."

'Was the butcher far away?'

Coming home from Hogg's butchery, meat wrapped in newspaper in a string bag hanging from the handlebar. I decide to go via St Johns Park School because of the downhill run. I'm racing past the school on the gravel road and the string bag is swaying, then it swings into the spokes and over I go, landing on my arms and knees. There is lots of blood and gravel in my skin. I look and thank God the meat is okay.

"The butcher, Hoggs, was about two or three miles. But we had chooks, of course. Everyone did, and when Owen or Eric called in, they brought rabbits."

'Owen?'

"Mum's other brother. They called in at least once every two weeks and brought food from Grandma's farm."

I hear the Chalmers as it comes along Edensor Road. "Owen's coming!" It turns into Booralla Road and grinds up the hill. I smell charcoal from the gas producer and run out to meet him.

He hands me a bran bag that is wriggling. He laughs. 'Rabbits. You can skin them yourself.'

I run in with the bag for Mum while he follows with a bucket of oranges and a gallon of cream to make butter.

'You're smiling.'

"Yes, Owen was special."

'How?'

"You know, we all took him for granted back then. But now all the cousins talk about 'Owie' in the same way. He was the perfect playmate we all wanted. He was the adult who never married, the playmate of our dreams – a real-life Peter Pan."

'What was so special about him?'

'Want to help me set the traps?' We head off with a bran bag of rabbit traps, a small mattock and Owen's special soil sifter. Hanging from his belt, he has a sheaf of torn paper about an inch and a half wide and four inches long.

We come to a burrow. He drives in the peg, then digs a furrow, scooping some of the dirt into the sifter. Then he depresses the springs on the trap between fingers and palm, flicks the plate with his thumb and places its catch in position.

The paper covers the gap between plate and jaw so dirt cannot drift under the plate that might impede its movement. He then sifts dirt to cover it all until it is invisible. 'See,' he says, 'I never touch the soil with my fingers. Rabbits know our smell.'

Next burrow, it's my turn. I need to stand on the springs to depress them, but he is patient and soon I can set traps without help.

"Oh, whenever we were at the farm, he always found time for us. We rode around the farm on his 'slides', and he let us drive the horses."

'What's a slide?'

"Oh! Maybe he invented the slide himself. I never saw one on any of the other farms, so maybe it was another Owen invention, but it was a platform mounted between the wheels of a car axle. The wheels were at the back and at the front in the centre was a single plank on edge that was shaped like a runner on a sleigh. A swingle bar was attached to the runner so that when the horse pulled, most of the weight was transferred to the wheels and when the horse stopped pulling, the front took more weight, and the runner acted as a brake. Simple but effective."

'Yes, indeed. So he made a few slides?'

"Oh yes, he had two or three that were used on the farm for general transport, but on one of them, he mounted a gas producer so that he could connect that to any of a few motors that drove pumps and a sawmill."

'Did he do anything with you that were purely fun and now part of his working day?'

"Yes. He took us swimming and made little rafts from car tubes in bran bags for us to paddle around. When I was older, he took me shooting."

'Was that wise?'

"(smile) I don't know. All country kids had rifles then. The legal age to shoot was fourteen, and I was shooting before that with Owen. But the main thing I remember is that he was always keen to do things with us.

"He would tumble me out of bed at first light in summer and we would spend a couple of hours shooting at rabbits before rounding up the cows for milking. Being with him was always fun, and I don't remember one word of criticism. I appreciate him more now that I'm an adult and wish I could have been more like him with my kids."

'Let's stop there. I sense there are issues in there we can discuss next time. Okay?'

I'm a little disappointed that we stopped when we did. Talking about Owen always feels good, but I look at the clock, pick up my sunnies, smile, and nod as I leave.

Session 2

She looks a little more relaxed than last time and I smile at that. She indicates a chair, and I sit. She moves from behind her desk, sits opposite me and looks up.

'You were about to tell me how you wish you had been more like Owen with your own kids. Can we start there?'

"I've had a think about that and realise that Owen had us for a few weeks, but I had the kids all the time. And I was so busy working away from home that I didn't have the time to indulge them so much."

'You think Owen did? Have the time?'

"No, he was always busy with the farm, and most of the things we did with him were part of his working day anyway. But he might have chosen chores that offered opportunities for us to have fun while he worked."

'Tell me about that.'

We stop the slide on the natural rock causeway on Eagle Creek Road beside deeper water. Owen drops the reins and the horse drinks while he takes two buckets to fill the two forty-four-gallon drums. He points to the water. 'You can have a swim in there if you like.' He starts to bail water into the drums while I wade in. I can see the bottom. Rounded stones and sand. I push forward and try to dog-paddle but haven't quite mastered it yet.

Water in my mouth tastes like sweet clay. Feet down and go again. Check on Owen. He is still bailing. I go further, then climb out to sun myself on the rock platform at the far end of the pool. There is a rustling. I look. A snake is slipping into the water. I scream. Owen runs around the pool to me and carries me back.

'It's only a grey snake. It won't hurt you.' He sits me on the slide and continues to bail. The drums are now full. We move to stand behind the drums. He hands me the reins. 'You drive home.'

"What was work for him was fun for me. You know, driving the horses, taking the milk cans up to the carrier, bringing the mail back to the house, collecting eggs, picking oranges. He would pick oranges and throw them to me to catch and put into boxes, so it was a game. He always found ways of making work into a game."

'So, in what ways do you think you failed your own kids?'

The little shit won't eat the banana. I hold his cheeks and push some in. He cries, so I give up.

What will Vera think when she sees that he hasn't eaten what she left for him?

"I loved David, and he got lots of cuddles. He was a beautiful baby and a lovely little boy, but I didn't have enough time for him, and I was stressed financially. He came along at a bad time."

'Did you take your frustrations out on him, do you think?'

"Maybe I did a bit. I remember when Vera was at work, forcing him to eat some banana. He refused to open his mouth, so I squeezed his cheeks and forced some in."

'Did he eat it?'

"(laugh) No, he spat it out, so I gave up."

'Was that a pattern, do you think – forcing him to eat?'

"No, it might have happened a couple of times, but I remember how Dad treated Eleanor, and I didn't want to be like him…"

'Your sister?'

"Yes. He made her sit in her highchair for what seemed to me to be hours until she ate her porridge. But she worked out a way to beat him."

'How's that?'

"She waited until he was close, cried, then held her breath until he grabbed her out of the highchair and put her head under a tap."

'Sounds brutal.'

"Yes, he was often brutal."

'Did you ever hit David? Your referral mentions beatings by your father. Most men who beat their children were themselves beaten.'

"No, I never hit the children. I gently slapped a bottom a couple of times, more like a push, but never in anger and never with a belt or a stick. I was always aware of their helplessness and any anger I might have felt was overridden by sympathy. Spankings were never a part of my kids' lives.

"Of course, by then I'd had teacher training and was pretty good at soft discipline. But the cane was still in use in schools, and I did use it a few times. Actually, it was expected."

'How did you feel about that?'

"You've been warned twice, so hold out your hand." I bring the cane down, not too hard, but enough to hurt. I feel elation and that frightens me. I put the cane away, thinking about what my father might have felt when he was belting me.

"I think I used it twice in two years, but never again after that. My boss, Bill Still, was often away from the school for two or three days at a time for bowls competitions so I had the whole primary school for that time, all eighty of them."

'Wow! So, how did you handle that?'

"He organised work for his own kids to do, so I just needed to make sure they were doing it. But there was a kid or two who took advantage, so I gave them a whack with the cane to let them know it was not on."

'How did you feel about that?'

"It frightened me that I enjoyed it and realised that was a problem for me, so that was the end of the cane."

She stares at me for a moment. 'Of course, that came from your father. He might have felt pleasure, elation, do you think?'

"Yes, I did think that, and that's one reason why I stopped it there."

'You did well to recognise that and control it.'

"No, I don't think it was only that. I just don't think I ever felt anger like my father did, and I thank my Atheism and maybe my mother's calm for that."

'Indeed. Now, I'd like to talk about your first wife Vera and the pregnancies. Did you ever wonder why Vera became pregnant when she did? Was she on the pill?'

I come back to the car empty-handed. 'He said he doesn't sell condoms and gave me a lecture on the evils of contraception.'

Vera runs into the pharmacy, and I can hear her from the car parked outside.

'You've got a hide, pushing your Catholic bullshit onto everyone. You run a pharmacy, not a damned seminary!'

"We used condoms up until we were married and for a time

afterward, then she used a pessary, but David got past that somehow. (laugh) He always was a determined little bugger."

'Are you sure she used the pessary every time? Did she want to become pregnant do you think?'

'

I've run all the tests I can. I've eliminated all the physical causes, like tumours or aneurisms, so the headaches must be psychosomatic. That doesn't mean they aren't real. But the cause? Well, it could be any number of things and the chances of discovering them are slim.

'I know you worry about your living conditions – the single room and begrudged use of amenities – but my advice as your doctor is, if you need to live in a tent so you can have a baby, do it.'

"I never thought of that at the time. I trusted her to be on the same team, but it destroyed any plans I had to keep the house and pay Dad back. She seemed more thrilled than dismayed. Thinking back on those days, I now suspect she married me to escape what was happening at home, and maybe the babies were insurance."

'Did you think so at the time?'

"No, it didn't enter my mind that she would get pregnant intentionally, and I presumed it was accidental. The thought that it might have been intentional came many years later, when I was trying to make sense of those years.

"She was a very organised person; she was runner-up in her final exam at teachers' college, so she was intellectually smart as well as being compulsively neat. It is now hard for me to believe the pregnancies were accidental. I think she tried it on me again, years later and for the same reason."

'What happened?'

David, Julia and I have been at Wollombi for a few months. David's drug use has not stopped. I am still working in Sydney on weekends and staying there in a bedsitter, dropping the kids off with Vera on Friday evening and picking them up Sunday night. The kids are in the car, and we are standing in the doorway. Her hand brushes my penis, and I know it was not accidental. She leans closer. 'We could have another baby, you know.'

"We had been separated for over a year. The kids and I were permanently at Wollombi, but I saw her every weekend when I dropped the kids off and picked them up. I had no woman in my life, and she offered to have another baby."

'What did you say to that?'

"I don't think I said anything. I was speechless that she should think I would want that, so I said goodnight and left."

'Do you think she missed the security, and maybe the companionship she had with you?'

"Maybe. But she had the house that was paid for and a car."

'How did she get on with her father?'

"I think her relationship with her father was problematic. We had a conversation about it once, but she stopped before she revealed the whole picture. I think he was a huge problem for her."

'What made you think that?'

"Well, her mother seemed to think she was not safe at home. Can you imagine her mother, a conservative Catholic woman, who remained married to a man who had been in an insane asylum in Spain for thirty years, living in sin with a drunk, sending her daughter to Sydney from Cairns to live with her Bohemian sister? There had to be something seriously threatening going on."

'Why do you say the sister...'

"Lydia."

'...was bohemian?'

"She came south from North Queensland in the depression to live in Kings Cross, and as rumour has it, made her living as a nude model. Who knows what else she did to survive, but the modelling was what she would admit to."

'Does that offend you?'

Lydia in shorts and loose halter top is gardening when we arrive. She isn't afraid to show her tits! Vera's mother is proud of her body too, but it's easy to see even now, why Lydia was in demand as a model.

"(laugh) Not at all. I spent quite a lot of time with Lydia and Ernie, her husband. We visited often before we were married, and afterward too. I must say, even in her late forties, she still had an amazing body, which she didn't try too hard to hide. Ernie was funny too, and I could see why Vera loved them."

'Did they like... did they approve of you?'

They tease Vera about her boyfriend in Cairns, Brian (Briney) Nacken, who was Indigenous.

'Nice to see she has the sense to latch onto a teacher. A cut above Salty Balls.'

"Um... I think so, and they knew I was a teacher, but they were also interested in my music. Ernie spoke with a cultured accent and loved books. I think he appreciated what I was bringing to the table, as they say. Not so much Vera's mother."

'What was her problem with you?'

Sitting at the kitchen table, one side, Vera's mother, Elvira, and her sister Amelia, wife of a judge of the Arbitration Court, dressed in traditional Spanish finery, complete with tortoise-shell hair combs and fans. Amelia, down from Brisbane, has driven Elvira out to quiz Mum on my prospects. They take it in turns to ask questions, then hide their faces behind their fans while Mum answers. We are nonplussed. I keep out of it. Neither Mum nor I have any idea why they are doing this but Mum plays along, making them tea and bringing out the biscuits.

"We didn't meet their standards. Not just me, but the whole family. Vera told me later."

'What did she say?'

"I think she was as puzzled as we were. The verdict was that we were 'white trash', which Vera took to mean basically that we weren't Spanish."

'But she agreed to the marriage?'

'We are sure we want to marry, and we are already lovers, so it might be a good idea for us to marry before something happens.' Vera lays it on the line. I am a bit embarrassed but am proud of her standing up to her mother. She turns to me.

'You seem to be determined to defy me, but I will not allow you to marry until you have somewhere to live.'

She knows that accommodation in Sydney is scarce and expensive, but I find a place in the classifieds.

"(laugh) Yes, but she made it hard. I had to find a place to live before she would give it her blessing. A single room was 'five pounds per week, shared amenities', and my weekly take-home pay as a teacher in 1958 was seven pounds fourteen shillings. The two pound fourteen wouldn't even cover groceries, and I was running a car.

"But I had music jobs that brought in another ten pounds or more, so we married and moved in with a retired man."

'How did the room work out?'

"He was a cranky old bastard. I was out working a few nights a week and Vera had no transport. There was no TV, not even a radio, so it must have been boring for her, particularly after she finished college and was home all the time, but as the summer holidays arrived, serendipity intervened, and we were saved."

'What happened?'

"At Mum and Dad's, a young couple Dad knew from the running club rented a room. The husband had a serious car accident and died, so the wife moved out. Dad agreed to us moving in, and we did before Christmas of that year."

'And that worked for you?'

"Yes. Dad had already put a door through the wall onto the veranda, so I enclosed the end of the veranda to make a kitchen and dining area, so we had a flat. We stayed there until we moved into the new house just over a year later."

'So did life become easier then, in the new house?'

"No. We had actually moved in before Dad gave me the bill. The house had cost almost three times the original estimate, and he made it clear that he wanted the money."

'That must have been a shock.'

"(laugh) That was only the start of it. Then Vera announced that she was pregnant with David."

'Whoops!'

"Yes. He came along at the worst possible time, financially. But I must admit, Vera loved being pregnant and I thought she was a great mum in the early months."

'And that changed?'

"To me, trying to manage the finances, it was a disaster. He was a beautiful baby, and I loved him dearly, but it blew our finances out of the water. Vera's income from teaching wasn't all that much, but it was on top of what I earned, so it made paying Dad back a possibility."

'Did she go back to work after the birth?'

'I'm not giving up this house. It's his bloody fault if it cost more than he said. Anyway, he should give us the house for nothing, the old tightwad!'

"If we sell it, we can start again with a house we can afford. He did spend the money."

'No, we're not moving. I'm not losing my house because he can't add up!'

"She needed to teach for two years to work off her bond. When she took maternity leave – there was no paid maternity leave back then, her income stopped. In fact, as soon as we married, the department withdrew her scholarship, so I had to pay for her last college term and that took all my savings.

"She had worked for just over a year by the time she had to leave work, so she only needed to go back for a few months when David was nearly one. But then she left for good, never to return."

'So, she never worked again?'

"No. She was already being treated for what was diagnosed as psychosomatic headaches and I remember when she resigned. She came home very upset that she had started menstruating at school and had bled through her skirt. On the way to the car some workmen had jeered at her, so she refused to go back, and that was the end of her teaching."

'Had she worked out her bond by then?'

"Yes, thank goodness. That was one debt that was behind us."

'That seems a good place to leave it. See you next week?'

As I leave, I have visions of two-year-old David, reaching up, smiling and again feel the never-ending grief of a parent that loses a child.

Too soon
Perfect infant
Born to children
Too soon.

Prodigy
In an adult world
Too soon

Making choices
Taking chances
Too soon

Addicted
Choices gone
Too soon

Stolen life
Ended today
Too soon,
Too soon.

Session 3

'How's your week been?'

"(laugh) I don't know if dredging up all that pain is a good idea...

Smiling, looking at notes. Wearing a pants suit. I like the skirt better. She has nice legs and it's a shame to cover them. The questions hurt, but she is easy to talk to and some of it is coming into focus.

...But I think it's working."

'In what way have things changed for you?'

"(smile) I feel more relaxed about where this is going. I was more apprehensive last time."

'Good. Can we talk about your beatings?'

"With the strap?"

'Yes. How young were you when that started?'

She has that smile that isn't a smile. Lips turned up but pressed together.

'This hurts me more than it hurts you,' he says, but I can't understand that. Getting the strap fills my mind and I can see it. Legs jumping, trying to get away from the pain. But a big, angry man is holding my arm, and I can't get away. I cry.

'Shut up or I'll really give you something to cry about!'

"I can't remember when it started. I can't remember when it wasn't a part of my everyday life. I remember thinking that if I had not had a belting for a week, that it was amazing."

'So, it was pretty constant?'

"Mum says not, but to me it was. It seemed a given that it would happen sooner rather than later whenever he was home, and it seemed to happen a lot."

'Come here! You painted the cat with blasted creosote!'
He's taking off the leather belt.
"*What creosote?*"
'You know what creosote, by jingo, and I'll teach you not to hurt the cat!'
"*I didn't paint the cat! I didn't paint the cat!*"
Hurting, trying to get legs out of the way.
'And here's a few more for lying!'
"*I wasn't here! I didn't paint the cat!*"
'Well, if you didn't paint the cat, you should have stopped it! You're the eldest!'

'So did that change your behaviour... for the better?'

"(laugh) I don't think it made any difference. Somehow, the beltings and whatever I did to deserve them rarely seemed to be connected."

'How's that?'

"Sometimes I knew what the belting was for, and even then, it seemed excessive, although I had nothing to compare it with. But more often than not, they came out of the blue."

'Did you try to explain, let him know you didn't understand?'

"(laugh) Of course. But he seemed to be angry anyway and had to take it out on somebody. I remember Uncle Eric, laughing, saying that he heard me yelling: 'Can't we talk about this?'

"No, his decision to strap me came from somewhere else."

'Did you ever come to an understanding of why he did it... to you? Did he belt the other kids?'

God sees everything. God knows what everyone thinks. The husband and father, the head of the family, is ultimately responsible for everything that everyone in the family does. 'Spare the rod and spoil the child'. Children are born to do evil and that must be driven out by the fear of God and fear of the rod. He saw that his son failed to stop his sister hurting the cat. The son is responsible, and I am responsible for him.

"I don't remember him belting the others. He never belted Eleanor, but he did bully her a lot, and Bill seemed to be always sick with something. I remember pneumonia and diphtheria, when we had to have the house fumigated. He was born as the war broke out, so there were other worries, like being called up. Then he was away a lot.

"Bill was two when Dad left for the army and by the time Jen arrived, there were less beltings, and I was more useful to him as a helper.

"Eventually I think I came to understand the immense pressure he was under to please his god and that included keeping us all sinless."

'(smiles) Mission impossible.'

"(laugh) Indeed. But it came in waves. Sometimes he didn't seem to notice us and at other times he was super vigilant."

'What about your mum?'

"Yes, sometimes I saw how he looked at her and sensed a deep anger. I think he would have belted her when he was like that if he could have gotten away with it."

'Did he ever actually do anything to your mother?'

"A couple of times, I saw him grab Mum by the shirt front as a sort of demonstration of what he wanted to do to somebody, but the intensity hinted to me that he was sending her a message, without going far enough to risk being called out by her."

'Do you think he suffered from a general state of anger?'

'The blasted thing! Why did it happen now? By cripes, I don't know why it had to be now!'

"I'm sure of it. When the car broke down, for instance, he would bellow his version of invective to the sky, and I would make myself scarce."

'Was your sense of danger worse when he was in that mood?'

"(laugh) Oh, definitely. But when he calmed down, it was me who helped him fix whatever it was."

'Did he appreciate your help?'

"I guess he did, and he sometimes included me in a report, like the day we poured ninety huge barrow loads of concrete in one day to make the floor of the patio for the Orange Grove Road house. I remember him telling Mum: 'We poured ninety barrow loads today, Madge. We got it all done in the day!' He did say 'we'."

'Did he ever compliment you, as distinct from including you in the report?'

"I don't remember that ever happening. He did express his general disappointment in me a couple of times when he said: 'You'll never be that man that your father is!'"

'That's a very hurtful thing to say to a child.'

"Yes, but he did trust me to do things that should have been beyond a child."

'Such as?'

'It has a new motor, put in since the war. The old one was ruined by charcoal dust getting into the cylinders, but I don't know what I can do about the wiring being burnt out.'

"I'll rewire it."

He looks at me for a minute and then nods. 'If you think you can do it, have a go.

Ask Mum for money for the wire.'

"I was probably thirteen when I rewired a '37 Chev truck he bought, so that would have been 1948. I was already driving the tractor and had been driving Dad's ute around the property for over a year. I had helped with numerous motor reconditionings, then testing spark plugs, coils, condensers, and so on.

"I was getting to know my way around motors and machinery by then. Aunt Ella turned up one day and complained that her little Ford Anglia was not running well, so I had a look at it, and after taking out the spark plugs and testing the compression, decided it needed a valve grind."

'How did you test the compression?'

"(laugh) I didn't have a tester, just took out the plugs and as she spun the starter, I blocked the plug holes with my thumb and noted the different pressures. Anyway, I went to town and bought a new head gasket, and by the end of the day, she had a de-coke and valve grind done and dusted."

'So, you did a fair bit of mechanic work as a young person.'

"Yes, I did. I never seemed to doubt my ability to fix things, and some were a bit creative, like the 1924 model Morris 9 that had a burnt-out clutch. I couldn't get a new clutch plate in 1957, so I glued slivers of cork onto the old plate with Tarzan's Grip and that worked fine. But it was my confidence around vehicles, and the skills I had accumulated, that might have averted a nasty accident that could have derailed a train."

'A train! What happened there?'

"Dad had sent me to Swain's Hardware for something, and as I turned from Cabramatta Road into John Street where they meet in a V shape, I had to swerve to avoid a truck reversing from the John Street kerb. When I came abreast of the cabin, I saw there was no driver, so, I dropped the bike, leapt onto the running board, opened the door and climbed in.

"By this time, it was picking up speed downhill toward the railway, but I stopped it with the footbrake, applied the handbrake, pushed it into gear and left it there in the middle of the road, continuing on to do the shopping."

'Did anyone say or do anything?'

"You know, it seemed like the street was deserted. Nobody came over to me, nobody seemed to notice and maybe that was lucky."

'Why lucky?'

"(laugh) Can you imagine what the driver might have thought, seeing a skinny kid in bare feet and shorts apparently driving off with his truck?"

'(laughs) Yes, I see your point. All right. Now take me back to Owen and your dad. Did your dad ever play with you like Owen did?'

"(smile) We would sometimes listen to the radio together. He was interested in cricket, so, particularly when Australia was playing England, the ABC broadcast the match in the evenings, and we would listen. We also listened to fights. He was interested in boxing, so I knew the names of the great cricketers and boxers of the day. I'm not interested in boxing, but still like to listen to cricket, or watch cricket."

'Did he play cricket with you... in the back yard?'

"I'm getting to that. I remember cutting a branch from a melaleuca tree and shaping it into a cricket bat. I knew it should have been willow, but we didn't have any of those, so tea tree it was. Anyway, I spent hours shaping the bat with saws and spoke shaves..."

'Spoke shaves?'

"They were a type of small wood plane with a blade between two handles and, I guess, were first used to shape wooden spokes for wagons. But when I had finished the bat, I took a spade and cleared the grass from a chain length, twenty-two yards of a paddock to make it smooth for a cricket pitch. I then cut some straight round stakes from wattle trees for stumps, and when I had the stumps in place, I asked Dad to come and play."

'Did he?'

"He did come down for a look, but that's all he did. He looked at the ground and the stumps, lifted the bat, dropped it and walked back to the house, leaving me standing there."

'What did he say? Anything to excuse himself?'

"No, he just left me standing there, feeling miserable."

'What happened after that?'

"For me, do you mean?"

'Yes, did you ever include him in anything like that again?'

"No. I made plenty of things but just went and did them. Anything we did together for my benefit was always his initiative."

'Did anyone in the family take an interest in what you did?'

"(laugh) Yes, there was the tree house. Eleanor and Ron played with me there, but I built it alone."

'Tell me about that.'

"Well, we had quite a few large melaleucas on the property. One was in the house yard and we kids climbed it a lot. I had read *Swiss Family Robinson* and wanted a tree house, so I nailed some three-bytwos across some branches and used fence palings for a floor and soon had a tree house, fairly high in the tree, where we had picnics. We also played at being spies, not that we could see much. Then, I decided that lifting stuff up for the picnics was difficult, and it needed a lift."

'You're kidding. (laughs) You built a lift?'

"Yes, luckily there were some sturdy branches higher up on either side, so I mounted a length of steel water pipe across the gap with an old motorbike wheel in the centre, cut a hole in the floor and threaded a rope over the wheel and through the hole so both ends reached the ground."

'Did you have all this stuff lying around the house?'

"(laugh) Dad always said that if you kept something long enough you would find a use for it. We had old motorbikes and truck bits lying around, and heaps of building materials, so finding resources was rarely a problem. Anyway, I made a wooden seat in a loop on one end of the rope to sit on while the other end was pulled to lift oneself up."

'Could you lift your own weight?'

"You know, I thought I would need to but was surprised that it was easy. If you know anything about pulleys..."

'I don't.'

"... then I can tell you that you need to lift only half your weight, so it was easy."

'Did anyone else try the lift?'

"Eleanor and Ron both used it, so we had picnics with the lift as a dumb waiter to bring the sandwiches and drinks up."

'Did your dad try it?'

"No, I don't think he was there. He must have been away somewhere. It was probably while he was in the army. Mum's younger brother Eric tried it, and it nearly killed him."

'It broke?'

"Make sure you sit on the board and have that rope inside your arms when you pull on the other rope." He's trying to stand on the seat! He doesn't have the rope inside his arms!

Crash! He must be dead.

"(laugh) No, it didn't break, but he stood on the seat, against my advice, and started up. When he was about a metre off the ground, his feet went up and his head came down and he crashed head-first onto hard dirt."

'Was he seriously hurt? I hope not.'

"He was knocked out. Mum was there, watching. She ran inside to get a tumbler of brandy, which she produced within seconds and tried to force it between his lips. He wasn't having any, so she upended the glass and drank it herself."

'So, what happened to Eric?'

"As I was being dispatched to the Christian's house – because they had a phone – to ring an ambulance, he opened his eyes and asked what happened. I couldn't help myself and pointed out that he had not used the seat to sit on and that was the trouble. He just stared at me, then got up and walked into the house, asking for aspirin."

'I'm surprised that a good Brethren had brandy in the house.'

He comes to the back yard where Dad is working on something and I am helping, as usual. Dad says he is a Polish Jew. He is carrying a shovel. He is hard to understand, but the story takes shape that he makes fruit brandy using a still in the shed where he lives. It is illegal in Australia to make brandy but is common in Poland.

He doesn't understand why it's illegal in Australia, but is afraid he might be caught, and, I now suspect, sent back to Europe where the war is still raging. Dad was persuaded and agrees that if he sees the police coming, he will throw the still into a hole in our scrubby back paddock that the Polish man is offering to dig, out of sight of the road and his shed, and Dad is to throw dirt over it, burying the still.

"It was toward the end of the war and our next-door neighbour, a Polish refugee, asked Dad to hide his brandy still if the police came."

'Did your father agree to that? Seems a bit against the religion, I would think!'

"(laugh) Dad was a bit anti-establishment, and I also suspect that his mother, Mary Steadman, was Indigenous, so…"

'Are you sure of that?'

"No, but there is evidence. Dad was always sympathetic to Aboriginal causes when it definitely was not cool to be so. He could recite Henry Kendall's poem 'The Last of His Tribe' with great drama and gusto and that didn't come from his schooldays."

'Did he ever say he was Indigenous?'

"No, and Mum told me when I was nursing her that he could have been, but if her father had suspected he was, she would not have been allowed to marry him. Grandma Ray was quite dark-skinned, so there was always the question, but it never was definitely answered."

'Did you make any other life-threatening contraptions when you were a kid?'

"(laugh) I made a lot of those, not that I thought of them as life-threatening at the time. The lift was quite safe if used according to directions, but it was demolished shortly after while I was at school, by Dad, I think. Or maybe it was Eric on Mum's instructions."

'Did that upset you?'

"No. I can't remember being upset by its removal. I think I was more interested in the construction than its use. I made many contraptions throughout my life. Most worked, but only a few of them survived long past the first use."

'What are some of the contraptions you made?'

"I always seemed to have a bow and arrows and a shanghai, but they were common among kids then. I did make a series of elastic-powered pistols that could shoot a bit of lead or a stone quite a way. But they all worked. I made a bull roarer several times, and once tried to make a miniature circular saw."

'How did that work?'

"It didn't. But have you ever pulled a thread through a button to make a loop that makes the button spin when you pull on the ends of the loops?"

'Yes, and it hums too.'

"Right. Well, Dad and Eric had a sawmill at our place from about 1944, so I was about eight going on nine, when I thought I could make a small circular saw using that principle. Unfortunately, I spent a lot of time filing teeth into a can lid before I could try to mount it on some sort of spindle. Of course, there was not enough power being transmitted to the saw blade to cut anything, so that was a fail."

'Did many fail?'

"No, most of them worked, and some worked so well that I patented them, but that was much later. The most spectacular fail was my steam-driven canoe."

'Oh my goodness! How did that work?'

"It didn't, but maybe it would have if I'd had better materials to work with. Anyway, I first made a canoe from an old sheet of corrugated iron, where I pulled each end double, then nailed both sides through a piece of timber, probably a piece of fence paling, and sealed the gaps with pitch. At the centre, I spread the sides with part of a tomato stake and mounted a four-gallon oil drum on bricks inside, leaving a space underneath for a fire. At the top of the drum, I drilled two holes and soldered short pieces of steel tubing to the drum, the right diameter to attach some hose pipe. Under the waterline at the back of the canoe, I strapped a short piece of steel tubing each side and joined them with hose pipe to the steel bits soldered onto the drum.

"After pouring about a gallon of water into the drum, I lit a fire underneath to create steam."

'This sounds dangerous.'

"It wasn't dangerous yet, because as the water boiled, the steam coming out had no pressure. The steel pipes were of too large a diameter to concentrate the steam into a jet, so I shaped two pieces of wood and drove them in to block up the pipes, then drilled a quarter inch – about a centimetre – hole through each and stoked the fire again. Pretty soon I had a good spurt of steam coming from the jets and I was thinking of taking it to the creek for a real test when the drum exploded, blowing out one end, sending superheated water splashing over the canoe and the fire. If I had been sitting at the back of the canoe, I might have been killed. End of experiment!"

'What did your mother have to say about that project? She must have known what you were doing.'

"At that time, Dad must have been away. Uncle Bill and Aunt Violet had left and gone to Werombi, so Mum was responsible for looking after three children, keeping the poultry farm going and making do in an unfinished house. I think she was just glad I was out of her hair."

'I'd like to ask you about other inventions of your childhood, but you are paying for my time.'

She is interested, and I have never thought about this part of my childhood as being extraordinary. Am I trying to impress her? Probably.

"I'll pay for you to hear about a couple and leave it at that."

'Okay.'

"When I was about seven, I attached a box and a wheel to my scooter to make a sidecar and that worked. I took Bill for rides in it down Booralla Road hill, and we had no mishaps, so that is of less interest. But, about five years later, the one that killed his trust in me was the sprung trailer on the back of my bike."

'Do tell.'

In Owen's shed is a Chev sedan that needs doing up. He calls it 'Mother's car', so we guess it is destined to be a more comfortable means of transport for Grandma than the trucks or the Chalmers.

I am intrigued by the front suspension and ask Owen about it. He says it is 'wishbone suspension', and I can see why. Instead of one axle, with leaf springs on either end, the wheels are attached by stub axles and kingpins. The system has a coil spring and an upper and lower arm, both pivoted from the chassis. I love this design.

"I attached a sheet of thick plywood to the front lower edge of a box, using hinges. At the open back end between the ply sheet and the bottom of the box, I nailed some coil bed springs (from the dump), which was my swinging-arm wishbone suspension. I think I had three springs and that was enough. I loaded a few bricks into the box and towed it. The box attached to the bike with a length of reinforcing rod; it handled the bumps perfectly and was ready for a human passenger."

'(laughs) Poor Bill!'

"Yes. All went well while we were racing along Orange Grove Road until we came to a rough patch. I kept one eye on the trailer and one eye on the road. The springs and the trailing arm suspension worked a treat until it started to rock from side to side. The rocking increased and Bill began to yell. Then suddenly, it gave one last lurch, snapped the rod off the bike and threw Bill into the stones and grass at the roadside."

'Was he hurt?'

"He had a few scratches, but that was not all that was hurt. From then on, he refused to have any part in the testing of my contraptions."

'You had more?'

"(laugh) Of course. One of the near misses involved my mate Dougie Noble and my billycart. My billycart was never going to be like Meggsie's, just a box with two wheels on the back and a swivel front axle with a rope to steer. Mine had to have a steering wheel. So, I built a frame at the front of the box into which I fixed a drum around which was wound the rope with a wheel attached to drive it.

"The problem was that I had wound the rope the wrong way, so to make a right turn, I spun the wheel to the left and vice versa. I mastered that and was soon hooning down Orange Grove Road hill at a fair speed, across the bridge over Cabramatta Creek, to stop and drag it up for another go.

"Dougie wanted a turn, so I gave him instructions and off he went. To my horror, at the bottom of the hill, where the road curved left onto the bridge, he turned the wheel to the left but went right, to crash into a bridge post. If he had missed the post, it was a long drop to the dry creek bed."

'I'm guessing there are more?'

"Yes, but you've probably heard enough for one day."

'(looking at her watch) Just about, and thank you for the engineering lesson. You certainly were an inquisitive child. Did you do particularly well at school?'

"I don't know. I was always struggling at school with my image. All the other kids seemed to be so good at everything and I wasn't."

'Was that fact or your interpretation?'

"My interpretation. When I finished kindergarten, I was promoted straight to second class, but I got a scalp infection that kept me out of school for six weeks, so I went back with my peers. Probably a good thing too."

'Why do you say that?'

"I'm a teacher. Most kids who are promoted beyond their years have problems socialising and become isolated. They often take up chess or music and they get kudos but feel different."

'Did you feel different?'

"Always."

'Still?'

"No, not so much. In fact, those experiences gave me a perspective that allows me to jump into anyone's shoes. I surprise myself."

'(laughs) You would have made a good diplomat.'

"Maybe, but my new-found self-esteem has been very recent. Too late for a career change."

'What got you there... to feel better about yourself? Was it any one thing?'

"Music."

'Okay. Next week, we should get into what really troubles you.'

"And what's that?"

'Sex and all that jazz.'

"A lot of jazz and not much sex, I'm afraid."

She stares for a long moment.

'Let's talk about that next week.'

Session 4

She is smiling, indicating that I should enter and sit. This week wearing jeans and a long-sleeved shirt, buttons done up high. I wonder if this is her androgenous look. She sits, opens her notebook and crosses her legs. She reads for a few seconds.

'Remember at the end of our last session we mentioned that we would be talking about sex?'

"Yes, and as difficult as this might be for me to talk about sex, it is where I have had most trouble in my life. I'm sure I married to have sex."

'So, no sex before marriage?'

'Carry that end with Pepsi.'

Pepsi, Dad's assistant maintenance carpenter, so named (Pepsodent) for his tobacco-stained and rotten-toothed smile.

He takes some of the weight.

'I bet you have fun with the girls! How old are you now?'

"Sixteen." I don't know what to say, I blush.

Withering glare from Dad. 'Nothing like that 'til he's married!'

Pepsi loses his grip, the big table drops onto my leg, damn near breaks it. Saves me from further embarrassment.

"At the time, it seemed the right time to get married."

'Why was it time to get married?'

"That was what we did then, although I now think the deal was that you married, and sex was a given and a man needed to marry to get it. If I'd been asked, I would have said I married for love. Everyone else seemed to be having sex and some seemed not to need to get married, but I was always too terrified to go past kissing."

'So, you only kissed girls up until... what age?'

"There were incidents with other children playing sexual games. You know, 'I'll show you mine if you'll show me yours' sort of stuff, simulated sex and that kind of thing."

'At what age did that start?'

"Hard to remember, but I might have been eight, no later, and it started with Ron showing me condoms he'd found hidden in a hollow tree stump in the bush."

Sweet musk, earthy smell. Rubber streaked with white. Sniff them, put the used ones back. Take two new ones away.

'How did he know they were there?'

"Some had been used."

'Okay. How did Ron know?'

"Now isn't that funny! In all these years I never asked that question. He might have just come across them, but I doubt it. He must have been shown. He said they belonged to his brother and were for him and Hildegarde. She lived on the other side of 'the bush' and she walked past our house after work in the afternoons. A strange walk. Up on her toes."

'Okay, so what did you do with them?'

"Well, we took two."

'Were they in a package?'

"No, they were loose, so we took one each, then found our sisters to show them."

'And how old were they?'

"Two years younger, both of them. I was a few weeks older than Ron and Jill was a few weeks younger than Eleanor, so they were probably six, maybe going on seven."

'Who was running the show?'

It looks so pink. She is lying back on the pile of feed sacks. It is hot and I have the condom on. It is loose, not a real erection, so I guide it to the opening. I can see white tissue covering most of the opening, so I put the end of the condom at the entrance then take it away.

Then we swap sisters and try again.

"Ron led me to the condoms and seemed to know what to do with them."

'Seems like it was Ron.'

"Probably, but I never thought that. All four of us were keen to try the condoms."

'What does that suggest to you?'

"I don't know, never thought about it much... but I always felt responsible for everything, still do in a way, but they were both keen to be in on it. There was no question of anyone saying no or running to tell our mums."

'So, was there intercourse? Penetration?'

"If you had asked me then and for some time later, I might have said there was, but..."

'What you were doing is sin! You will be punished forever by fire for your sins!'

"...But no, we didn't really know that's what you did. We just placed our penises at the opening and laughed ourselves silly. There was no thrusting or penetration, and we had no intention, or at least, I had no intention of doing that again."

'I see, so what happened to make it such a big deal?'

"I don't know really. I do know we had a boarder named Hazel Harrison, who saw me and Ron flashing our condoms to each other as we walked past the side of the house. She called out 'I saw that!' So, I guess she told Mum, who must have told Dad. Next thing we were being grilled and Eleanor says Dad was so graphic and invasive of her body, she now insists it was sexual abuse."

'I might come back to that, but when did you get past the taboo... get past kissing?'

Friday night, Engadine, walking down the road toward the Woronora River, holding hands, singing, me harmonising, loaded down with sleeping bag, guitar, food in the knapsack. Glenda and I are early, others expected later.

In the cave, we start kissing, lying, she on top, erection aching. Going on for a long time. Then the others arrive, and we start the fire to cook dinner, snags and boiled potatoes.

Sitting around the fire, Glenda is in her swimmers, my hand accidentally brushes her breast. I am mortified and mumble an apology. Her quizzical look leaves me confused.

Funny, I have never noticed her breasts until now, and later, can't remember much about her body, except that she was slim and athletic, a tomboy. I guess a sexy body wasn't what I was looking for in a girlfriend. I just felt good around her. Later, she declared she is gay, and that fits with what we did. It was genderless sexual arousal, no undressing, no skin on skin, no wandering hands.

'That Jonathan is always trying to get his hands into my pants. Bastard! Anne too.'

"(laugh) Not until I was almost finished college, I did venture further once with a girlfriend. I guess I just wanted to know what she felt like. There was no thought of intercourse, at least, not from me."

'Did she touch you back?'

"No, and that didn't seem strange to me then. I had an idea that it was the male who initiated everything to do with sex."

'I see, so with Vera, she didn't touch you?'

"No. She tried once, after we were married, and I pulled away."

'She never tried again?'

"No, not really. As I mentioned earlier, she did once long after I'd left."

'Okay, was she a virgin up until your first time?'

'What are you doing?'
"Having a look."
'Why?'
"I just want to see what it looks like."
'Stop it. I don't like it!'
"Okay, sorry, I was just curious, that's all."
'Well, don't!'

"She wasn't a virgin, although I didn't realise that until years later."

'She told you?'

"No, I knew nothing about virgins and what that meant... (laugh) except the Virgin Mary of course... I don't know what children are supposed to make of that, when they are shielded from any knowledge of sex, but I remember, thinking back on the first time, there was no resistance, no hymen to break, no blood, no discomfort for her, but I didn't know that meant anything until later. I was just so over the moon to have finally had intercourse at last. I had a gig that night and the boss asked what had happened to make me play so well!"

'So, you felt good about it, but you weren't married then?'

"No, but we were only a month or so away from the wedding and I did have condoms."

'(smiles) So, you were prepared.'

"(laugh) I'd been prepared for years. Geoff Cawthorne, he was my roommate at college, was a bit older. He used to buy them by the gross and hand them around. So, I had one in my wallet where it stayed as a tell-tale ring in the leather until it went into the bin with the old wallet!"

'All right. Now can we go back to the first time you remember being aware of your sexuality?'

I am looking out of the window into the back yard. Noel Groves, Mrs Groves, Mum and Dad are still at the dining room table with Eleanor, and Bill in the highchair. They are talking about a particular point in scripture and discussing its meaning in their lives. I am bored, so I go to the window and see Patricia, our pedigreed Irish Setter, and another dog stuck together, bum to bum. I am amazed and a little frightened. 'Dad! The dogs are stuck together.' He runs outside yelling at the dogs: 'Get out of it, you mongrel!' He throws brickbats at them. They cry and pull apart. The other dog runs off, penis dangling. The Groveses are at the window. Dad comes in and smacks me on the behind. 'Get outside and play.'

"I was about six, I think, when I saw our dog and another dog mating in the backyard."

'How did you feel, seeing that?'

"A bit scared, interested, naughty."

'Why naughty?'

"When I told Dad, he threw bricks at them and then smacked me. So, I felt that seeing what they were doing must have been sinful."

'How do you feel about that now?'

"(laugh) Noel Groves and his family had come for lunch, and they were talking about the scriptures as usual, when the dogs were..."

'Fucking? It's okay, I've heard everything, and I won't be judging you, no matter what you say. It's important that you get all that stuff out. That's what I'm here for.'

"Okay, fucking. Dad must have been embarrassed. (laugh) We weren't allowed to talk about anything between the navel and the knees. I soon learned to keep quiet about anything to do with my penis, defecating or urinating."

'So, how did you cope with communal toilets, like in the army?'

"I was at Grandma's place once when I went to the outhouse. The door was closed as it usually was, so I just pushed it open and there was my cousin Wally sitting, just sitting staring at me. I ran away into the bush and hid."

'Who were you hiding from?'

"Shame, God, I don't know."

The tent was there with four camp beds already made up. I'd camped plenty of times, but this was two weeks near Holsworthy Army Barracks with a communal latrine. Just a long plank with holes over cans. People will see me wiping my arse.

"Hello!"

'Hello, where are you?'

"I'm at the camp, and I want you to pick me up."

'When?'

"Guard duty starts at six. Come along the side road just past where you dropped me off this morning and I'll be there at about six-thirty, okay?"

'I guess so. What's wrong?'

"I just can't stay here, okay? Please."

'Okay, but how will you do it?'

"I'll just tag onto the guard detail and after the last guard is posted there will be me marching along with my rifle, and I'll just keep marching on as if there is an extra guard post. They won't know how many guards there should be. You can drop me back just before six in the morning, and I can join the guard detail and follow them back in."

'That's silly!'

"I know, but please do it!"

'Private Ray, this bed hasn't been slept in!'

"No, sir."

'Where do you sleep?'

"At home, sir."

'Why's that, Private?'

"My wife isn't well, so I go home to take care of her, sir."

'I see. You're a teacher aren't you, Private?'

"Yes, sir."

'Okay, say we don't report you AWOL and you can come to my house every day and coach my kid in maths? Lunch supplied.'

"Yes, sir, I'd like that."

'All right, take your bedding back to the store and start tomorrow. Not sparrow fart (smiles), arrive about nine. How's that?'

"On my first camp with the army reserve after Nashos, you know, National Service? About half the men from my year at college were called up for six weeks of full-time training. Then after college we were required to spend a day a month, then three weeks a year full time for five years.

"At this camp we were expected to sleep in tents and use a communal latrine, and I just couldn't do it. The tent bit was okay, but I couldn't do the latrines. Vera picked me up every evening and dropped me back next morning and I held it in until I got home. It was that strong."

'Did you get away with it?'

"(laugh) No, but the sergeant bent the rules for me, so I was home at night and coached his kids in maths during the day at his house."

'So, you never had to explain your aversion to shared latrines?'

"No. At all other camps they had toilet cubicles."

'How do you feel about communal toilets now?'

"Nothing's changed, I'm still very shy about that. Poor Mum (laugh)."

'Why do you say poor Mum?'

"(laugh) Oh, I wiped poor Mum's bottom for a couple of years after she suffered a stroke... I didn't mind it so much, and I tried to make light of it so she would be okay with it too. And of course, I changed the babies often. It's just me and my own bum (laugh)."

'So, if you never talked about anything between the navel and knee, as you say, how was sex explained to you?'

"Dad had a pedigree chart for Patricia, which he displayed for us to see, and had planned to breed pedigreed pups to sell but neglected to explain the detail of how the pups happened. After Patricia produced a litter of mongrel pups, he bought a pedigreed dog. But he never restricted their movements, so when she was on heat, dogs from miles around were there mating with her."

'Did you ever get a pure-bred litter?'

"I don't remember ever having pure-bred pups, but that was not the only one of his ventures that failed at the business end. One year, he decided to grow chrysanthemums for Mother's Day. He ploughed a patch of ground, worked it up with harrows, planted the seed, then left it. He might have weeded it once, because the plants grew and right on time, flowers burst out, but he never picked them."

'Why was that do you think?'

"That was one of many ventures he began but never cashed in on, like he made felt hats for a while, then fake flowers, but sold none."

'Were they any good?'

"I remember wearing a fake carnation to a ball when I first started work and it fooled most people, and it even had a carnation scent. No, he was very clever and made some amazing things but failed at the marketing. I suffer from some of that too."

'I would be surprised if you didn't, but let's put that aside for another day. We were talking about sex education. (smiles) Yours to be precise.'

"Yes, well, I remember not long after that, he took me to see the cow being serviced. We always had a cow for milk..."

'And how did you feel about that?'

"(laugh) It was pretty intense. The bull was huge and excited. He was moaning, frothing at the mouth and when he mounted her, I could see his penis go in. It seemed to go on forever, and I was aroused by watching that."

'How aroused? Did you have an erection?'

"No, just tingling. Then he gave a bellow and slid off her, his penis disappearing into his belly."

'Did your father say anything to you about that?'

"No, we just led the cow home and put her in the paddock, then probably had a cup of tea."

'And what about sex and humans? Sex and you?'

'Wesley does this thing with his dick. He rubs it and this white stuff comes out.'

I'm interested to see that, so Ron organises it. We are in the shed where the Polish man would come to live later, so it is maybe 1943. There are tubs with rotting tomatoes pickling for seed. They smell yeasty but sweet. Wesley sits on an oil drum and pulls down his shorts. His legs are really hairy.

His dick is sticking up and he is spitting on his hand. He is rubbing his cock, up and down, spitting on it. Ron and I are standing on either side, watching. He keeps rubbing, then shouts: 'Grab my balls!' Ron grabs and squeezes his balls, and white stuff shoots from the end of his penis. There is a smell. Musky and thick. Ron stands back, and Wesley mops up with his handkerchief, then we leave.

"I watched a wanking demonstration when I was maybe going on eight."

'How did that happen?'

"I think Wesley was about sixteen when Ron asked him to show us his ejaculation."

'How did you feel about that? Were you frightened? Excited? What?'

"I wasn't frightened, but when Ron told me about Wesley's trick, I was keen to see it and when it happened, I was amazed to say the least, and that was when I started masturbating."

'I'm not surprised. So, you had erections at, what, eight?'

"Yes, I started masturbating in the bath, but we only had baths once a week, and I didn't masturbate every time."

'How did you feel about masturbating?'

"Oh, it felt good, but I knew it must have been a sin because it was about sex. I mean, just watching the dogs fucking got me a slap, so this must be really bad. I was always ashamed."

'But you kept doing it.'

"Yes. By then the connection between doing anything and the strap seemed so arbitrary that I pretty much did as I wanted, expecting a strapping at any time."

'I'm wondering if that disconnect between the transgression and the punishment had any impact on how you related to other authority figures in your life.'

"You know, it took me quite some time to see how that worked for me. I've always had a physical fear of teachers, police, and to a lesser extent officers in the army, so I was always compliant unless my rights or those of someone I was close to were being infringed, then I was able to confront them."

'That must have been hard to do.'

Milton hands me fifty dollars and I stare at him. "Mate, that's way below the award. It's got to be worth seventy-five."

He looks at me a moment. 'It's cash in hand. I'm happy with that.'

I see the manager.

"G'day. I'm Ford, the bass player in the band today and I wish to make you aware that the pay you are offering is below the award. I guess you didn't know."

'I see. The way it works is that I pay Frank Crisafi a lump sum for the show, and he's responsible for payments.'

"Okay, thanks."

I confront Frank and he says there isn't enough to pay us scale and there is nothing he can do, so I go back to the manager.

"Me again, I talked with Frank, and he says there isn't enough to pay the musicians scale, so I guess the buck stops with you."

He glares from behind his desk, then sighs. 'Well, I'm not paying any more, so you know what you can do.'

I stand for a moment but have nothing to add that would help. "Okay, then I won't be seeing you next week." I walk out.

"Strangely, not that difficult. I always came to the boss from what I thought was a reasonable and considered position, but nine times out of ten, I was fired. I have sometimes said that if you want to be a pro musician, you need to get used to being sacked. (laugh) The first hundred times is the hardest, then later, I realised something that made it almost welcome."

'Really? What's that?'

"I was offered a gig at Gosford RSL with two mates, so I didn't ask the fee. When pay time arrived it was way below the award, so I complained to the manager, who sacked me. Then, barely a week later, I had a call from Tony Rossi, who ran a music and raffle show at Toukley RSL. He offered double what was paid at Gosford, so I rang Jack Grimsley and Laurie Thompson, Little Pattie's husband, who took the job, and we were together for almost ten years, with occasional pay rises, until Tony died, as did the gig.

"I realised that while I was employed at a particular time and venue, other musicians knew I was working and if a gig came up, they would get someone else. But as soon as it was known that I was free, the phone would ring and it was usually a better paid job, simply because the employer knew he or she needed to beat the price of the previous gig."

'I guess that worked in a situation where the number of players of a certain ability were limited.'

"Yes, the Central Coast was a defined area, and we all knew each other, but in the Sydney professional scene that worked too, maybe not so intensely, but it worked."

She is writing, reads for a moment, then lowers the notebook.

'You mentioned Hazel Harrison. Who was she?'

"Hazel Harrison remains a mystery, and I regret not asking Mum about her when I was nursing her in Eden, and we had the time to talk about the old days. Hazel arrived from Tamworth, near where Dad was stationed with the army at Werris Creek, perhaps four or five months pregnant, and stayed with us until a few weeks after the baby was born. Then she left as mysteriously as she came, so maybe she was there under sufferance."

'Do you think the baby was your father's?'

"I have wondered that but doubt it. I think the more likely scenario is that a Brethren daughter became pregnant and the parents asked Dad to hide her away from the local Brethren until she could give birth to the baby and have it adopted. There was some talk about adoption at the kitchen table, so Mum must have helped with that."

'Intriguing.'

"Yes, but we'll never know."

'So, was the condom event the last of the sex games with your sister?'

"I remember about the same time kneeling on all fours while I was 'milked'. I only remember that happening once. I think I expected 'milk' to come out like it did with Wesley, and maybe she tired of the game, or I did, because within seconds it was abandoned, and we were distracted by something else. But that was the last of our sex games together and I never was inclined to try anything else with Ron or our sisters."

'So, they were the last sex games for you and her together?'

"Yes, and it seemed that unless Ron initiated something, I didn't think along those lines."

'How about your sister?'

"Mmm... Many years later, Eleanor claimed that she was sexually abused by Dad. We, that's her siblings, have talked about what she claims, and remembering she would have been six, maybe going on seven, we cannot discount the chance she has been a bit creative in describing the scene, but we agree he would have been so upset that he would have used everything he could to stop it, scaring her and shaming her into compliance."

'Do you think that was sexual abuse?'

"Depends what you mean... I think the whole Brethren attitude to sex and how sexual information was passed on, or not passed on, was a form of abuse.

"Lack of sexual reality led to fantasy, and in my case, a warped sexual awareness was assured by the cryptic answers to children's questions, particularly in the secret society of the church. The shame attached to anything sexual was so intense as to prohibit sensible questions.

"Sex was for procreation only, and there was no room for fun. It seemed to me that there was no healthy pathway to knowledge and any natural inquisitiveness led to damage. There could be no calm discussion. It was always couched in terms of sin, Satan and retribution. There was always shame and blame."

'But for you, was that the last of the sexual games?'

"I wish. No. I guess it must have been through Ron again, because there was no other kid I spent time with. There was certainly no other boy who knew so much and was keen to share his knowledge. He told me about homosexuality and that was my undoing for years."

'Did you have sex with Ron?'

"No, I have never had sex with a male. Maybe if I had, it would have been kept secret, but I didn't and it wasn't, and that is probably why it became such a problem."

'How did that happen?'

'Come into the toilets and I'll show you something really funny.'

Kevin drops his pants, and I mime fucking him up the anus. I can't see his bumhole, and I am not looking to see it. It doesn't interest me. There is no contact. It is the absurdity of the whole idea that is so funny to us, and we are laughing ourselves silly. It is just a joke to me, as it is to Kevin, but our laughter attracts other boys who gather around for a look.

"He told me that males had sex together, and I thought this was so interesting that I couldn't wait to share that knowledge with my mates at school. They too were intrigued. So, Kevin and I went to the toilet and put on a demo. There was no contact and no intention of actually doing it, even if we could have, which I doubt. We were miming the action in front of an audience. A repeat was demanded, so I did the same show with Peter. By then, quite a few boys had seen it and, of course, it was too good a story not to tell a teacher, and that's what happened."

'How did they react to that. Do you remember?'

'Whose idea was it to do it?'

"It was Kevin's. He made me do it."

'Stand over there.'

He talks to Peter. Calls me back.

'Peter says it was your idea, and it was your idea with Kevin too. I might have expected this behaviour in a big city school, but not here. I'll need to tell your parents.'

I'm back in class and Mrs Johnson says nothing, but I feel the fear of retribution, terrified of what will happen at home. If that would be the end of it, a belting would be a blessing.

"I remember it all very well. At the time, I believed that whatever we did, it must have been so sinful that what followed was deserved. Many years later, I came to understand that the headmaster had imagined full-on homosexual sex and that was what he acted on and reported to Dad. We were never really asked for the details, and I can't see how any teacher could really go to that."

'As a teacher yourself, did you ever have to deal with something similar?'

'Ford, Herb here. Have you got a moment?'

"Of course. What's the problem?"

'It's a bit delicate, but Hannah said my son and your daughter were caught playing... er doctors and nurses... We don't worry about that too much, not as Jews, but we want to get the facts.'

"I wouldn't worry about it either. I'll have a word with her, so forget it."

'No, we think my son is being blamed, and I want to ask her a few questions. When can you bring her up here?'

"No, I'm not letting anyone question my daughter. What are you trying to do? Trying to establish blame? Believe me, you will do more damage making this into a big deal. So as far as I'm concerned it never happened, and you can do the same. Okay?"

'No need to get defensive, we were just going to ask who started it, that's all.'

"I'm not being defensive. I don't give a shit who started it. I just don't want a couple of kids showing each other their bits and pieces being made to feel ashamed of it. The answer is NO!"

"Not as a teacher, but as a parent a situation came up where a friend wanted to quiz my daughter about something sexual that he thought might have happened between her and his son. Being Jewish, I suspect that it was the reputation of his son he was keen to protect."

'What happened?'

"I just refused to give him access to her. She was only eleven, and I was acutely aware of the damage it could do. He was insistent, but I was adamant, so it didn't happen."

'Pity you couldn't apply that wisdom to your situation when you were young.'

"Yes, the shame was excruciating and that stayed with me for years. It wasn't until I was near middle age and thinking about it that I ran the memory tape and realised that I had actually not indulged in a homosexual act, as an adult would understand it."

'What if you had?'

"I've thought about that too, and I hope not to offend my gay friends when I say that I realised later that what we did was actually expressing the opposite of being gay."

'Can you explain that?'

"(laugh) I'll try. As you know, I did actually try to have heterosexual sex with my sister and Ron's sister some time earlier, and that was fairly serious business to start with, and I am sure we would have succeeded if we could have, although we also thought it was funny. I had seen dogs mating many times and there were bulls servicing cows, so I knew what went where in the traditional sense, and I was aware of the pleasure I got from masturbating, as shameful as I thought that was."

'Why did you think it was shameful?'

"It was a sexual act, ergo, shameful."

'Oh dear! Poor you. And what were the repercussions after the school episode?'

'Come into the bedroom.' Dad's voice is not unkind, but I dread what is coming. He sits on a chair and motions me to sit on the bed. He opens the Bible and reads to himself for a bit then says, "If boy lie with girl, he will be forgiven. But, if boy lie with boy, they will surely die." Do you understand what that means?!'

Wait, go numb. Wait. It will be over soon.

'Answer me! Do you understand?'

"Yes, Dad."

'It means when you die you go to Hell, and you burn and burn forever. Do you understand what forever means! Not a day, not a year. It never stops. Never, never, never! You burn, and you burn, and you burn!'

He leaves and I lie back in horror. I have a picture in my mind of what Hell is. The old men at the Gospel Service on Sunday evenings have ranted about it incessantly. I don't know what brimstone is, but it must be worse than fire in "fire and brimstone", and I certainly know what fire is. I'm feeling worthless, hopeless, terrified, and profoundly ashamed.

"(laugh) Repercussions! That bit of silliness caused me grief that I now believe set me up for difficulties and pain for much of my sexual and social life."

'How did you handle the shame?'

"I now know it was my father's shame that I was forced to feel as my own. How did I handle it? I prayed. Despite being given no hope of forgiveness and the terror of imagining an eternity of burning in Hell with no reprieve, I prayed constantly for forgiveness, and luckily it all happened near the end of the school year, and I was packed off to Grandma's."

'Did she know?'

"I don't think that shame would have been broadcast beyond Dad and Mum and my class teacher, so she could watch out for deviant behaviour, but nothing more was said at school or at home, and life continued as before, on the surface."

'So, it never came up again?'

Lindsay and I have been to the urinal for a piss after lunch and we are walking back to where we play marbles. Is he talking to us? I look up and it is Mr (Kanga) Ruse, our Phys Ed teacher, and he looks angry. 'I know what you dirty buggers were doing in there!'

I know what he means and the shame hits. It has been at least three years since anyone has said anything, and I was beginning to feel it was over. I look at Lindsay and he just appears puzzled. We walk on and he never asks what Ruse meant, so it passes, and I calm down.

"It must have been on my school record card because one teacher, when I was in what is now called year eight in high school, saw me and Lindsay together after we had been to the toilet. He let me know he was watching, and that he suspected we had been doing something sexual."

'Had you? There's no judgement here.'

"No, it never occurred to me to do anything like that, not even when we did that miming thing in primary. Anyway, by that time, in fact, since I was five, or maybe even before that, I remember being romantically interested in girls."

'Did you have a girlfriend?'

"Yes, I had a girlfriend, but she was a girl and a friend. I think the most intimate thing we did was hold hands. But I felt good being with her."

'So, you had no desire to have sex with her?'

"No, by that time I was about fifteen, and it was like sex was off limits and that's how it stayed into adulthood."

'Were you ever sexually aroused by girls about that time?'

We are visiting the Groves family at their place. She is there, and we are alone. She looks lovely and I would like to ask her for a fuck. I do notice her breasts, but that is not what I focus on. She just looks nice, so I go inside and say nothing, feeling ashamed.

"I had thought I wanted to try sex with a girl, and that started in primary school, but as I said, by fifteen... well, probably by thirteen, I didn't think of it as something I could actually do. Dad seemed to have no friends outside our family except the Groveses, who visited maybe every other year. I remember the visits well, because he was diabetic and each time they came, Mum prepared a special lunch. It was the only time we got to taste celery (laugh) split into florets and we dipped the stalks into salt."

'Did you ever visit them at their home?'

"Once, when I was about twelve."

'What do you remember of that visit?'

"Not much. I do remember looking at their girl. She was about my age, maybe a little older and felt the urge to ask her for a fuck."

'Did you?'

"No, I never asked anyone for a fuck. Not after the first and last time in fourth class when I passed a note to a girl who I had no particular yen for. I don't know why I did it because if she had agreed to it, I know I would have panicked. The note just said: 'How about a fuck?' I watched her take the note to the teacher, expecting serious trouble, but she just tore it up and told me to 'not be silly'."

'So, except for the high school teacher's remarks, I'll call it the homosexual incident had passed by, and you were feeling less, um... unforgiven?'

Gentle Jesus, meek and mild, look upon this little child. God bless Mummy, Daddy, Grandma and Owen, and please forgive me for my sins. I will never do that again, I promise. Oh, please God forgive me. Please, please forgive me.

"No, I never felt forgiven. Over the years it gradually took up less of my consciousness and eventually there were times late in my teens when I didn't think of it for stretches of time, maybe a day or two. But it always came back to renew the terror.

"I imagined that, except for Grandma Turnbull and the others at Coromandel, everyone knew. My uncle Eric knew and let me know he knew, which gutted me at the time, so it's hard to imagine that he kept that to himself. Remember, that was the age of gossip as entertainment.

"In the Brethren, gossip and judging of others was the essence of most adult conversations that I heard. But maybe they regarded it as a passing phase. In any case, nothing was said at Grandma's, and Owen was his usual loving and fun-loving self.

"More to the point, God knew, and God had spoken through the Bible. In fact, in Leviticus, it says that homosexuality is punished by death, so I am lucky I wasn't born into those times when I am sure the subtlety of miming the act for fun versus the real thing would not have been appreciated, as it wasn't with me!"

'(laughs) Yes indeed!'

"Then, after Christmas, I was picked up from Grandma's by my older cousin Wally and taken to where he and his mother were living in Roseville. I remember particularly, the train stopping at Canley Vale station, near my school. I sat on the floor, heart in mouth as they say, while the train was in the station. I was terrified that someone might see me through the window. I don't know what Wally made of that, but he didn't ask, and we continued on, arriving at his place after dark. It was my first visit to their home at Roseville, and I remember the walk from the train station and was amazed that he knew the way."

'Did the pressure come off while you were there, at Roseville?'

"Yes, it did. We were kept busy, and I can't remember the terror being as intense as it had been. My clothes and my bike must have been delivered there because I don't remember having luggage on the train, and my bike was there when we arrived. On most days we rode to Roseville baths. I am not conversant with Roseville's surroundings, but I do remember riding through the edge of a golf course, with cicadas almost deafening, and the long hill down to the baths."

'So, you enjoyed the baths?'

"Yes, that was the year I learned to swim. I had turned nine in the previous November."

'You hadn't tried swimming before that?'

'Just lie on your back and float'. I am about five and Dad has his hand under my back. I try that and my head goes under. I cough and he turns me over, his hand under my stomach. 'Paddle like a dog.'

I get the arms and legs moving and he removes his hand. My head goes under. 'He's a sinker,' he laughs. He picks me up and dumps me on the side of the pool.

"Dad had a couple of tries, but he said I was a sinker and gave up. At the baths with Wally, I could walk across the smaller pool. It was only about waist deep, so I pushed off from the edge and put my feet down at the end of the glide, then gradually, I got the hang of paddling with my arms and doing some sort of frog kick with my feet. By the time I went home, I could swim in the deep pool."

'What was the attitude to you when you were back home?'

"Life seemed to go on as before, but I can't remember seeing much of Ron after that. My closest buddy was Mark Smith, and I spent a lot of time with Mark until high school."

'Was there any sexual stuff with Mark?'

"No, we just rode bikes around and probably played board games at his house. We just did the sorts of things I imagine most kids do. No, the curiosity had been well and truly squelched by then. I can't remember ever needing to stop myself thinking about doing sexual stuff. I just didn't think about it. Then we moved to a new place in Orange Grove Road, Cabramatta on twenty acres."

'So, did you ever see Ron again?'

We dig down a foot back from the creek bank between it and a thick blackthorn bush. The soil is loamy, and we make good progress. When we are about five feet down, we dig a tunnel under the thorn bush with a foxhole on the other side. We place logs across the top, cover them with corrugated iron sheets and hide all that under soil and the turf divots we saved.

We dig a small round window through the creek bank so we can see people going past along the path beside the creek. Then we think it might be a good idea to have a fireplace, so we dig into the side of the underground room and create a fireplace shape. We dig a round hole down from the surface and above that, we embed a yard-long hollow

log as a chimney, and we're ready for the fire.
We get paper and twigs and light it up.

"Yes, once. Ron came for a holiday of a week or so. It must have been before we got the first tractor, or I would have spent the holiday mucking around with that."

'So, none of the sexual stuff came up?'

"No, we spent most of the holidays building an underground house."

'(laughs) What else! How did that go?'

"Nearly killed us. The house was fine. It had a tunnel to a secret entry out of sight on the other side of a thorn bush. That all worked, but we decided it needed a fireplace.

"It looked as if it should work, but the chimney didn't draw, and the room soon filled with smoke. We were probably lucky we weren't asphyxiated but were able to skedaddle out of there, and I don't remember ever going back in. Then I took Ron home, towing him behind my bike in the billy cart with the steering wheel."

'Had the steering been fixed by then?'

"Yes, I fixed that after Dougie's accident and added a trailer. It was probably in the August school holidays."

'(laughs) Of course you added a trailer! Did the masturbating stop with the move to the new place?'

"No. I suffered a mild stutter from early on, but after the homosexual event, that became much worse, and I started wetting the bed regularly."

'That must have been hard. Did it happen every night or occasionally?'

"Before we moved to Orange Grove Road, it was rare, I think, but as soon as puberty arrived, the bed wetting became worse. And I was afraid to sleep away from home."

'Did you ever sleep away from home, and what happened?'

"I never wet the bed at Grandma Turnbull's or at Wally's, and they were the only two places I stayed overnight until years later. But I was always afraid that I might, and that fear still lingers."

Walking down from the bus. Had an erection brought on by the vibration of the train. Stayed on the train, couldn't stand, or my dick would have been seen. The lap of my school shorts was covered by the school bag. The train terminated at Liverpool, then came back. By Cabramatta it had come down, and it stayed down on the bus but was still tingling and the erection is up again as I walk down the road. I continue past the driveway into the bush in the gully, spit and wank... out it comes, just a little. Feeling elation. 'Mature. I'm mature!'

"It was more difficult after I started ejaculating. It made more sense to masturbate to avoid wet dreams, but I didn't understand that either, so I tried not to masturbate at all."
'What did you think when you had wet dreams?'
"I thought it was a punishment. A judgement. Really ashamed."
'You didn't know it was natural?'
"No, not until much later. I was upset by the dreams but devastated by the ejaculations."
'Did you think you should have been able to control them?'

The car is tooling around the bends, fast, centreline streaming under the bonnet, and here comes the build-up. It rises and rises, then I come, waking to clag in my pyjamas. So ashamed.

"Yes, in a way. There was part of my mind that knew it was a dream. It was like wetting the bed. Usually, I was in a dream where I would be somewhere where it was appropriate to be urinating, like in a real toilet, or behind a bush, but there was always something not quite right about the situation and I began to think it might be a dream. This was all in the dream.

"Then sometimes, I would think in the dream that it was not a toilet or a place to wee and look elsewhere, but eventually I would let go. But it never felt quite right. Then, partway through, I would wake and find myself wet."

'That must have been embarrassing. When did that stop? (laughs) I presume it stopped.'

"No, occasionally I still have the dreams, and I still let go, but I wake up dry and don't wet the bed. In my sleep I recognise it as a mind-trick and wake up in time."

'So, you still have the dreams. That is extraordinary. Were the 'wet dreams' graphically sexy?'

"No, well, sometimes but not usually. One was a car speeding, another my aunt hanging out washing."

'Did you use pornography to stimulate yourself?'

They are out for the day. Go through the drawer to find the photography book with the nude. There she is... and here's another book. Father and Son: Sexual information for Boys, by Lord Baden Powell. I open the book at the contents page and see 'Self Abuse'. I read and remember it went something like this:

'Self-abuse, or masturbation, rots the mind and damages the penis. However, if the boy stops masturbating, he will heal his body and mind. Masturbation is an abomination in God's eyes, being a temptation from Satan as he undermines God's will by corrupting the holy spirit of his people.'

I read on.

'Scouts avoid weakness following ejaculation by tying a cotton reel to

their backs so they will not sleep face up, the position that encourages the distressing occurrences of nocturnal emissions and masturbation.'

"No, there was no real pornography around our house, only one photography book of Dad's that showed a naked female torso in black and white, but I can't remember that being what aroused me. I didn't need anything, it just seemed to happen, jiggling on the train. It still happens while I'm driving, but not often. (laugh) I am a bit older now, you know."

'I know how old you are (laughs). It's on your card. Do you still have wet dreams?'

"I had one recently, but there was no ejaculation. It was quite pleasant."

'(laughs) And it didn't weaken you?'

"No, and despite what Baden Powell wrote in the Scout book, I learned that having sex didn't weaken men when I read about Roger Bannister."

'Roger Bannister?'

"Sorry, Roger Bannister disproved the long-held idea that ejaculation weakened men. He disproved it by having sex in the morning with his wife, then immediately afterward running a four-minute mile."

'Yes, I do remember that, so masturbation was a problem for you. Was it the shame or was there more?'

'Blisters... Huge blisters! Shit!'

"Yes, I masturbated, not that often, but it sometimes causing swelling of the skin, like blisters..."

'(laughs) Shame you weren't taught to use a lubricant!'

"In the bath I used soap."

In the bathroom cubicle at college. Deep warm water, wash the hair, face, body, then start to lather up for what I'm really here for. Get the pressure down. Aware of movement and look up. A ring of faces watching over the wall. They know I have seen them, so they leave. I finish the job and get out. Nobody says anything.

'It is very common for boys to masturbate in the bath. There, or in the toilet, both private places. Did you ever masturbate with someone else? A boy, a girlfriend?'

What is a young woman doing walking along the roadside at two a.m.? Hitchhiking! She could be in trouble. I stop, roll down the window.
"Are you okay?"
'No, I'm not. Can you drive me home? It's not far by car.'
"Okay, hop in."
She opens the door.
"Where to?"
All the while, glancing at her, she is staring straight ahead, giving directions, otherwise silent. Hair messed up, clothes a bit dishevelled, sexy image, showing a lot of cleavage.
Shit, I'm horny!
'Here we are. Stop here.'
"I hope everything's okay."
'Thanks, I'm right now, thank you.'
"Take care, good night!"
I watch her go in, porch light goes off. I drive, stop in a dark spot. Hand cleaner in the boot. Sit back in the car with the tissues.
Doesn't take long.

Feel bad, drive home, guilty with memories of lustful thoughts but relaxed after wanking.

(laugh) At least I have a clean penis!

So weak, so sinful.

"No, I never masturbated with someone else. It was too shameful to share. It just felt bad, really weak."

'So, you didn't enjoy it ever?'

"Oh, I enjoyed the physical sensation while it was happening and the release, but even before, I felt the shame and after the orgasm I always felt... always feel it is a character flaw."

'When did you actually do anything sexual with a girl?'

"(laugh) On my twelfth birthday, and this amazes me. At the end of my primary school days, my parents threw a party and invited most of the kids in my sixth-grade class. We played spin the bottle, and I kissed all the girls there."

'How did that feel?'

"I enjoyed it, but don't remember it being sexual, in that I was not aroused. Dad and Mum were there, so I got the impression that kissing was okay. Then I can't remember kissing a girl until Glenda, over five years later. I probably did, but like at the party, sex wasn't the motivator, and I didn't feel any urge to take it further."

'Tell me how you met Glenda.'

"So, you're the new girl in the blueprint room. I'm Ford." I go in to deliver drawings and at lunchtime seek her out and we talk. She lives close by, invites me home. I meet her mother and brother, and she offers me a cigarette. I try it and choke but keep trying until I can hold the smoke in without coughing. She plays the guitar for me, then I play her guitar, and she plays a ukelele and we sing; I can manage a simple

harmony. That's fun, and I go back often.

Pay day, collect my pay packet and sign for it at the paymaster's window, open the packet and buy tobacco, rolling papers, plus twenty 'tailor-made' cigarettes, about five shillings all up. Glenda rolls her own, has nicotine-stained fingers. She is a few months older than me, and I am led by her.

"I met Glenda Bain shortly after starting my first official job at Coote and Jorgensen. They made gears and gear boxes. I started work as a cadet draughtsman and she operated the blueprint and dyeline machines, which were in a separate room but adjacent to where we worked as cadet draughtsmen. She played the guitar, as I did, so we had something in common right away."

'Tell me more about your relationship with music.'

"I made most of my income playing the guitar and electric bass, mainly the bass, and music probably saved my life."

'Saved your life! That's a big claim. So how did you get to play the guitar in a Brethren household?'

"(laugh) It was one of those lucky coincidences that changed my life. Mum had started work at Cable Makers in Liverpool and became friends with Beryl Pearson, a fellow worker living just down the road who had a son named Greg.

"I had always loved singing and knew most of the pop songs on the radio. Then, one day, Greg turned up with a white round-hole guitar. It was set up as a Hawaiian guitar and came with finger picks, a 'steel', a lyrics book and directions. The kit was sold as the Tex Morton Guitar Method for five pounds."

'Who was Tex Morton?'

"Tex was an American originally, who did radio shows in Australia, playing the guitar and singing cowboy songs. Dad loved cowboy songs and anything to do with cowboys. He read all of the Zane Gray books and anything related to the Wild West, so he knew Tex Morton's music and thoroughly approved of me learning any music that had Tex's name attached. Anyway, Greg asked me to see if I could work out how to play it and left the guitar kit with me. I won't go into technicalities but suffice to say that it was very simple to play an accompaniment to any song that used only major chords. A book came with the kit that had lyrics and chords.

"I seemed to know intuitively when the chords changed, and within a few minutes, I was playing and singing the songs in the book. I don't think I did much else that week but play that guitar, so by the next weekend, when Greg came back, I could play with some fluency and attempted to show him how to play."

'How did that go?'

"He had no idea when to change the chords or which chords to use, even with the book and in any case, I don't remember him singing, so he gave up and took the guitar home."

'And there you were, with the ability but no guitar!'

"Yes, but Dad found a guitar somewhere for a couple of pounds and I set it up as a Hawaiian guitar. So, I was soon singing away and then took it to the Opies, when they were having a musical weekend, which happened often."

'That's your friend Lindsay's family?'

"Yes, Lindsay's father, Bert Opie, was trying to make it as a market gardener. I have no idea how successful he was, except to say that he often complained that the family got no support from his brother-in-law, referred to as Uncle Doug. Uncle Doug being Doug Gilmore, who owned Gilmore Products and ran a fleet of vans that home-delivered groceries and other non-perishables, as my dad did for Rawleighs. Apparently, Uncle Doug was quite wealthy, and as Communists, the

Opies saw Doug's wealth as wealth that should have been shared.

"Anyway, I think Lindsay's mother was Dame Mary Gilmore's daughter, so there was literary talent there and social weekends with poetry and music were common. I often stayed over and was welcomed into the Communist musical fraternity that gathered there."

'Did your dad know they were Communist?'

"(laugh) No way. That is something I didn't share with him, and I am sure he never knew."

'All right. We might leave it there, and next time I'd like to go back to Glenda. She seems like an interesting person, and a big influence.'

"Yes, she was."

'But before you go, it might help you to know that children who are abused often respond by masturbating more than is usual and being defiant. So, in that way you were reacting normally to the abuse.'

I stand and look at her. She is smiling and I smile back, feeling lighter. Knowing that my masturbating had a link back to being belted was somehow a relief, as was getting the homosexual stuff out, and I'm looking forward to talking about Glenda.

Session 5

I'm running a bit late, not like me. I like to be early. The door is open. I walk in, she glances at the clock behind the chair where I will sit, smiles but says nothing.

She has had her hair cut. I liked it longer, but it is neat and makes her face look more angular, more severe. The smile is welcoming. I glance at the clock, then sit.

'You said you made most of your money playing music. How did you get into that with the Brethren looking on?'

Arriving at college, I dump my bag and guitar on the bed and see that both other beds have been taken. I know one is Stan's, but the other one has the sheets removed and folded at the end of the bed. Maybe it hasn't been made yet. I learn later that Geoff Cawthorne never slept in sheets. He never said why, and we didn't ask. The door opens and two men enter. One is slim and intense, and the other is taller, has a dark, pock-marked face and is holding a clarinet. He points to my guitar. 'Can you play that thing?'

His manner is aloof, but I have been working with some pretty tough blokes out on the dam, so I smile. "Depends what you mean. I can play a few chords."

'Do you know "Five Foot Two, Eyes of Blue?"'

"In C?" I ask.

'Let's hear you then.'

I get the guitar out and run the pick over the strings, sounds in tune and he counts off pretty briskly in 4. I play one chorus with him, then he stops, nodding his head. 'I'm Ray,' he says. 'And this is John. Band practice in the common room, seven o'clock', and they leave.

"Yes, there were a few times in my life that serendipity intervened and changed my expectations and opportunities. One of them was when I met John Speight. John was one of the best organisers of anything I have ever met, and he led the college band.

"That band was good enough to be offered paid gigs and in fact, along with Sandy Bourke, a girl in my year singing, we opened the first leg of the first Johnny O'Keefe tour in Bathurst Hall, 1955."

'History in the making. So, you met Johnny O'Keefe?'

We have come backstage to collect our instruments at the end of the show. O'Keefe is there talking to half a dozen groupies. He is openly 'auditioning' their breasts. 'You come back to the motel, you come back to the motel. Nah, not you. You come…' I'm shocked and we get out of there. He doesn't speak to us.

"Yes, I met him, and I wasn't impressed. He was monsterising young girls."

'Monsterising?'

"It looked like he was organising an orgy, and I guess the expectation was that some of those girls would be sexually compliant. I wasn't ever into the rock scene and had only one experience of a groupie jumping into my car."

'Was it that blatant?'

'Can I come with you?'

I can't help smiling. She's very pretty!

'Do you have a car?'

"Why? Why do you want to come with me?"

'I just like you, that's all. Do you have a car?'

"Yes, I have a car."

'Where is it?'

"It's right here."

She opens the door and climbs in. I'm a bit flustered.

"What would you like to talk about...?"

'Would you like to kiss me?'

"Maybe, but I'm not about to. I'm married and have a little boy."

'I don't care, you're cool.'

"I don't feel cool. Can I drop you somewhere?"

'Aren't you going to kiss me?'

"No. Listen. You're a very lovely young lady, but I'm happily married, and I don't want to muck that up. Can you understand that?"

'You're boring!'

"Yes. I had one or two latch onto me after concerts, but I was never really interested in one-night stands and even less interested in teenagers."

'What about the sex?'

"(laugh) No, not in that context. I felt pity, and also saw them as trouble. That night, I was unhappy that some of those girls left with O'Keefe's troupe. I always wondered what people saw in him, but then, I wasn't a girl seeking thrills, taking risks with pop stars.

"I worked with him many times as a professional some years later and was impressed with his ability to know what made records sell. He had the knack of for inserting hooks into songs; hooks that made them stand out and become hits. I developed a respect for his ability as a producer, so the last time I saw John it was sad."

'How so?'

"He had booked a large orchestra to record a backing track in Festival's new studio, sometime around 1974. Festival now had the best equipment, not like the old house in Pyrmont where they started.

"We played the chart. I didn't hear any goofs, but he wasn't happy, so we played it again, and he still wasn't happy. Unlike previous sessions I'd done with him, this orchestra was too large and complex for him to insert his little bit of magic, like in 'Get a Little Dirt on Your Hands' for the Delltones, where he picked up the drumsticks and showed Johnny Blevins what he wanted. 'Here, John,' he said. 'Like this,' and played a simple beat on a tom-tom: dubba-dubba-dum, and that became the focus of the track.

"Anyway, at that last session, he was getting through a bottle of Johnny Walker and eventually went to sleep on the floor of the control room. So, the guy on the panel told us to put it down again and when that was done, he asked if there were any errors and as there were none, he sent us home, leaving John there asleep.

"But there was a second round of good fortune in that first week of college that helped me become more socially adept and, I guess, that was a by-product of being in a college with about two females for every male."

'So, what happened?'

"One afternoon, soon after my arrival, I had settled in the common room with a coffee, when two senior girls rocked up and asked if they could sit with me. There were plenty of empty tables, so I knew they had an agenda, and I was amused by their approach. It turned out that they didn't like their chances of finding partners for the college ball, so they offered to teach me to dance if I partnered both of them.

"I agreed. So, after many free periods with a wind-up gramophone and Fred Astaire records, I could get around the dance floor with some skill and confidence."

'That must have been an asset.'

"Yes, at college I was able to dance at all the do's, and after college, on some Friday nights if I was not playing somewhere with John, I went to dances."

'Were there many places to dance back then?'

The room is hot. Girls are already seated along the walls. I go downstairs for an orange juice. From there, huge coil springs can be seen under the steel beams. This dance floor is regarded as one of the best in Sydney. I go back and the barn dance is starting. I pick out a free girl and ask her if she'd like to dance. Of course she says yes. This is where I get to meet the girls and arrange to have other dances together and maybe sit together later and then, after the dance, perhaps walk home together or make arrangements to meet at another place and time.

"Yes, there were. Most Fridays and every Saturday night there was a dance on somewhere. Most communities had a hall where fifty-fifty dances were held. In the early sixties, there were 2,600 venues in NSW that had a live band, employing over 7,000 musicians' union members in the Sydney Branch. Newcastle and Broken Hill had their own union branches, with maybe another 1,500 players. I was working most Saturday nights with John, so my favourite was Friday night in a hall where the Sydney University Union is now. It had a good band, a sprung floor and punkahs."

'What's a punkah?'

"In India, it is common for there to be punkahs. They are rectangles of canvas that pivot at the ceiling and wave to create a draft and are operated there by punkahwallahs."

'(laughs) Did your dance hall have a punkahwallah?'

"(laugh) No, this one was mechanically operated, but it was effective. My reason for going was to dance, but I had no girlfriend then, so I was open to the idea of meeting someone special."

'Did you succeed?'

"(laugh) Yes and no. I had many dance partners, and I loved that, but there was one girl I fancied who lived in Terrigal on the Central Coast and caught the train down for the dance. I took a shine to her and asked could I visit on Sunday. She agreed and gave me her address, so I drove up there and spent a couple of hours at her house with her family.

"When I was leaving, out by my car, I attempted to kiss her goodbye. She pushed me away and was quite angry. She said she was not that kind of girl and stomped off. I think that was the end of my Friday night dancing."

'(laughs) So you gave up?'

Tony Furness leads the new band. He suggests we go to Club Eleven to see the best musicians play. I arrive with John Speight and Ron (Rowan) Welsby. Tony has brought two girls along, Carole Tarlington and Vera Fearns. They are students at Sydney Teachers' College, so they are about eighteen. This becomes our regular table. I am fascinated by Carole. She is tiny, voluptuous, has dark blue-grey eyes that suggest some Oriental influence and is funny. Her friend Vera is the 'straight man' in their conversation. Neither Tony nor John has a car, and I offer to drive them home. They accept. I drop Vera off at Earlwood and take Carole home to Cronulla. We talk in the car for a short time, then she goes into the unit she shares with her mother.

"No. John and I had joined up with Tony Furness, trumpet, and Ron Welsby on drums. At that time Ray DeLangre was still in the band and we were busier with gigs. A new jazz club had opened called Club Eleven that offered the best jazz musicians on a Thursday night, so that became our night out. That's where I met Vera, who I would marry a year later."

'But she wasn't your first choice. Who was?'

'So, you want to marry our Jill?'

"Yes, she accepted my proposal, but she says you need to agree to it."

He is a huge man with some sort of profession. Sitting off to the side is Jill's mother and their toddler daughter. It is not a big family by Catholic standards, with two boys and three girls spread over almost twenty years, and I wonder how they managed that. He is standing while I sit at the kitchen table with a cup of tea.

'You will have to join the Catholic religion.'

I gulp.

'You will have lessons in Catholicism with the priest and sign an agreement that all children of the marriage will be brought up Catholic. How do you feel about that?'

I feel gutted. I have escaped from the damned Brethren and now am being blackmailed into another paternalistic, self-centred and oppressive regime.

I sit for a while saying nothing. Mrs Speight speaks, 'We really like you and would like you in our family, but we can't agree unless you convert to Catholicism.'

"Yes, I was in love with John's sister, Jill. But she was Catholic, and I wasn't prepared to take on their religion. Her parents wouldn't give permission unless I did, so I walked away. I had escaped from the

Brethren, and was still wounded from that, so I was determined to stay away from all religions."

'That must have been hard.'

"Yes, it was. Sometimes we are lucky enough to meet the perfect match. I felt that Jill was that and we had a ready-made family in her and her siblings that I knew and liked."

'Did your feelings for her linger on? Or were they replaced?'

"Funny you should ask that, because my friendship with John went on until he died, so one day, about three years later, I was visiting him at his parents' house when Jill turned up. She had two children by then and I was surprised at my reaction."

'Were you resentful?'

"No, the opposite. I felt a surge of love for those children and had to hold back the urge to hug them."

'Wow! So, your love for Jill was that strong.'

"Yes, but I had to move on and knew it. Her attitude to me then was a friendly indifference and that helped me turn the page."

R.C. Priest's Prayer

Give me, O Lord, my daily bread.
I promise I'll sleep alone in my bed.
I'll keep myself celibate
So I can celebrate,
Life's fun and games when I'm dead!

'You mentioned escaping from the Brethren. How did that happen?'

Dad spends all of Saturday with me up on the rafters, nailing battens into place. After dinner, we all go to the Cabramatta cinema to see one of Dad's favourite musicals. I think we have seen all the musicals that came there, particularly those set in the American wild west. But this would be his last. Dad loves his musicals and has mentioned that his mother used to take him to the circus and to movies, so the Brethren were either less restrictive then, she defied them, or joined them some time into the marriage to my paternal grandfather.

On Sunday morning Dad is keen to finish off the battens, which we do by lunchtime. After lunch, Dad takes me to the little shed to make another batch of a hundred concrete roof tiles. I mix the sand and cement, while he gathers and stacks the moulds.

We are just getting into the swing of it, with me shovelling in the cement mix and Dad forming them with the steel shaping tool, then colouring them with the powder box.

I am always in awe of Dad's ability to work with wood.

The powder box has a fine gauze base, fine enough that the yellow, blue and red coloured powders do not run through until it is shaken. Each colour has a compartment, so when shaken over the wet cement, it drops enough powder for one swipe of the shaping tool to impregnate the tile with a pattern in three vibrant colours. A frame holds the moulds in place while the cement mix and colours are combined, then a foot pedal lifts the mould from the frame to be removed and placed on a drying rack. We have finished about fifty tiles of the hundred when three black cars trundle up the driveway.

"Dad and I were making roof tiles one Sunday afternoon when the elders turned up. Dad and I watched from the little shed where we made the tiles. Dad needed to use up the mixture of wet sand and cement before it set, so we didn't go to meet them right away, but we watched them talking to Mum.

"She was clearly becoming upset, picking up Jen and clutching her tightly, so Dad hurried down, followed closely by me.

"Mum turned to Dad. She was crying. I had never seen Mum cry. She was saying that the elders had ordered her to take the 'lambs', that's us kids, and leave him because he was 'of Satan'.

"He was seen, the night before, leading us into Satan's house, the cinema.

"We were still walking toward Mum when she said that, and I will be forever proud of Dad because he did not hesitate. He must have known what the repercussions would be, but he picked up a hefty stick of timber and advanced on the elders.

"They stepped away from Mum as he bellowed at them to 'Get off my property!'

"They were not about to confront a strong, angry man wielding a big piece of wood, and couldn't get into their cars quick enough to skedaddle down the driveway and so, we were 'withdrawn from'."

'Withdrawn from? What does that mean? Is it like excommunication?'

"Pretty much. None of the members of the church would be permitted to have anything to do with us from that moment."

'So, what was the evil movie you saw at the cinema?'

"Oklahoma, one of Dad's favourites."

'How did you feel about being excommunicated?'

"I didn't feel anything then. I was an observer, but later I felt relieved and much later thankful that I was free of the Brethren, their spying on each other, the gossip, their vindictiveness, and most of all, their nasty restrictive rules that never did make sense to me. I was able to escape from their God and to me, with my history, it was a partial release from the past and the start of a new lease on life."

'You could say you escaped God through Oklahoma.'

"(laugh) Yes, I guess I could."

'And what about your father? I would think he was shattered.'

The letters start to arrive from family and people we thought of as friends. Then, just after we were withdrawn from, Aunt Clarissa died from complications following an operation for a brain tumour. All the letters bore the same message. Dad's sins had made God so angry with the family that He had taken Dad's favourite sister in retribution.

"Yes, and he remained shattered until he died at sixty-three from a massive and unexpected heart attack. His sister died shortly after we were chucked out and the family blamed her death on him. It was particularly cruel because she was his favourite sibling."

'Did none stick by him?'

"Yes. Dad's brother Frank was never in the Brethren, so he and Aunty Beryl were always there for Dad, as were Mum's brothers and sister. But, except for Grandfather Irwin Turnbull, I don't think her family was ever that judgemental. But Dad's family were extremely so."

'Did they hurt him and you in other ways?'

We hear through cousin Eddie Ray that Uncle Bill Chesterfield has died, and his funeral will be held at Warwick in South Queensland. I am living on my boat in Mooloolaba Harbour and Dianne lives close by, so we decide to drive up for the funeral. It takes us almost three hours, but we arrive well before the service is to start.

We find Pam Chesterfield, the only one of the Chesterfield cousins who has kept in touch, and we're introduced to a few others. Then we head off to find Aunt Malvie (Malvina). I remember Malvie as a bit crazy, as in zany-funny, but I haven't seen her for over sixty years and calculate that she's in her late nineties. I presume that the anger at Dad due to his sin of entering a house of Satan would have faded, but I am wrong. Dianne and I find her in a wheelchair and walk up.

'Who are you?' she wants to know, her tone not welcoming.

"Hello, Aunt Malvie, we're Stafford's children," I answer.

It is as if I have slapped her. She makes that noise that is described in literature as 'Harrumph!' and turns away. I am tempted to laugh at the silly old goat, who is so trapped in her bullshit that she can't even acknowledge her brother's children after all this time. We walk away and find her son, Colin. He is standing with his wife and daughter, clearly upset. He tells me that he is not allowed into his father's funeral service either. I know how unyielding they can be, so I suggest that the five of us repair to the nearest pub and have our own little wake.

"When uncle Bill Chesterfield died, my youngest sister Dianne and I showed up for the funeral, but we weren't welcome. I might have been tempted to go to the gathering afterwards, to say hello to cousins I had not seen in sixty years. I knew we would be offered tea and cake, but when I realised that they wouldn't mix with us while we ate and drank, requiring us to take our cake and tea to another room, away from them. By then, I saw their whole shtick as pathetic, and declined.

"Then, when I learned that even his son, Colin, had been barred from the service, I became angry and took Colin and his family to a pub for a few drinks and a chat. We managed to have a few laughs, but Colin was deeply hurt by the rejection."

'So, tell me about your father…. His death. Okay, I see that's difficult for you. Take your time.'

"No, it's okay, I just seem to cry when anyone talks about him, sorry."

'Okay, so how long before you started to grieve, to cry?'

"Oh! It was years. Many years. Twenty or more. It wasn't until I began to understand him; to understand what he went through with his family, with the Brethren. Although I knew the facts, I hadn't put myself in his place to understand what he felt.

"Unlike Dad, who imagined that God was watching his every thought and action, along with those of his family, I never felt the need to take responsibility for what my wife and kids did as he must have."

'Do you remember him ever putting himself in your shoes... to understand how you felt?... There's a box of tissues there. Take your time.'

"(sobbing) That's a good question. I don't really know. I suspect he was beaten as a child but no, I don't think he ever tried to get to know me as an individual person. I don't think he saw that as an option. His job was to control and discipline. I always felt he didn't like me, and I had to earn his affection, such as it was."

'Do you often break down when someone is kind to you, or says something kind?'

"(laugh) Yes, often. And I cry when I see kindness anywhere, even on TV."

'(smiles) That's showing empathy. Don't feel bad about it.'

She leans over and pats my knee.

'I'm delighted that you have come to understand your father. That is important. But next time, I really want to take you back to Glenda. She seems to have been an important influence.' She stands. 'I'd like you to tell me more about her next week.'

Suffer the little children

Born into Genesis,
raised by the rod.
Threatened with Hellfire,
a cruel, jealous God.

*Childhood of guilt
and mindless submission,
pleading with Jesus
for sweet intervention.*

*I argued my case.
I asked my god why?
He ne'er deigned to answer.
I wanted to die.*

*So, year after year,
after year of despair,
then came realisation:
"There's nobody there!"*

*A god manufactured
by ancients to hold
their people in thrall
and under control,*

*The god of the cross,
the star and the crescent;
a god of extremists,
terrorists nascent.*

*So, believe what you want,
and say what you must.
I've eyeballed your god,
And left in disgust.*

Session 6

The door is open, and I glance in. She looks up from her notes and smiles. I sit and wait. I am more relaxed now than I had been. I sit as she lifts her eyes from her notes.

'Let's get back to Glenda. I feel there is more to tell. You suspected she was gay but loved being with her anyway.'

"Yes. My friend Lindsay had joined the navy. We corresponded by mail but that was slow, so Glenda became my best mate, and as I have said, except for Lindsay, and later Greg, I preferred female company most of the time. I have only fond memories of Glenda. She was good for me."

'Tell me more about the sorts of things you did together, and please don't edit out anything to do with sex.'

"There was no actual sex. We've already covered the overnight stays at the Blue Pool at Engadine on the Woronora River. She organised the food, and I remember taking a sleeping bag, my guitar and not much else. I do remember wearing a Hawaiian shirt that was a bit loud, as they used to say, and I guess that said something about my changing confidence.

"I got on the train at Cabramatta, and she got on at Fairfield, two train stops along. We took up the end of the carriage where there were bench seats on either side, and we sang songs all the way to

Engadine. When we got there, it was a fair walk down a dirt track to where there was a ford, in what I suspect was the first iteration of what became Heathcote Road. Just before the river, we turned off to the left where there was a cave. We set up in there, then we usually lay down on the sleeping bag and kissed."

'Yes, you said that. But it never led to sex?'

"No, and that seemed to satisfy her too."

'Did you find that odd? Then? Now?'

"No, not then. It was fine with me and that is what we did for sex until I came home from college for the first holiday. I told you about her friend who she referred to as 'bloody Anne', who, she used to complain, would bother her. She eventually hooked up with Anne and as far as I know, is still with her. They played country music together, recorded albums of original songs and maybe still do."

'So, what happened when you came home for your holiday from college?'

"I missed Glenda a lot and thought then that maybe we would get married someday, so I took her for a motorbike ride to the Burragorang Valley, and there I was prepared to have sex with her, but she didn't even want to kiss me."

'That must have been disappointing.'

"In a way it was. But it also answered the question for me. She talked about being with Anne, and that let me know she was gay and although we remained friends, I lost interest in any romantic relationship with her and felt free to explore available females at college."

You said you met Glenda at Coote and Jorgensen, so tell me how you got that job and what happened to it in the end.'

Watching Uncle Frank at the lathe, soluble oil running over the steel as the cutting tool eats into the edge, a curl of swarf dropping away.

He finishes that cut and takes me to the turret lathe, shows me how to centre the blank in the chuck to make a pulley wheel for a V-belt drive, set up the tool and cut the 'V' shape and the boring tool to cut the hub. I am soon making belt pulleys as well as he does, and we get through the work. We knock off for lunch.

Beryl has made sandwiches. She brews tea and brings it to the table. Frank tells her how well I'm doing, and she grunts and mumbles: 'I hate boys.'

I feel bad and leave the table. This is not the first time she has made it clear that she doesn't want me there. I grab my jumper and take off on my little Waratah motorbike, the 'Wog', heading home. Frank overtakes me in his car and pulls me over, convinces me that she doesn't mean it, and I go back.

I love the job, love working with Uncle Frank and love the lifestyle. We start early and mid-afternoon, we knock off and go to the beach. Aunty Beryl loves the beach and is nice to me there.

Frank is talking about an apprenticeship, and I like that idea, so we go on, through the Christmas holidays and into February. I suspect that Dad looks at the unused tractor, thinks of the foregone contracting cash and comes to take me home.

I don't want to go. I don't care about the money, but he is upset that I'm not being paid.

"After school and Christmas 1952, I went to stay with my uncle Frank at Shelly Beach on the Central Coast. Then, it was still mainly scrub and his workshop was the only building on that section of Shelly Beach Road. He had a contract to do the turning and fitting of parts for, and the assembly, of air compressors.

"He had two lathes, and he showed me how to operate them, and I loved it. It was intended, I suppose, that I was to come home after the school holidays and get a 'proper job', but I loved working with Frank. He was a bit like Owen in that he was clever and did interesting things with metal, and he gave me a lot of encouragement, which I never got from Dad."

'So, you wanted to stay and work with Frank?'

"Yes. It just seemed to follow that I was a natural with the lathe, so why not follow on with that as a career? But Dad had other ideas and brought me home. Beryl had three boys and always wanted girls, so another boy in the house annoyed her, and she was not afraid to say so. Dad was also aware, no doubt, that Frank was not offering me any theory training, unlike TAFE would, so I would end up like Frank with a skill that might not always be recognised.

"Anyway, when I came home, Mum got the Herald Classifieds and found a position she thought would interest me. She came with me, and I got the first job I applied for, in the drawing office of Coote and Jorgensen, Engineers."

'Were you good at drawing?'

Look in the Herald. Leaving Certificate Results, and there is my name, four passes, one distinction and one fail. The fail is in technical drawing. That can't be right. I had topped the class for two years, me and John Bolton. If he came first, I came second and vice versa. Dad knows I had been doing well and takes me to see my teacher.

We discuss the paper, and he says I had answered all the questions correctly, as well as he could tell without seeing the actual paper. Dad asks for, and pays for, a remark. That's done and there is no change to the mark, with a comment that I had not answered any of the questions correctly. I suspect that I was given another student's number and he mine, if that is possible. But there is no further avenue for appeal, so the result stands. Mr Richardson, my teacher, writes me a glowing reference and with that and some sample drawings, I am accepted as a cadet engineer.

"Yes, I was good at technical drawing and liked working with my mentor, Karl, who gave me lots of room to innovate and innovate I did, catching the eye of the boss, Ray Soady, who complimented me a couple of times on how I had thought outside the box and improved an original design, so I was happy, and of course, there was Glenda right there to have breaks and lunch with, but I was not keeping up with the uni work."

'How do you mean?'

"The job eventually required a Bachelor of Engineering degree, so I was doing a part-time degree as part of the deal. That meant four nighttime lectures and one afternoon lecture per week."

'You could handle that.'

"Yes, if it was just the lectures. But it was the time of the lectures that brought me undone. Some went from 8 until 10 in the evenings, so I was not getting home until maybe 11:30 or midnight and then I needed to be up by 6 the next day to be there by 7:30. By the time winter came, I was catching colds, and in the winter, I was always cold."

'Why were you always cold?'

When I was your age, I walked to school in bare feet through the snow.

"It seems that our comfort was not considered, once we were no longer babies. I remember not having warm clothes in winter but never thought to question it or ask for anything. To be warm in bed, I remember piling on old coats and sometimes going to bed dressed. I remember mixing fowl feed in the mornings with bare hands. The water was so cold the tap sometimes iced up."

'How old were you then?'

"Just before I started school, maybe four or five, but it was my job for years until the shed burnt down. That was the end of the chicken growing part of the farm."

'How did the fire start?'

'Get up! The shed's on fire. Run down to the Brazels and get Stan!'

I run out and Mum is hosing our two-storey shed, the chicken brooder end well alight, fibro exploding. I start down the road, but there are men arriving dragging hoses.

'Bloody stupid connectors! The hoses won't fit. Get the car out!'

They drag open the wooden double doors. Fire whooshes towards the car and the men.

'Shit! It's on blocks! Can't save it. Get out!'

One small chicken runs through the flames, feathers on fire, and Mum catches it and smothers the flames. Hands it to Beryl Brazel.

Stan plays the one hose on the house wall. It is steaming.

'Get the kids out. The house could go too!'

"We think the cow tipped over a brooder to get at the chicken feed. We had hurricane lamps keeping the chickens warm. Dad was in the army, the car was on blocks, and Aunt Ella's furniture was stored in the loft. We lost the lot, including those of Dad's tools that weren't in the unfinished lounge room where he worked when he was home. It was a huge setback."

'Were you insured?'

"(laugh) Insured? You're kidding. Dad believed God ran everything. He wouldn't even vote."

'I will overthrow the throne of kingdoms, and I will destroy the strength of the kingdoms of the heathen'.

"We were taught that we were the only people who really knew what God wanted of us, so engaging with the community was not what he sought, and I suspect that taking out insurance was in that category.

"Of course, he worked for wages sometimes but was never happy working for other people. "All his family members were self-employed whenever possible. He was very independent, and he seemed to resent spending money on anything that was not income-producing. Although we always seemed to have plenty to eat, he did let us know we were lucky."

'When I was your age, the youngest got the top off the boiled egg, then the middle kids got half the rest, and it was only the working adults that got a whole egg. We had bread and butter or bread and jam, but not both. If it rained, we got wet', Dad is fond of telling us, so I don't feel entitled to ask for a coat or shoes.

We need decent shoes and respectable clothes to go to Meetings, so Mum takes me to Mark Foy's to get shorts and shoes. She makes my shirts and knits socks and jumpers and gets hand-me-downs from Wally until Wally stops growing and his clothes are too short in the arms and legs for me.

"Second-hand stuff was given to us sometimes, but I rarely wore shoes, even in winter. At our school, very few boys did. In fact, I can't think of any boy who wore shoes to primary school. The girls did, but maybe it was because of the war and clothing was rationed, but until I had my own money, and that didn't really happen until college, I never had adequate clothing.

"I remember walking down George Street with John Speight in that first winter after I started teaching, and he asked if I was cold.

The street was funnelling freezing air right through my shirt and light jumper. John wheeled me into a men's clothing store and insisted that I buy an overcoat. I had no money, so he lent me the twenty pounds.

"At Parramatta High, I never had a uniform."

'Were uniforms not compulsory?'

'Ray, this is a first-class high school, so the least you can do is wear the uniform and those sandals are not to be worn to school. By next week, have the uniform or you will be on detention. Understand?'

"Yes, sir."

"(laugh) Yes, they were compulsory, and I was the only boy not in uniform, but somehow, I knew that if I brought up the question of a uniform at home, that would be the end of my schooling and I did like school, particularly in those last two years. There were no students there who knew me from before, so the shame dropped a quantum. For some lessons, my stutter was less pronounced, and I could debate points with my classmates and teachers.

"By then we were not permitted to attend Meetings, so I didn't really need good shoes, and I had no closed shoes that fitted me. When I was pulled up again for wearing sandals, I said I had tinea and needed to air my toes."

'Did you have tinea?'

"Yes, but that wasn't the real reason I wasn't wearing shoes. I was pretty good at lying, so I said that to get them off my back. For the tinea, the closest I got to treatment was Mycosol powder. I'm not sure if it did any good, but it did poison me once."

'How did that happen?'

We are travelling by train to Armidale. At Central, I buy a chocolate. It is July and cold. I eat a few squares and put the rest in the pocket of my old army greatcoat with the can of tinea powder. I doze off. It is hot in the train. I wake and reach into the pocket for some chocolate and eat some more. It is very soft from the heat and doesn't taste too good, but I'm hungry and eat it anyway.

Dad meets us at Armidale train station, and we walk to the Dodge truck. I have a splitting headache. I complain. Mum tells me to shut up and stop whinging, so I climb onto the tray of the truck and sit. We get to the sheep station where Dad and Uncle Walter have been working.

They lift a tent-shaped corrugated iron frame onto the truck and tie it down. Under the 'tent' they throw some blankets and there is a box with plates, mugs, cutlery, and a billy can. There is food, like bread and potatoes, tea of course, and some bags of straw for beds and we set off for home via Ebor.

"I put a bar of chocolate in the same pocket as the tinea powder. The train was hot, and some powder got into the partly melted chocolate. In the dark, I reached into the pocket for the chocolate, ate it and poisoned myself. I had the worst headache I have ever had. I was nauseous and felt wretched."

'What did your parents do?'

"(laugh) I was told to shut up and stop whinging."

'Did they know you had ingested the Mycosol?'

"No, and I didn't know either until later, when I took the chocolate from my pocket and saw the powder embedded in the re-formed chocolate. But I suspect that even if they had known, the response would have been the same."

'Did they often show disregard for your safety? Was that a characteristic of your upbringing?'

We get up early and go to Dunker's in the Dodge. All of us go: me, Eleanor, Bill and Jen, Mum and Dad and Lindsay. Mum has brought food for a couple of days and there are blankets and pillows. Dad ties a rope to the back of the Dodge and to the front of a 1928 Reo truck. Dunker assures Dad that the motor is 'in good nick' and that is all that matters. The plan is to tow it to Springwood where the motor will be repurposed to power a new breaking-down saw.

Lindsay and I are to steer it and apply the brakes when necessary to prevent it running into the back of the Dodge. It has a timber-framed cabin with no doors. We get in. The gear stick has been broken off just above the floor, and I try the footbrake. Even after furious pumping, there is no footbrake. We have only the handbrake.

Off we go. Lindsay has the handbrake in both hands, his feet against the dashboard. We are going well until, coming into St Marys, a motorcycle cop waves Dad over and stops his bike in front of the Dodge. The Dodge's brakes have always needed pumping, and we can see it jerking as he pumps. It is a race to see if he can stop before running down the cop's bike or with Lindsay pulling as hard as he can on the handbrake, we can stop before running into the back of the Dodge. We manage to avoid a double accident and the cop walks up to Dad's window.

'How far are you going?'

'Just up the road,' says Dad. 'Not far.'

'Okay,' says the cop. 'Take it easy.'

Up Lapstone Hill and I can imagine the rope parting. There is no way the handbrake will hold us going backwards on that slope. I have decided that if the rope breaks, I will rear-end the Reo into the shale cliff on the other side of the highway. But it holds, and we are okay until we are on Hawkesbury Road and going down the Golf Links hill.

We are catching up. Lindsay is losing the fight to hold it back. We *can see Eleanor and Bill at the back window of the Dodge and imagine them yelling at Dad to go faster. I am sure Dad has the accelerator flat to the floor, as dust rises around us, and the tailgate of the Dodge comes closer, closer, almost touching. I have given one hand to help Lindsay – and at this speed, the steering really needs two hands. At that moment, the road flattens out and the gap widens.*

"There used to be what we called Dunker's Junk Yard in Prairie Vale Road, Bossley Park, when all around were paddocks with cows and the occasional horse. That's where we bought our spare parts.

"Dad bought a Dodge truck from a bloke named Jack Snarball, near White Cross Corner where Winmalee is now, in the Blue Mountains. I went with him to look at it.

"Jack had run off the road and hit a tree, stoving in the front. There were broken wooden slats in the roof where his head hit, and I wondered how he didn't break his neck.

"Dad reckoned it only needed a new radiator, a grille, and maybe a water pump, so he bought it for twenty pounds.

"When we pulled it apart, the water pump axle had pushed a hole through the number-one cylinder, so the motor was wrecked too. We found an engine block at Dunker's and rebuilt the engine. When the engine was going and Dad tried to drive it, he found that the differential housing, the banjo, was also cracked, so it needed a new diff.

"Eventually he fitted a diff from an international truck. The diff gear ratio was lower, which meant that the Dodge was slow but strong. Anyway, he needed to tow an old Reo that he and Eric wanted to use to power a breaking-down saw to Eric's property at Springwood, so Lindsay and I steered the Reo with only a very inefficient handbrake and rickety steering. Any one of a dozen calamities could have befallen us on the way, but we made it intact."

'That seems a bit careless of them, to put you in harm's way. Was that the only time he did that?'

"(Laugh) No, he had me and Lindsay in a roof space of a house he was building during the heat of January, painting all the timbers with creosote after borers had been found. We were probably in danger of suffocating. We survived, but Lindsay suffered from creosote poisoning due to cuts in his hands, which took months to heal. Dad wasn't interested in that.

"When I was about twelve, I remember him loading an old car onto the Dodge tray that could have ended up with the car upside down with me underneath.

"He had backed the truck as close to the side of a steep slope as possible, then, because the car had no tyres, he put two sticks of four-by-two from the front wheels onto the tray and I was given the job of steering it over the gap and applying the brakes when it got there. I remember the timbers under the wheels bending alarmingly, but they didn't break, and we all survived.

"He once had me dive down about six metres through a fallen tree that was underwater in the dam to retrieve a canoe. There are too many to mention them all. But, somehow at those times, I trusted him."

'(laughs) Maybe you shouldn't have.'

"Maybe not, but what could I say? I was ordered to do these things, and I did them. There were never any arguments tolerated. It was 'Do as you're told or get the strap'."

'Do you think those situations led to your own risk-taking behaviours?'

The Dean kid is sitting on the disc harrows. We are coming toward the house. I put the tractor into top gear, and we are speeding up. He is bouncing and crying, but I keep going for a while. I stop and he runs to his mother. She says nothing, but that will be the last time he comes over to play.

"I did a couple of things that could have killed somebody. I gave a kid a ride on a set of disc harrows once. If he had fallen off, the discs would have cut him into slices. I wasn't really emotionally competent to drive such potentially deadly machines, and I certainly took risks."

'So, why were you driving tractors at such an immature age?'

"I first drove the Dodge on my own when I was about eight."

'How did that happen?'

"On the night before, it had rained, and Dad couldn't get over a clay section of the Booralla Road hill, so he left it where it stopped. There were no other vehicles in that very short street, so he could do that.

"Next day he rode his bike to work and by that afternoon when I got off the school bus, there was the truck sitting on dry ground, so I started it up and drove it home. Mum couldn't see my head because I could hardly see over the dashboard and ran outside to see the truck turn into the driveway and stop. Then I got out."

So, you were handling machinery from a very young age?'

Dad wants to plant fruit trees come winter, so it is time to plough the patch to root out the blackthorn. I start the old steel-wheeled Fordson, and I know the wet multi-plate clutch will not work for at least ten minutes, but I have learnt to ram it into first gear and while it warms up, drive it to where I want to work, thus saving the time the clutch takes to warm up and become operational.

It won't go into first gear, so I pull the gearstick back. It goes into reverse, but I can't get it out. It is idling but has a governor, so it is slow. It starts climbing a vertical post, which is also part of the back wall of the dunny, as its power increases.

I wrestle with the gearstick, but now it is under load it will not budge. The dunny wall is over halfway to being flattened, so I pull the 'kill knob' and the wheel slides slowly down and the tractor is still, but the dunny is seriously out of kilter. I go to get Mum who first of all laughs, then says we could get a chain and try to pull it up again.

We do that, and it works to a point. The wall is almost vertical and the dunny seems no worse for wear, and that remains our secret.

"Yes, as I said, I now know that I was not really mature enough to be trusted with potentially dangerous machinery. I once almost destroyed the dunny, basically because I was not strong enough to force the tractor out of gear. Another time, coming home from a ploughing job at Hoxton Park, I could have killed myself.

"I was on a fairly steep downhill grade, when I became impatient with the speed of the tractor, so I threw it out of gear. That was okay for a while, then the tractor started to bounce sideways on its big balloon tyres. I could see that bouncing would only get worse, until it overturned, so I gingerly applied the turning brakes with my toes, and little by little brought it back under control."

'You were barefoot?'

"I was always barefoot unless I really needed to wear shoes."

'Did you ever tread on something sharp and hurt yourself?'

"(laugh) If I had been wearing shoes when I was out of control on that hill, I would not have had the dexterity to use those brakes to slow the tractor. But there were a few times I had serious injuries from not wearing shoes. Once at Coromandel, that's at Grandma Turnbull's, I trod on a piece of rusty wire, and it went right through my foot behind my toes."

'Ooh, I bet that hurt!'

"Yes, it hurt but that was not the worst of it. Remember, this was a dairy farm, and the wire was rusty, so I was a good candidate for tetanus."

'Did you get treatment?'

"(Laugh) Yes. Grandma bathed my foot in Condy's Crystals and when I cried from the pain, she told me to 'shut up'. It didn't become infected, so I survived that one."

'There were more?'

"Oh yes. We lived on land that was infested with blackthorn."

'Which place?'

"Both. I haven't seen such blackthorn infestations anywhere else since. Not like it was there and then. Of course, as I wore no shoes, my feet were forever being pierced with thorns."

'What did you do about that?'

"(laugh) I now wonder at my suppleness. I could sit on the floor and have the sole of my foot facing me so I could dig out the thorns with a needle. There were no thorns in the house yard, but there were always nails sticking out of timber and all sorts of hazards, but the worst wound was self-inflicted. I was splitting blocks of wood for the stove."

'How old were you then?'

"I must have been eleven, but I had been splitting blocks of firewood for a few years before then. One of my jobs was to keep the woodbox full. I must have been a bit careless, because the axe ricocheted off a block of wood and sliced my left big toe on the knuckle. Dad bundled me off to Liverpool Hospital where the wound was stitched after a lot of carrying on."

'Carrying on?'

"Yes, my skin was so tough the doctor couldn't push the needle through and had to send for a pair of pliers, which he used to stitch my toe. Unfortunately, the wound became infected, and the stitches opened up."

'So you had to go back?'

"No, I was given a bottle of Dettol and treated it myself. It healed eventually, but there is a pretty impressive scar there.

"Then, once I was riding my motorbike on a road that was being graded. The grader was on my side of the road, so to overtake it, I had to ride through a ridge of soft dirt thrown up by the grader blade.

"I had no shoes, and my feet were hanging off the foot pegs. What I didn't see was a fair-sized lump of rock in the soft dirt and I crossed at the exact spot, crushing my toe back against the peg, breaking the knuckle.

"I was fairly close to Parramatta, so I went to the hospital there and had them look at it. I don't know what they thought of this grubby urchin with no shoes claiming his toe was hurt on a motorbike, but they said there was nothing they could do and sent me on my way. That knuckle never did heal properly, and at times, is painful to this day. There were other foot injuries, but I reckon I have fewer foot problems than most people my age."

'(laughs) I was hoping to explore your early sexual experiences. There is a big gap between sixth class and Glenda. So, were there no special girls in those years?'

I get off the train at Cabramatta and in front of me is a girl about my age. She has short, very black hair peeping out from under her Parramatta High School hat. It is near the end of the school year. I am in the middle of the Trial Leaving. I know she is not in my year, so maybe she is in the year behind. Next day I look for her and sit on the train where I can watch her.

She seems unaware of me.

I go up to a girl who had been sitting with her and ask her name and next afternoon, I follow her home. I knock on the door. A man answers. He has her features, clearly her father. I introduce myself to Mr Timmins and tell him I would like to visit his daughter, Nancy. He is a bit nonplussed.

He asks: 'Here?' I say yes, and he calls her to the door. She doesn't seem surprised to see me there, so maybe she was taking notice. The next day is Saturday, so her dad invites me around for afternoon tea at three. I drive down in the Chev and pull up outside. The curtains twitch and when I knock, I am ushered in by her father, introduced to Granny and told to sit beside her.

Everyone else seems to be engaged in the kitchen, so I talk to Granny. We chat for a few minutes, then she stops talking and starts to choke. She becomes worse, so I call to Nancy, and she runs in. Nancy calls her mother and very soon everyone else is there and Granny has stopped choking. In fact, Granny has stopped doing anything.

"I once tried to get to know a girl from school who lived near Cabramatta train station. I was about to have afternoon tea with the family, when her grandmother, who was speaking to me seconds earlier, dropped dead in the chair beside me. I was forgotten in the melee that followed until the ambos left. Half of the family was crying, and I was still sitting there like a stunned mullet until Mr Timmins said: 'You'd better go.' And that was the end of that romance.

"Nancy did send me a telegram of congratulations when the exam results came out, but I was totally spooked and never followed it up."

'Oh dear! That must have been traumatic. So, you never saw her again?'

"I must have seen her at some other time, because I remember playing tennis with her at home, where I had pushed the dirt around to make a tennis court shape and size, the lines marked with used engine oil. We did put up posts for a net, but we made do with a length of fencing wire stretched across with no net, so maybe that was before I went for afternoon tea. In any case, the romance didn't get started."

'Were there others?'

"Early in my last year I had a crush on a girl in my class at Parramatta High named Peggy, but she had a boyfriend who played football and was a bit of a hunk. They went to college together and eventually married, so that was a fizzer too."

'It's a shame about Nancy. Next time, I would like to go back to the job at Coote and Jorgensen and what happened there to make you choose to go to Teachers' College. Okay?'

I smile as I leave. Teachers' College was one of my happiest times and just the mention of it brings pleasant memories.

Session 7

She meets me at the door with a coffee in hand. I glance at it and up to her eyes. She is smiling.

'I'm running a bit late today, so I missed my coffee break. (laughs) I must have my coffee.'

She moves inside and hands me the coffee. There is another coffee on her desk. I thank her.

'I thought it would be mean to drink coffee in front of you. You're a "flat white" person, aren't you?'

I take the coffee and sit.

"How did you know?"
'(laughs) It's the most popular coffee among men of a certain age.'

She moves her coffee closer and turns to me.

'What happened that caused you to finally make the break with Coote and Jorgensen?'

I am so sleepy, but the rattle of the points coming into Cabramatta Station wakes me, until they don't. I look up at a black guy in a uniform. He has the other hand on a broom. He is shaking me. I sit up, and he looks relieved.

'*You frightened me, man. I thought you were dead!*'

"Where am I?"

'*Hornsby, in the marshalling yards.*'

"Shit! What am I doing here?"

'*(laughs) I'd hazard a guess and say you were sleeping.*'

"I must have slept through the Cabramatta points."

'*Cabramatta! (he laughs) A bit more than that, man, you've been to Liverpool and back to Central then up to Hornsby. You must have needed that sleep!*'

"I guess. How do I get out of here?"

'*You can go to the edge of the lines (he points) and find your way to the station. (He points again) That way.*'

My bag is beside me, and my wallet is still in my pocket. I stand and walk to a door. There are steps at the door, and I can see the station.

"Soon after I started there, it was sold to Borg Warner, and we moved more into automotive gears for Holden and Ford mainly. I suspect that's when work ceased on a stepless speed-change gearbox we had been developing – when the ownership changed. But in the drawing office we were doing the same sorts of work. It wasn't the work that was too much for me. I loved the actual drawing but was constantly tired from travelling to and from lectures and lack of sleep. I was catching colds and at one time had tonsilitis that required treatment with sulfa drugs."

'So, did you resign then?'

We are handed our exam papers for physics. I light up a Gauloises and read the questions, understanding about half of it, and feel beaten. The old lecturer looks around the room and must have read the mood. 'If rape is inevitable, the best thing to do is relax and enjoy it.' We laugh, but there is no jollity and even some embarrassment, including mine. I go through the motions but know I have no chance of passing, and passing is a condition if I am to keep my job. I feel hopeless and don't see a way forward.

"No, I don't remember resigning then, but about six months before I did resign, I was approached by one of the 'checkers' to join him in a new venture."

'Checkers?'

"Two senior draftsmen checked our drawings to make sure there were no errors, like the steel type stipulated, the diameter of bolts, their strength and loads, all that technical stuff. They were senior engineers and were called checkers, so the paper drawings went to the checkers and then to the tracers who would reproduce the drawings in ink on tracing paper, which we called 'onion skin'. 'Onion skin' was, as you would expect, a transparent material, so the drawings could then be reproduced as blueprints or a less permanent method called 'dyeline'. Dyeline was quicker but would fade in time."

'How technology has changed!'

"Yes. Anyway, Frank Wooden, the senior checker, approached me to work with him in a new business as his apprentice. His business would be housed in an old garage at Ulamambri, near Coonabarabran and would be set up to recondition machinery, tractors particularly, in the paddock if necessary."

'I bet you went for that.'

"Yes, I did. I was a bit desperate because I was not handling the uni work. The idea of living in the country, working on tractors, away from people who might have known me, and my shame, was ideal. By the way, my very first love, when I was five, turned up at our office as my boss Ray Soady's secretary. She had been in my class from kindie until sixth class and was also a neighbour, living in the house just past Rawlings' shop.

"She recognised me, but we never spoke, and her presence, along with her refusal to recognise me, was a painful reminder of my shame from primary school days. So, I resigned and off we went. Frank with his new wife and his wife's brother in two 1928 model Dodge cars that Frank had reconditioned to be like new, and me on my Wog. One of the Dodges was set up as a mobile reconditioning workshop."

'Clearly, it didn't work out, because you ended up as a teacher.'

"Right. It was very hot, early January, and at Coolah, the Wog spat out its piston rings, so I sent it home to Dad by train and rode with them the rest of the way. We arrived in Ulamambri at an old farmhouse that was in a lane with neighbours opposite and on the other side, an acreage where an older man was living with a younger aboriginal woman.

"A comment was that she worked for 'two quid a week and slept with the boss'. I remember feeling dismayed at that remark, but I had a room to myself and was keen to start work, so soon forgot about it.

"We opened up the premises in Ulamambri and waited for business. We did sell petrol, but that was all we sold. I started going out to shoot rabbits to eat, which I did a lot of the time because if it was not my turn on the petrol pump, there was nothing to do."

'What did you do for fun?'

"Frank's brother-in-law took me to visit the nurses' quarters at Coonabarabran Hospital a couple of times, where we sat around and talked to half a dozen nurses for an hour or so, then went back home.

I don't know if he made any contacts, but I didn't.

"There was a big water hole in the river near the house where I swam and met an older girl who lived across the lane. She invited me over."

'Did you go?'

"Yes, I went over to see her, and it must have been after dinner because she was already in bed where she slept on the veranda. I had seen her in her swimmers earlier that day and made some stupid remark that she 'had nice legs'. She laughed, pulled back the bedclothes and invited me in. That scared me off, so I politely declined and left."

'Was the offer repeated?'

"No, and within days I was gone. With no money coming in, Dad must have phoned Frank because Frank put me on the train home. Dad must have also spoken to the boss at Borg Warner, because they welcomed me back. But that didn't help with my failure to succeed with the uni work."

'Was it then you decided to go to college?'

Stan picks me up at Merrylands Station on the Matchless and we head to town for our Thursday afternoon lecture. We have plenty of time to eat our sandwiches, so we head for the far end of Hyde Park, north along Elizabeth Street towards St James Station, and it begins to rain.

Stan turns right, but the front wheel catches in tram tracks, and we go down. The bike looks okay, but I am bleeding from the arm, and we are shaken up. Nobody steps from the kerb to help us, so we push the bike over to Hyde Park and sit. I wind a handkerchief around the wound, and it stops bleeding, so we eat lunch, and decide that we are finished with uni.

"I had made a friend at uni, Stan Nightingale, who shared some lectures with me and was having similar problems with study. We both had friends who had gone straight from school to Bathurst Teachers' College and were happy there. So, one Thursday in July 1954, we skipped our afternoon lecture and presented ourselves at the NSW Department of Education to apply for a teaching scholarship. They were very happy to have us and signed us up to start in February of 1955."

'Did you stay with Borg Warner until college?'

"No, my pay there was about three pounds ten, and as most of that went on board and travel, I had very little for myself. Our friends at college let us know they were receiving almost as much in pocket money alone, with accommodation, food, and tuition free.

"My old Wog was dead, and I wanted a motorbike for my time at Bathurst, so Stan and I took off for his parents' place in Hill End."

'What was at Hill End?'

"I'd been there with Stan to visit his parents, so I knew what it was like and before we left Sydney, Stan had lined up a job with Bush Leaf Dick."

'Bush Leaf Dick! Now I am intrigued. What did he do?'

"Bush Leaf Dick, I don't know his real name, had a still mounted on a semi-trailer with which he extracted essential oils from the leaves of native trees.

"We were taken out to properties on a truck and our job was to collect leaves from a particular species of stringybark tree. There were no chainsaws in those days, so we first chopped down a tree, hacked off the branches, then with a machete, stripped the leaves, collecting them on a tarpaulin. We then bagged them up, identifying which bags were whose with coloured beads. Mine were blue.

"At the end of the day, our bags of leaves were weighed, and we were paid two-pence-farthing a pound. For me, that worked out at about eighteen pounds a week – good money in 1954."

'How long were you doing that?'

Stan is yelling something and holding his wrist. Mike and I run over and see he has sliced his wrist with the machete. The wound looks deep, and blood is spurting out. Mike grabs the first-aid kit from the truck, and I use my limited knowledge from a short course at uni to stem the bleeding and dress the wound. I bandage it tightly, but it is still bleeding.

I apply a tourniquet to his upper arm. The bleeding stops, and we get him into the truck. It takes us almost an hour to reach Sofala Hospital. I take the tourniquet off a few times, but each time the bleeding starts again.

We deliver Stan to the nursing sister, the only senior person there. She examines the wound and assures us she can 'stitch him up', adding 'you boys look a bit shocked, so a couple of beers might help'. We have two schooners each, then pick Stan up at the hospital and head back just in time to knock off. Stan is on compo until Bush Leaf Dick leaves.

"We must have started in about late August because I remember frosty mornings and warm days, but by the time that job ended it was hot. I was paying Mrs Nightingale a couple of pounds board, but I was banking most of it. We continued until late November, then Bush Leaf Dick said he had enough stringybark oil and was moving to the north coast to harvest corkwood leaf."

'Do you know what the oils were used for?'

"Yes, the stringybark oil was used by dentists to stop bleeding, and the corkwood oil was used by ophthalmologists and optometrists to dilate pupils."

'Interesting. Did you and Stan go straight from there to college?'

"No. I still didn't have enough to buy a motorbike, and Stan's wrist had healed. There were no other jobs in Hill End, so we approached what is now Centrelink, the Labour Exchange in Bathurst. Asparagus picking had just finished, but the Department of Works was looking for labourers for pick-and-shovel jobs at the Perthville River Dam, now called the Ben Chifley Dam, near Bathurst."

'I'm guessing you took it?'

"We'll take anything. We just need work until college starts in February." He looks in a ledger and runs his finger down a list.

'Nothing here that suits your qualifications, but we do have vacancies for some labouring jobs that pay fifteen pounds plus four pounds living allowance. Interested?'

"What is the living allowance for?"

'You bring your own food, but they supply you with a place to sleep, a place to cook your food and eat it and four pounds to make up for the discomfort. But that shouldn't worry young coves like you.' He smiles, expecting us to agree. We nod.

"When do we start?"

"Yes. By that time Stan had traded in his Matchless for a BMW."

'Car?'

"(laugh) No, a bike, but a bit posher than the Matchless scrambler he had been riding since I met him. So, we arrived with just about all our worldly possessions on the back of a motorbike and were shown to our huts."

'Did you take your guitar?'

Seen all the sights of Hill End, tried fossicking, no luck, tried fishing, no luck. Really miss music. Find a one-gallon oil drum and attach a piece of two-by-one, shape it, carve a bridge, drill holes for tuners and carve them. Stretch fishing line from the end of the neck to the back of the oil drum and glue on matchsticks as frets.

"No, I left that at home, but I did make a ukelele from a rectangular oil drum, some scrap timber, fishing line and match sticks for frets."

'It worked?'

"(laugh) Yes, but tuning was too difficult to maintain, so it went into the dump eventually."

'So, you left Hill End for Perthville?'

"Yes. Next morning, we started. The job was to dig vertical shafts to anchor what would become the concrete spillway. It was steamy hot down those shafts, so we needed to drink a lot. Water was provided by a spring nearby that oozed clear water and silicon flakes, but we drank it.

"The shafts were big enough for about four of us to work together. The first week went well and we celebrated with a couple of beers in the Perthville pub. We also discovered a paddock of unharvested potatoes on a farm that had been resumed for the dam, so we had free potatoes done every possible way. We spent some time over one of the early weekends gathering rose hips from the roadside, from which I made syrup that resembled extract of malt to have on our toast."

'Sounds like you were enjoying Perthville.'

"Yes, we were. But there was no entertainment at the camp, so we cooked nice meals and even had dessert almost every night."

'What did you have for dessert?'

I am baking chips and have chops grilling on the stove top. I have opened a can of peas, so that's the meal. Stan is cooking a pot of custard and is opening a can of peaches. I am watching the chops but turn around as he yells. The peach can is on the floor, peaches and juice running between the planks and he is holding his hand, blood dripping. I turn back to the stove, push the chops and custard off the heat and lift his hand for a look. Clumsy bastard!

He had pulled at the jagged lid of the fruit can and sliced right through the web between his forefinger and thumb. I have heard that such a wound is serious, so I help him onto his bike and drive him to Bathurst Hospital.

Apparently, it is serious, because he comes out with his hand plastered, his arm in a sling and a certificate to say he is not to use the hand for three weeks.

Back at work, he is given a job in the office – one finger typing and answering the phone.

"(laugh) We weren't there a week and Stan had sliced his hand opening a can of peaches. His hand was encased in plaster, so he was given a job in the office while I was digging myself toward China. I worked hard, but there were two older men who must have been sent there to keep them off the dole. One in particular smoked constantly and coughed pitifully and could barely lift his shovel. But he was tolerated by the foreman who sat all day on a fold-up chair reading comics."

'Did that upset you?'

Bert is leaning on his shovel, a home-rolled smoke dangling from his bottom lip. He digs in the shovel and lifts a few grains of dirt and throws them out, then coughs, leans on the shovel again and has a puff of his smoke. He lifts a few grains again and coughs. The big boss arrives, and the foreman stands and comes over. Bert digs in the shovel and lifts a good load of dirt and throws it out. The boss moves away, and Bert leans on his shovel to roll a fresh fag. I just keep going at my usual pace.

"Not really. He seemed to not pay us any attention, but one time I was chipped for being a bit slack. I didn't put on a show for the boss when he came around while some of the others did. But the foreman must have known that I did as much work as most of the others put together, so I thought he chipped me because he had to show he was doing something for his keep."

'Yes, sitting reading comics doesn't set a great example.'

'Hey, Ray,' the foreman yells as I climb out of the shaft at knock-off time. 'You're a farm boy, aren't you?' I go over. The others have gone back to camp or home, and he leads me back to the shaft where water is oozing in. 'What do you know about pumps?'

"He was perhaps a bit more observant than I gave him credit for because he came to see me after work and offered me overtime if I came down early and pumped water out of the shafts."

'So that was a bonus.'

"Yes. I dropped a hose into the hole, primed the pump and started the motor. Once it was drawing, I could leave because when the pump sucked air it cut out. Then just before we started digging, I came back, and if there was more than an inch or so, I would give it another short burst. They paid me for two hours at time and a half, but really, it took me fifteen minutes max. I pointed that out to the foreman, but he just winked and said it might take longer some days, so 'cop it sweet'."

'Did you have a break at Christmas?'

No pay for me over the holidays, and still not quite enough to buy a good bike. I look for a short-term job and find one at a parking station that is in the basement of the first building up from the tram sheds at Bennelong Point. Eight pounds a week for five days a week. I tell them I can do only three weeks, and they are happy with that because it fills a holiday period for another employee.

"I got a job for three weeks in Sydney, parking mainly doctors' cars. They would toot at the kerb, and I would drive them to their chambers in Macquarie Street."

'I bet you got to drive some nice cars.'

"(laugh) Yes, there were Jags, Bentleys and Austin Healeys, but many had a compact English car called a Lanchester that I have never seen anywhere else before or since. It featured leather seating, a pre-selection gear box and had automatic greasing, with tubes radiating out to all grease points from a tank under the bonnet. Between deliveries and pick-ups, I serviced the cars."

'Were you the only one doing that?'

He looks like Jimmy Edwards, with huge moustaches, but is tall and lean, with a military aura. We are taking a tea break. For him, it is a break from what I can't imagine because I have never caught him doing anything physical. He is the manager.

"Were you ever in the army?"

'Boy, when I was in Kenya, we had the Mau-Mau to contend with. A more murderous gang of bastards never walked this earth, and I knocked over a few of them, I can tell you. Look.' He opens a drawer and there is the biggest six-shooter I have ever seen. He closes the drawer. 'And if any of those savage mongrels show up here, I know how to deal with them!'

"There was a manager who came over from Kenya and he directed my work, telling me which cars needed a grease and even checked that the parked cars were no more than an inch apart. He had them organised so the nearest to the door went first. He was a bit of a cheat too.

"When I ran out of distilled water for the batteries, he filled the dispenser with tap water. If the owners knew, they would have been horrified, but Sydney tap water is a bit acid, so really it probably didn't matter as much as I had been told by Dad and Owen, who went to great pains to catch rainwater in glass bowls for their batteries."

'So, after the break, did you go back to Perthville?'

I ride up on my bike, a second-hand Royal Enfield five-hundred twin and park it beside my room. Stan is here already, and his hand is out of bandages.

"How was the holiday?"

He looks a bit sheepish. 'I went to Melbourne, and I have to tell you they have the best beer.'

"Melbourne? How could you afford that?"

'They pay the office staff holiday pay.'

I stare at him and shake my head. We have been working together since August and he has managed to avoid hard yakka for most of the time. I can't believe it.

"Only for a few more weeks. I had the bike. But it took all my money, and I really wanted a few pounds in the bank for clothes. I only had working clothes and knew I would need more for college.

"Would you believe it, while I was parking cars, Stan was in Melbourne on full holiday pay. Because he worked in the office, he was classed as staff and was on full pay for the three weeks, seeing shows and drinking beer!"

'(laughs) That must have hurt.'

"I did think it was a bit unfair, but there was another story concerning Stan that sort of fits the pattern. About ten years after we graduated, I got a call from him. I had left teaching so I could do daytime music work and was working as hard as possible, taking anything that came my way, plus running a new business.

"I was always pleased to hear from him, but the reason he rang was that he had been appointed to a school with no kids. Imagine that! He was receiving a principal's salary with no kids or staff for two years. (laugh) Only Stan could do that."

'What was the business you started? Was it to do with music?'

I look at the clock. "It's a long story."

'(laughs) Yes, you're right. Let's talk about it next time.'

They are good memories, and I leave smiling.

Session 8

I am trying to remember the layout of my office and how it all worked when she walks in and hands me a coffee, smiles and sits, crossing her legs. She is wearing red shoes.

'You looked deep in thought.'

"I'm thinking back over fifty years, trying to remember the exact layout of the office. It was unique because it had to be super-efficient to work as I had envisaged, and that required some special equipment that I needed to build."

'It seems you were already busy, so why start a new business?'

"Good question. I was in the Musicians' Union Committee, and we had been looking at the performance of the Union Booking Office, now with a telephonist and a manager. It was probably August or September, and it was brought to our notice that for the whole of July that year, the Booking Office had sent out only one musician. That one musician would have been paid scale plus ten per cent, and that ten per cent, probably about five dollars, coming back as commission was the total income for the office for one whole month."

'That isn't viable.'

"Of course not. So, I put together a proposal to fix it.

"I told the committee the story of one gig, in about 1959, when I was booked through the union to play guitar in a band at St Marys

Golf Club. When I got there, I found myself working with three other musicians I had never met, and none of them had met any of the others, which, had it been a reading band and there were charts, might have worked, but it wasn't.

"It turned out that the pianist played only in the key of C and the saxophonist played only in standard keys, so that meant that for about three-quarters of the time they couldn't play the same tunes together."

'Goodness! What did you do?'

"Well, for songs in C we just played the songs, alto first chorus, piano second chorus and if it was a bit short, guitar third chorus and then the alto played it out, but for the others, I played the first chorus with the alto, then I modulated to C for the piano to have a chorus, played one myself, then modulated back to the standard key to play the last chorus with the alto. It was hard work, but it exposed a basic flaw in the union's booking service.

"It made more sense for the office to book a bandleader who could bring along people he or she could work with. So, when I saw the results for that month, I put forward some solutions to the problem that could make the booking office more attractive to potential employers. Unfortunately, those ideas included the need to prioritise the more skilled of our members and leave the personnel up to bandleaders.

"That part of the proposal was what killed it. The other committee members pointed out that such an approach would let non-union musicians in to do union jobs, and that some members, those not in a band, would get no offers at all. So, we were stuck.

"The problem of gigs going to incompetent musicians stayed in place because they were all equal as members and had the same rights to offers. You can see the problem."

'Of course. If incompetent people are turning up for jobs booked through the office, employers will go elsewhere to find bands, and it looks like that's what happened.'

"Correct. So, I worked out a system that would offer any employer a choice of the best available, and a booking system that showed at a glance whether that person was available at that time. That meant that any employer who rang my office could be guaranteed the best available, and in the same call, could book that person or persons."

'Did you have a computer? When was this?'

"About 1973."

'So, no computer?'

"(laugh) That depends on our definition of a computer. I made displays that showed every musician's name and every booked gig, divided into morning, afternoon and evening for every day for four months in advance."

'How big was this thing?'

"Not as big as you might imagine. I made displays that looked like huge cotton reels, about 75 centimetres high on axles. The ends were round, but inside the ends, there were four vertical flat pin board panels, about 40 centimetres wide, covered with paper and lined to show the musicians' names, instrument, day and time of day booked for one month on each face.

"We used coloured pins – a red pin to show the request had come in for that person at that time, then that was replaced by a green pin when the booking was confirmed with the musician.

"There was a separate reel each for woodwinds and brass. Guitars and bass shared one, as did keyboards and drums, so there were four reels mounted on top of a horseshoe-shaped desk, with two rotary phones, so that anyone ringing in never had to hear a busy signal.

"When someone rang to book a musician, or in some cases twenty or so for a big session, I could read off who was available and jot down the name of each one they chose. That usually took ten minutes tops, unlike the days it took to book a session before I set it up.

"The next step was to see where the musicians were and often they would be working, grouped in a few recording studios. So, I could call those studios and confirm the bookings. I would also need to call the odd one at home."

'How did the Union feel about that?'

"They weren't all that happy. My nomination for the committee for the following year was found to be ineligible because I was late paying my dues. (laugh) Anyone standing for re-election was usually informed beforehand if they were not financial, so they could fix it, but I wasn't.

"I also kept ghost diaries of all the musicians so that bookings further out than four months could be entered, but the main reason was so I knew where they were during the day and could contact them. There were a few over the years who had no phone, so my office became their vital connection to their employers.

"Just a short time ago, Paul Baker, who was a very busy session musician back in the day, reminded me that when he moved to Colyton, he had no phone and called in several times a day to get his bookings."

'Did you run this by yourself? How did you find the time?'

"(laugh) I did run it myself for most of the first year. We charged only two dollars per week to belong, so it was cheap, particularly for those who received many bookings through it, but with the numbers rising, it became profitable, and as soon as it was profitable, I could afford an operator and hired one.

"The first one was Dot Gavenlock, a delightful personality who left for a sailing adventure with Alby Mangels that was filmed and became a documentary. She was replaced by Gael, who I lost when she married George Golla.

"Gael would beat me to the newspapers in the mornings and have the cryptic crossword half done before I got to the office. When Gael left, I stole Mary Cockley from EMI with a fifty per cent rise in salary and she stayed until Vera's overdose, when I moved with the kids to Wollombi.

"Mary found it difficult because the office was in the basement of the house. It had a separate entry, but I think she began to feel some responsibility for Vera, and I can't blame her for not wanting that."

'What happened to the business in the end?'

"Vera wanted the business, so she got it in the property settlement. She had help, but within a year or two it died."

'That seems a shame.'

"Yes. For the first year or so, I came down to Sydney on weekends for gigs and spent part of Saturday checking the bookings and doing the books, but when I got the job at Long Jetty, I no longer came down and I think it was too hard for Vera, particularly the out-of-hours calls."

'Were there many of those?'

"Not many, but when they happened, the problem was urgent for somebody and therefore important to me. I had one call in the early hours of the morning from a ship in Bass Strait. Apparently, their alto player had jumped ship in Perth, and they needed a replacement for the Melbourne to Sydney leg, so I waited until a reasonable hour and by mid-morning had David Glyde on his way to Melbourne."

'Impressive!'

"Yes, but to do that, I needed a good knowledge of what was required and of the abilities of anyone I sent. Vera knew the musicians socially but lacked knowledge of their abilities and limitations. It needed an experienced musician or someone like Mary who worked constantly with studio musicians to make it work. Like anything else, one mistake brings down the reputation and we couldn't afford mistakes.

"I also started to write a news sheet that went out with the bills, so that was fun and gave me something to do while the phones were silent, which was a lot of the time."

'Can I take you back to your relationships? It seems to me, and I think you now get it, that in most of your relationships, you were chosen by your women. Was there any time you had that 'across a crowded room' encounter where you were clearly the instigator?'

"(laugh) Yes, except for Nancy Timmins, there was one, and I will not use her real name because it would cause problems for her, and I don't want that.

"It was at a Daly-Wilson party. I can't remember where or why, but I looked up and saw a young woman who immediately tugged at me. I just had to go and say hello. She looked like Morticia from the Addams Family, with a slim figure in an ankle-length black dress and shoulder-length straight dark hair. There was no way I could have picked up on potential co-dependency this time, but there was something that drew me to her, and I went."

'Did that come to anything?'

"Yes and no. There was no doubt I was in love at first sight, and she responded with enthusiasm, so it was a love affair. We saw each other as often as possible, usually after gigs, and I took risks to be with her. That went on for maybe a year, but Vera was becoming unstable again.

"I sensed that she thought there was someone else. On the other hand, I knew she was having sex elsewhere and even had a letter from a colleague warning me, saying that she tried to seduce him while I was asleep in the next room.

"But there was always the worry that she might overdose again, and I was not sure that if she died, I could survive that, and that was the conundrum. I knew it was a toxic relationship and we needed to separate, but I was terrified that she might succumb to a fatal overdose.

"At home, we went through the paces. I brought in the money; she kept house and cooked. The kids were fed and clothed and sent off to school. My clothes were always washed and, I blush to say this, shirts ironed, but it was becoming clear that I would need to break from her and separate if I was ever to have a satisfactory sex life and a relationship where I could relax knowing we could trust each other.

"There was one incident when we were still at Orange Grove Road, when Ken Bennett was working in Green Valley and stayed over. We had dinner and sat around having a drink, then we all went to bed. Much to my surprise, Vera initiated sex, so of course that happened, but I had an uneasy feeling and stayed awake afterwards.

"She waited until she thought I was asleep, then got up and I heard her go into the room where Ken was and close the door.

"I was torn between leaving it to Ken to handle it or getting up and interrupting. In the end, I knocked on his door and he said to come in.

"She was in her nightdress, sitting on the side of his bed. His look said it was not his idea, and Vera scrambled back into our bed. Nothing more was said, but Ken never stayed over again.

"Anyway, I was really dreading another of Vera's overdoses and called it off with 'Morticia', telling her I was extremely worried about Vera's state of mind, and she accepted that.

"By that time, I had bought the Wollombi property and spent most of my free time there fixing fences and getting the house ready to move into."

'Next time, I would like you to think of anything that happened that caused you great regret. I know you take anti-depressants, so I'm looking for causes of your depression. Okay?'

"I can think of a few, but one stands out and that's the death of my much-loved uncle, Eric."

'The same Eric who landed on his head trying your lift?'

"The same."

She stands and hands me my sunnies. I nod, smile and leave.

Session 9

The room is open. She is not there, but I walk in and sit. I have been thinking about Eric for most of the week and it still brings great sadness. She enters carrying two coffees and hands me one.

'I bet you have been going over the events that led to Eric's death. I hope it hasn't been too hard. How long ago was it?'

"1973, so a long time ago. In a way, it followed my dad's death, and that was the third from that generation within a few months. Before we got home from Dad's funeral, we heard that Ella, Mum's sister, had died of a heart attack too. So, for Mum and Eric that was another shock to contend with.

"Then, in the Christmas holidays, Owen, Eric and I decided to bring Dad's trailer-sailer from Tewantin near Noosa to the Maroochy River for one last sail. From there, I would take it home. Mum had no use for it and as it was in the water all the time, it needed to be antifouled, so it made sense for me to have it.

"I had never sailed Dad's boat and in fact had very limited experience of ocean sailing. Eric and I had helped Eleanor and Dmitri sail their old yacht from Clontarf to Botany Bay, so we had that short exposure. We were ignorant of so many basic rules that the trip was foolhardy in the extreme.

"We had the weather forecast, which was favourable, and we took a blow-up mattress for a life raft. But we had no life jackets.

"In all my years of sailing various dinghies and small yachts, I had never worn a life jacket. It was as if the need to wear one did not apply to me. There were none on Dad's boat, so maybe that's a clue, and nobody suggested that we should get any."

'Was it just you and your uncles on the boat?'

"No, and the potential for an even greater tragedy was set up when David and two of Mum's friend Val's sons came along. They were in their early and mid-teens.

"We left Noosa and raised the sails, but I soon found that the sails were not professionally made, and they were very unbalanced, which made steering under sail difficult. But we had the motor and plenty of fuel if we needed to motor all the way. With an onshore breeze and low seas, we felt safe enough and were on schedule to get to the Maroochy River well before dark.

"The plan was to hug the beach and slip in between the beach and the bar, but a fog came in that made it difficult to know how close in we were, so Eric was at the bow looking out for the bar.

"By thirty years later, when I was sailing my 54-foot steel ketch, *Heavy Metal*, around the coast I had learned a few tricks, such as crossing bars on an incoming three-quarter tide is ideal. The inrush of water pulls the bottom out of waves, so they flatten remarkably as the water shallows. But we came in on a low, outgoing tide and in the mist, Eric could not see the bar, and we came in right over it.

"The first I knew anything was amiss was when the boat lifted on a breaker, and I could see the bottom through very shallow water. The centreboard was not one that pivoted, so it dug in, and the breaker rolled the boat over.

"The rigging snapped, and within seconds, the boat floated out, upside down, the tide pushing it back into deep water. I was thrown clear and surfaced to see that David and the two boys were okay. David was close by, but Eric was further out to sea with Val's boys. Owen was still in the cabin where he had been sleeping, so I dived in and guided him out.

"By the time I had Owen out, David and Val's boys had clambered onto the upturned hull, but Eric was nowhere to be seen. The boys said that Eric had told them to swim over to me, and he would follow.

"It was still misty, and we were in deeper water, still being carried further out to sea, so I took the fuel tank for flotation and swam to where I had seen Eric earlier. I kept at it until I was so tired that I was in danger myself and swam back to the boat.

"By this time, there was a rubber duckie there and we sent it to search for Eric, but they came back to ferry us to shore and then tow the boat up the river where they beached it.

"Norma was there by then, and because we couldn't believe that Eric, who was the strongest swimmer in the family, could have drowned, she persuaded the pilot boat crew to look for him. Norma and I went too, and we searched until dark with no luck.

"Next day, Norma took the Volvo, which they had only just bought, to a reserve overlooking the river mouth and was scanning the sea when the Volvo rolled down into a gully, stoving in the front.

'Was the body found?'

"Yes, he washed up on the beach at Alexandra Headland three days later, and I volunteered to identify him. (pause) Sorry, he looked like he was asleep, apart from some skin discoloration.

"The cause of death was drowning, but some of us think he must have had a heart attack that incapacitated him but didn't kill him outright. That would explain his disappearance when we all knew he could have swum to the boat easily and the fact that I couldn't find him."

'How awful for you all.'

"Yes. It was a tragedy for his family and for the family fortunes. They had bought the Volvo on the promise of the sale of some of their Springwood land for a subdivision, although by then, they were living in a house on a block that was Eric's but part of the Coromandel property.

"When Eric died, we think the developers and their real estate partners saw an opportunity to get the land for less. I don't know the details, but I think the land deal was withdrawn, and the land not rezoned, so Norma sold it at a much-reduced figure.

"The land was rezoned after the developers had bought it. I know it sounds pretty low, and it probably was."

'So, how was your relationship with Eric's family after that?'

"Mmm. Well, the girls pretty much treated me the same, as did Norma, but Geoffrey was cooler for a while. But I stayed at his farm near Nundle with Sally and the kids a couple of times, and he has been okay with me at various family occasions over the years."

'What happened to the boat in the end?'

"I did take it home and it sat in the front yard at Earlwood for a few months until I decided that the repair job was beyond me, and in any case, there were too many traumatic memories attached to it, so I sold it with the trailer and sent Mum the money."

'So, what did you draw from that tragedy?'

"Not much. I was too emotionally devastated to look at it properly, so the mistakes I made did not become clear until I did some courses in sailing in the early 2000s and then sailed *Heavy Metal* along the coast, using that knowledge to safely navigate bars.

"Going north from Sydney, there are many harbour entrances with formidable bars, but even the entry into the Sandy Straits, which is one of the most difficult, became easy. I still have the occasional nightmare that features me on a capsizing boat, so it never went away."

'What about Owen?'

"(laugh) I have no idea. He said he was asleep until he was tossed off the bunk, then found himself kneeling on the cabin ceiling, chest deep in water, surrounded by cushions from the cabin seats. He never came sailing with me again, not that I asked him to."

'Do you think they trusted you to know enough for the trip?'

"Yes, and that is what haunts me. I didn't know nearly enough, but ignorance is bliss, as they say."

'Yes, indeed.'

She looks at the clock, then at me, and smiles.

'We have a bit of time left, so tell me something that happened that was a magic moment. You know, something attached to a memory that makes you smile.'

"(laugh) Well, there were many magic moments, but if we are talking about romantic moments, there are two, with one so magical that I sometimes think I must have dreamt it.

"But it did happen and at a time that I knew the marriage was over but hadn't yet taken the decision to move out. There was no sex at home unless Vera initiated it, and that was extremely rare, but I hadn't thought, or had the opportunity, to get it elsewhere. There was nobody else."

'So, this was before "Morticia"?'

"Yes, maybe six months, and I had been touring with a show from Japan called *Tokyo by Night*. The lead was a singer who was a big star in Japan. Her backup acts were two young men who dressed like the lead characters in a popular TV series at the time, *The Samurai* and *t*heir female partner was so exquisite that she took the breath away. She dressed in just enough to hide very little but keep it classy.

"Remember, this was in the 'Hair' era of stage nudity, so in the background were two topless models and a chorus. So with the band of three, Barry Stewart, Warren Ford and me, we filled a bus, crisscrossing New South Wales for about three weeks, finishing up in Taree at the RSL.

"For much of the time on the bus, some of the girls sat with me to practise their English. They knew a lot of the language, but pronunciation was what they were working on.

"The 'magic' happened at the end of the last day of the tour. One of the managers suggested that I take one of the 'samurais' fishing, so I hired a boat and some fishing gear. We spent most of an afternoon catching nothing, but it was lovely out on the water.

"On the way back, the young man stopped me to ask about the obelisk that sits just below the RSL in the park beside the river. It was a war memorial, just like others to be found in parks right over Australia to commemorate our war dead. He wanted to know what it was for, and I explained that it commemorated servicemen and women who had fought against Japan in the Second World War.

"The look he gave me was one of complete disbelief, and he said, 'No. War with US, not Australia!' He had no idea that Australia was involved."

'For young people like him it might have been all about Hiroshima and Nagasaki.'

"Hadn't thought of that. You're probably right. Anyway, that night was our last show, and we were all sitting around afterwards having a few drinks when I felt I needed to go to bed. A day on the water always makes me sleepy, so off I went and was soon asleep.

"Something woke me, probably the door closing. I looked up and there was Eco (Etchko) Namazawa, the exquisite creature I had watched dance for three weeks and helped a little with her English translation, undressing beside my bed. I didn't say anything, maybe because I knew that of all the girls, she was the least proficient in English, but mainly not to break the spell.

"When she was totally undressed, she pulled back the covers, slid in beside me and snuggled up.

"Of course, I was aroused, and she soon took care of that. I expected her to maybe sleep there, but she rolled out of bed, dressed and was gone."

'Did you ever get a hint as to why she did that?'

"Next morning Barry gave me a knowing look that suggested he might have had something to do with it, but nothing was said, and it remains a mystery to me and always will."

'So, all of your sex was not transactional.'

"(laugh) No, that certainly wasn't, and because it happened at the end of the tour, I never saw her again, although I have thought of her often and wonder what she did after show business, what her life was like."

'As you would. Well, that's enough for today. Next time, I want to go to your time at college and your sexual experiences there.'

"Not much sex happened there, at least not for me."

'Okay, but it was two years of your life spent in close proximity to a lot of females, and by sex, I don't necessarily mean intercourse. But if not much happened, that's interesting too.'

She stands, and so I do. I pick up my sunnies and walk out as she says,

'Sometimes the absence of something tells us something that is as important as if it had been present.'

Eco Namazawa
Stage doll of Nippon
Dancing through my
Nights of magic.

Body of grace and
Exquisite face were
Beyond lust.

But while I slept,
She came once unbidden
To my room.

Waking to soft hands,
I should have, but could not
Send her away.

Session 10

I am right on time. I knock and open the door. She is sitting in her chair, reading notes, and there are two coffees on the desk.

'Hello, right on time.'
I point to the coffee. "For me?"

She nods, places her notes on the desk and picks up her notepad. I take the coffee and sit in the usual chair, take a sip. She rests the notepad on her knee.

'It must have been easy for you to find a girlfriend at college, with so many females to choose from?'
"Funny you should say that, because girls were far less on my mind than the music we were playing in the band. In first year, I did have a couple of friends who were girls, and we hung out together, but the relationships were less sexual and more companionship, not that we lacked companionship in the dormitories."
'So, there were no offers of sex?'

Karen is pretty and has a lovely figure. She is in second year and has a bit of a reputation. Her boyfriend, Joe, is a big guy, blonde and handsome, and I would have thought a real catch, so I suspect there must be a problem when she asks me to take her for a ride on my motorbike.

I am more curious than keen, but I don't refuse. I get the bike, and we meet outside her dorm. She has swapped her college blazer and skirt for a loose-fitting jumper and jeans. I can't help thinking of Marlon Brando in the The Wild One. She climbs on and hugs me tightly.

I can feel her breasts against my back, and she is not wearing a bra. I'm more uncomfortable than aroused. We ride a few miles, then I stop at a small park, and she slides off. I prop the bike on its stand and as I turn around, she kisses me on the lips and holds herself against me.

"Yes, a very sexy second-year student, who was publicly in a relationship with someone else came on to me out of nowhere."

'How did you handle that?'

"(laugh) I took her for a ride on my bike and we had a chat. Frankly, I was very uncomfortable. She was not wearing a bra under her loose-fitting jumper and clearly wanted me to do more than look, but there was still Glenda in my thoughts, and I had never gone past kissing. I was also loath to be part of a plot to hurt her boyfriend, Joe."

'So, did you do anything?'

"She kissed me, and that was nice, but I wasn't ready for even that, so it stopped there."

'Did she ever try again?'

"No, she went on seeing Joe and married him after college, so I still don't know what that was about."

'Were there any other offers?'

Sitting sideways at a table in the dormitory common room, reading and smoking. Ron comes up and starts to chat. He is in his pyjamas, which is not unusual in itself, but then he leans against me, and I can feel his penis against my arm. I am uncomfortable but don't want to hurt his feelings. He's a nice guy. I wait and he talks for a few minutes longer, then when he sees that I'm clearly not interested, he leaves.

"There was one guy in my year who I noticed was a bit effeminate and he let me know that he fancied me. I managed to keep him at arm's length, and he eventually gave up. He wasn't the only gay man there, but he was the most obvious."

'How did you know of others who were gay?'

Mark Kelly's flat. Bathurst Radio 2BS crew Christmas party. Steve is there. That's a surprise. What's his connection? Two women, eight or so men and we are playing 'Cardinal Puff' – drink a tumbler of wine from the two-gallon cane-bound jug, say a tongue twister, make a mistake, start again. A way to get pissed really quickly.

I'm not comfortable. It feels like I might lose control. I'm not a drinker. I go to sleep on the lounge.

Wake. Look around. Lights low, no women. Just blokes moving around nude... what are they doing? Steve is there in the middle of it. He sees me looking. Need to piss. Stagger into the toilet. Mark follows.

'What would you do if I kissed you?' He's close as I wash my hands. I turn, and he grabs me.

"Don't, Mark, not interested!"

He just walks away, then Steve is there, dressed, inebriated, haggard, defeated.

'Can you give me a lift back to college?'

I don't see Mark until ten years later in the canteen of ABC Channel 2 TV. He is walking toward me with a coffee. He still looks the same. I'm glad to see him... fun, late night recording sessions at 2BS.

"Hi, Mark, how you doin'?"

'I'm not Mark!' He hurries past.

"Sorry!"

What happened to him? Jail? At that time, homosexuality is still a crime.

"There was one other student, Steve Schaffhauser, who was gay, but not openly, and I suspect Greg Katahanis might have been gay too."

'What was your relationship with them?'

"As you know, I was not gay, so they were just friends. But Steve, in particular, was important to me in a couple of ways. He was the editor of the annual student magazine and encouraged me to write for it, which I did."

'Do you still have the magazine?'

"Yes, and it is really cringeworthy, but after I discovered he was gay when we both attended a party that ended in a nude homosexual orgy, which I escaped but he didn't, we found in each other a person we could confide in.

"I talked about the pretend homosexual stuff at school and the ongoing shame. He understood how I felt right away and advised me to write it all down, then burn the paper. I did that, and it helped me forgive my younger self and was the start of real healing."

'Did Steve stay on as a teacher?'

"No. As far as I know, he worked off his bond, then went to Germany where he became a film producer."

'How about Greg?'

"Greg was a fine artist and came from urban Sydney so his choice to teach in rural Papua New Guinea is an odd one and there is a story I must tell you that is attributed to Greg, although he never mentioned it in letters to me, so maybe it's a myth. The story goes that he reported for duty, was flown to a remote bush airstrip, and left there with the only sign of civilisation being some aviation fuel drums and an assurance that the Australian ranger 'would be along shortly'.

"So, Greg waited with his bags of school textbooks and personal stuff, then just on dusk, a khaki-clad figure emerged from the forest leading a gang of Highlanders carrying loads of tools and camping gear. 'You must be Greg,' the ranger said, and I will call him Martin for the story, 'I'm Martin.'

"Greg was relieved to see him, looked around and asked: 'Where's the school?'

"Martin laughed and waved an arm to indicate the bush all around. 'Where would you like it?'

"Greg's letters suggested that he would not last long there, but later I learned that he went on to bigger things, eventually lecturing at Port Moresby University, so he must have adjusted, then thrived, which I'm very happy about. He was a very caring human being, and I liked him a lot."

'(laughs) I can't imagine the shock, being dumped into the middle of nowhere with his background.'

'Now back to you. Did you have any significant sexual events at college?'

We are on the back seat of an FJ Holden, being given a lift back to college by a couple I don't know, and we are kissing. She is wearing slacks and a jumper. It is becoming pretty intense, and I slip my hand down the front of her pants. A sweet musk scent wafts up. It is a pleasant, exciting smell, but I am aware that the other two in the car can probably smell it too, and I withdraw my hand.

"There were two, one potential and the other happened."

'Tell me about the one that happened.'

"I had partnered up with a girl in my year, a redhead with brown eyes. Again, she was a friend rather than a sexual partner, as I would now define it, but one night when we were being given a lift back to college by friends of hers, I remember we were in the back seat of their car, and we began kissing and that became more intense. For the first time, I wanted to take it further and felt for her clitoris, not that I knew then what that was and its importance."

'So, how was she with that?'

"She was pressing herself against me and kissing harder, but the scent rising from her was strong and I feared the couple in the front seat would recognise it and know what was happening."

'So, you stopped. What did your friend have to say about that later? Anything?'

"Yes, when we were back at college, she asked me what I thought of that, and I said something like it was just like touching another part of me. I didn't mean that it meant nothing, but rather that it was comfortable."

'So did that, er, friendship continue on?'

"No, not then, and I don't know why. In fact, there were long periods when I had no special female friend and was more interested in the music and of course, I went back to Sydney for many of the weekends to play in John's band, when couples were more likely to go out or spend time together.

"Very late in life, I realised that if I had married her, my life would have taken a much more comfortable trajectory."

'What makes you think that?'

She is showing off her skill as a baton twirler, and I'm a bit embarrassed by it. There doesn't seem to be enough difficulty to make it exceptional. It appears to be an activity that leads to no practical use. I say I'm impressed, but I don't know that she believes me. We look at photos of her wearing a crown in a pageant of some sort, but she is not that sort of pretty. We seem to be together by default. I'm looking for something more exciting, more edgy, more interesting.

"I just didn't go on with it, lost interest."

'Was she too "ordinary" for you?'

"Funny you should say that. Maybe that was it. I seem to have needed to be special and mix with special people. People who were not 'run of the mill', and I probably saw her then in those terms."

'But you changed your mind?'

"Yes, but not in time to do anything about it. She married a nice bloke and went on with her career."

'So, you never saw her again?'

"(laugh) Oh, I saw her again all right, and there were a couple of incidents involving her that I now smile at, but at the time were risky."

'Do tell!'

"A few years later, one of my colleagues was best mates with her husband. We met again at social events, then she turned up as a teacher at the girls' school next door, and we were thrown together, producing a musical for the kids.

"I had trained a few of the teachers to play instruments, and there were a couple who were already skilled, so we formed a band to accompany the production. I think it was *The Mikado*. She did the directing, I ran the music, and it was a great success."

'How long after college was this?'

"About eight years."

'That's quite a while. Was it still awkward?'

"Not until I made it awkward. I hope it isn't my ego talking, but I got the impression that she had taken that position because I was there. There were signals, so I rang her one night when I knew her husband would be out and we arranged to meet, basically to finish what we started at college and have a fuck."

"Hello!"

'I was wondering if you'd ring. What are the other guys doing?'

"Playing the pokies, I never do."

'Me neither. I was hoping you would contact me. We never did get to do it, and I always wondered...'

"Me too, we could meet maybe..."

'Yes, Tuesday nights he goes to his lodge meeting, and we could meet near home. We would have a couple of hours at least. Meet me at the corner of Henry Lawson Drive at eight. Okay?'

"Yes. No gig Tuesday, eight is fine. I'd better get back."

'See you Tuesday.'

'How did that go?'

"(laugh) Not as well as we had envisaged, I'm afraid.

"We went to a beach on the Georges River, near where she lived, and after a bit of kissing and fumbling, she lay back on the sand and I dropped my pants. Then, and we had been too distracted from our environment to notice, it started to rain. We ignored it until I got sand on my penis and the attempted entry was impossible. We just laughed at the absurdity of it and went home."

'Was that the end of it with her?'

"No, an opportunity came up and we did it. We found ourselves in a car, doing some shopping for the group of friends I had joined on a skiing weekend near Cabramurra."

'I didn't know that was a popular ski area.'

The group arrives at the old farmhouse on Lake Eucumbene we have hired for the Easter weekend to fish for trout. We sort out the house space, get the fires going, and then it starts to snow. By next afternoon, there is enough snow to ski, so we take off for Smiggin Holes and hire skis. There are no lifts operating, so we are limited to trudging up the hill and skiing down. I have an idea and suggest we come back another time and by then I will have built a rope tow.

In my garage, I put it together. I have the old Wog motor, a Villiers two-stroke, rebored and I fit new rings and bearings. I use part of the frame to attach it to a plywood slide and above that, the rear wheel minus its tyre as a windlass, and it's ready. I find a large pulley wheel for the other end, and one of the guys splices a rope, so it is endless. By locating the motor and winch at a high point above a steep grade and tying the pulley to a tree at the other end, we have a thirty-yard rope tow.

"It wasn't, but for some reason, maybe because we had no money, we needed to do the ski holiday on the cheap. We stayed in the same old farmhouse, and we avoided ski lift charges, which were significant for us, by me building a portable ski tow. That meant we could ski wherever there was snow, free of lift charges."

'Your own ski tow. Did it work?'

"Yes, to a point. It worked fine, but it was a little too slow, and the rope was too short for it to be satisfying. I had underestimated the speed it needed to go, so even at top speed, it felt slow. At the end of the holiday, we left it there because nobody was prepared to cart it back to Sydney.

"Anyway, there we were, just the two of us, returning from shopping. There was no traffic, and she turned to me and said: 'Are you thinking what I'm thinking?'

My answer was to pull off the road, and we did it there."

'How did you feel about that?'

"Wonderful. Firstly, she wanted what I wanted and that took away the fear of rejection, a constant in my marriage. Then in the middle of it all, she says: 'Give it to me!' I took that to mean she wanted my sperm and that was a revelation. She didn't want my money, my house, or the security I could offer. All she wanted was my love and my sperm."

'That begs the question. Why didn't you go on with it?'

"We never discussed it. We both had marriages, we both had children, and I think it was understood that we didn't want to destroy all that. But we had answered a question.

"We liked sex with each other, as far as I understood it, and we left it there. She never brought it up, and I never pursued it, so that's where it stayed. I felt good about it, and I think she did too. The big change was that I felt that maybe I was not the 'dud fuck' Vera said I was."

'Can we go back to the college years. Did you form any love interests outside college... in Bathurst?'

1956 in the Continental Restaurant, singing for our supper with John Payne. Spring, but cold. We stop for a break, and he moves to join the mob around the open fire. By the time I get the guitar off, the circle has closed, and I would need to push in, so I walk outside for a smoke.

It's cold, but I sit on the step, then look up to see a red Citroën Light 15 parked at the kerb right in front of me. New, glistening chrome and lovely lines. I stop smoking and let my eyes wander over it. I had never seen a car like it. White leather seats, sweeping mudguards...

'Would you like to drive it?'

She is tall, backlit by a streetlamp. I can't see her face as she waits. She can see me.

I stand up, toss the cigarette, and walk around the car, not to see more of the car but to see her. She has shoulder-length mousy hair, huge blue eyes, big enough to be a symptom of something medical, and a lovely smile that is shining out of her face. I hadn't noticed her inside, but she must have followed me out.

"Are you sure?"

She nods. Then, 'Yes, please do.'

She hands me the keys and walks to the passenger door, gets in. She is serious.

We drive slowly through the night, talking. Out to Orange, back through Blayney, stop at Blayney on top of a hill where we kiss. We kiss for a long time, then she drives back to college where she drops me as the east is beginning to glow.

I think that is the last time I will see her, then an invitation to her twenty-first birthday party arrives in my mailbox. She is a few weeks older than me and a hundred years wiser.

We spend a lot of evenings together with the car. She is almost naked, but I stop there. I feel a dread of going further, and she picks up on that.

Months later, I realise what I have missed and go back to try to continue the relationship, but she is engaged, and my chance has passed.

"Yes, there was one that maybe I should have married. She was wise and lovely, but I was a baby."

'Why do you say you should have married her?'

"She was such a wholesome person, (laugh) you know, no apparent hang-ups, no need to be saved and that was the problem, I now suspect. And she chose me."

'Was that how most of your female friendships started, or did you initiate most of them?'

"(laugh) I thought I initiated most of them, but now I doubt it. But I had never noticed her before, so it was clearly her choice. She invited me into bed with her too, and maybe that was what frightened me off in the end."

'Tell me about that.'

"It was nearing graduation time, 1956, and a town girl, Joan, offered me a drive of her Citroën Light 15. I loved the look of the car, gleaming red with chrome headlights and flowing lines. It had front-wheel drive, which I had read about but never experienced, so I was hooked and accepted the offer.

"She was great fun, and we hung out together for most of my free time, and most of my nights over the following couple of weeks. Then she invited me to her twenty-first birthday party and told me to bring my pyjamas and sleep over.

"Well, the most memorable part of the party for me was one particular LP on her record player. It changed my life in a way, but I annoyed everyone at the party by playing it over and over with my head in the speaker."

'What was it?'

"Downbeat Poll Winners, 1955, with Julie London, Barney Kessel, Ray Brown and Shelly Manne. That was guitar playing like I had never heard before, and I wanted to learn to play like that."

'And you did?'

"Well, to a point. I practised and studied, and I did work at music and got some recognition for guitar playing, but that wasn't what I became known for."

'Okay, so tell me what happened with Joan.'

"Not much to tell really. I stayed over and of course we had all been drinking a bit, so I needed a toilet in the early morning. I was totally sober by then, and on the way back she called to me. I apparently had her room because she was in a bed in a sort of nook, so I went in, and she invited me into her bed."

'Did you get in?'

"No, it was too public, and anyway, even when we had been alone in the car, we never went past kissing and cuddling, so I went back to bed and then it was graduation. I became quite ill again from quinsy, like when I was trying to do uni in Sydney.

"My immune system was weakened from all the late nights with Joan, and I might have died if it wasn't for the intervention of John Payne's mother.

"I had a raging fever and was passing in and out of consciousness when she saw me through the infirmary window and called a doctor. I missed my graduation and as soon as I was well enough to ride the bike, I was gone."

'So, what did you feel about her and sex?'

"I honestly do not remember ever making the connection between feeling aroused and actual intercourse with any girl I was with. Of course, I knew the mechanics of it, but it seemed too fraught, and I blocked it off.

"There was an iron door between being aroused and intercourse. I don't know why, but it was there then and stayed with me well into adulthood. I know I broke through eventually, but the scars were always there and still are."

'Can you tell me more about Carole and Vera, and what happened there. Because, as you say, the iron door was breached eventually, and I'm interested to explore what was different to allow that to happen.'

"Carole was my first romantic interest after Jill. It was romantic, but not really sexual. I was attracted to the sexy package and must have been aroused, but I can't remember ever kissing her. She was a bit exotic, and I was afraid to touch, I think. Now, in retrospect, it was closeness I craved, the cuddling, and I needed to be needed."

'So, you saw sexual relationships as basically transactional?'

Late Sunday afternoon, we have dropped Vera off, and I take Carole to her house. We go inside and she is throwing clothes into a suitcase.

'Can you drive me to Parramatta? I'll miss the night express if I get the train from here.'

I am wondering how anyone could be so slack not to have worked out the timetable, but I am here, I have the car, and it would be mean to refuse. I agree, and we race across the city to Parramatta.

At the train station, I help her with her luggage, but we have just missed the train. We think we can beat it to Penrith, but we are again too late, so I drive her all the way to Bathurst. A quick peck on the cheek is my reward, then I drive home alone, arriving just in time for a shower, then gather my books and race off to teach my almost fifty kids in three classes at Glenfield.

"I once drove Carole to Bathurst because she missed the train. I felt a bit of responsibility because she had been out for the day with me and Vera. I don't think I expected anything in return, as in a sexual favour, but when college holidays came around, we made arrangements to go out."

'You were living in Cabramatta, and she was in Cronulla. That wasn't just around the corner.'

I arrive at the appointed time and knock on the door. Mrs Tarlington comes out. She is an older version of Carole, smoke in hand. She knows who I am, although we had not been introduced yet.

"Hello, Mrs Tarlington, I've come to pick up Carole."

'Well, you're out of luck. She's out for the day.'

I'm puzzled. How could she forget? I leave. She is at the next Club Eleven concert and apologises for messing up the previous Sunday. I accept that and we arrange to meet on the following Sunday.

I arrive a little early and again she is not home. I take that to be a clear sign that she's not interested in a relationship with me and go home upset.

"No, it is a fair way, and she stood me up on the two consecutive dates. We had arranged to go out, but when I arrived, she wasn't there.

"These were times when home phones in south-west Sydney were rare. We had no phone, so the reaction to my terse message left with her mother that she 'could find another dope to drive her around' was not known by her immediately. But I'd had enough."

'I don't blame you.'

We are packing up to go home and she arrives unannounced at school. She looks dishevelled, so unlike her, and I think she is trying to look sexy, again unlike her. I am still angry at being stood up and can hardly talk to her.

"But that wasn't the end of it.

"Mid-week, Carole arrived at my school just as we were locking up. That required a lot of effort. Electric trains came only as far as Liverpool, so she needed to get there first, then fluke an appropriate steam train to get her to Glenfield on time. I was still furious, bundled her into the car and took her straight to Liverpool, where I dumped her unceremoniously at the train station. I didn't want to listen to apologies.

"At our next Club Eleven outing, Carole wasn't there, so I drove Vera home and had time to spend talking to her in front of her house before she went in, the end of the conversation prompted by movement of the Venetian blinds."

'On the rebound?'

"Possibly. There was no burning desire, no love at first sight, but she was intelligent and witty. A friendship developed, and we became an item at gigs and parties. After a few weeks, she invited me to meet her mother, a bustling multilingual Spaniard, narrow across the shoulders and two axe handles across the beam. She seemed to be battling to manage the family budget, keep Vera at college and her second child, Dan Junior, at university while her youngest, David, thought only of golf, having won the NSW Schoolboy Championship the previous year."

'Did she encourage you beyond just being a friend in the group?'

Just before I arrived, she had scratched her thigh. She lifts her skirt up to her knickers and shows me the wound. It isn't much, but I am impressed by her legs. She has inherited some of her mother's Spanish skin colour and maybe her legs too. Her mother is not amused but bathes the scratch with disinfectant while I watch. I suspect the show is for me, and I am titillated but a little startled and aroused.

"Yes, she made sure I knew she had nice legs. I guess she thought it was one of her best features, which it was, but she was lovely all over, really. What I didn't know about, and she didn't go into any depth about until we were married, was that the family was seriously dysfunctional."

'In what way?'

"Dan senior was rarely at home. When he was there, he seemed to spend most of his time staring into the distance and drinking beer. He and Vera's mother did not sleep in the same room. Much later, when Vera was pregnant with Julia, I got an insight into her attitude to sex in marriage and it was a bit confronting."

'What did she say?'

I arrive home from work, and she is looking anxious. I take the tea she has poured and sit opposite her.

'I think I'm pregnant again!'

She seems worried about what I might think, but even I'm surprised how good I feel about it.

"That's good. When will you know? Can't wait to tell Mum!"

'I know the timing's bad, but it must have been the pill I missed.'

"We have one, might as well have another one now, three years, it's a good gap."

Arriving at my mother-in-law's, excited with news of our pregnancy.

'Mum! Mum! Guess what? I'm going to have another baby!'

'What! You're not still carrying on with that stupid sex business, are you?!'

"She was surprised that we were still having sex. Apparently, we were supposed to have stopped after David was conceived, but it did answer a question for me about her relationship with Vera's father. Without making excuses for his drinking, maybe her attitude to sex was one of the reasons he was how he was."

'And how was he?'

"He was almost always away, and what kept him away is probably important in identifying some of the demons that pursued Vera all her life. Her anxiety may have been the other side of the coin to my need to be needed and that probably influenced our relationship."

'Were you ever told what happened in Cairns?'

We are lying back in bed, and she is talking about Cairns. She talks about floods in the wet season, watching out for crocodiles, eating mangoes, and that is when she tells me about her father masturbating in front of her. Then she switches to talking about when she was back with her mother in Earlwood. She thinks for a bit, then tells me about her mother ringing Lydia, then Lydia coming to their place and punching her father until he left the house. She doesn't tell me the specifics, or if it was about her. But it clearly made an impression. I feel there is a lot more to tell, but I don't press the point.

"No. I do know that her father masturbated in front of her, and maybe that was it, but before I met Vera, and before her mother moved to Sydney, for a few years she lived with her aunt Lydia and uncle Ernie in Marrickville. I mentioned them before.

"Lydia was a wonderfully eccentric woman who seemed to always manage to dress to show her shapely breasts, unsupported and still perky as she approached her mid-forties, (laugh) but ignored the raven black hairs sprouting from her chin and breastbone that tended to spoil the effect.

"After Vera's mother's death, a pack of cards was found in her box of trinkets. A family myth hung around that Lydia had been a nude model at Kings Cross during the depression and was regarded as the family's Bohemian.

"Vera's mother Elvira, and her other sister Amelia, had attended finishing school in Paris in their early twenties, so they were well educated and multilingual, considering themselves superior to ordinary mortals. Elvira worked as a court interpreter after she came home from Paris, speaking Spanish, French, Italian and English. Amelia married a man who rose to become a Queensland Industrial Court magistrate, while Lydia, on the other hand, was somewhat of an embarrassment to her sisters."

'Did you see the cards?'

"Yes, each card, fifty-two plus a couple of jokers, all showed pictures of young Lydia nude and gorgeous, not a hair out of place, or one too many, (laugh) not that I looked at every card."

'So, did Vera ever say her father abused her sexually, apart from the masturbation?'

"No. I have no direct evidence of sexual abuse, but the fact that she was sent away, three thousand kilometres by a mother as refined and haughty as Elvira, to live with the family rebel, suggests to me that she may not have been safe at home with her father."

'How did your parents relate to Vera's family?'

"They didn't. When we met, my family was living back in a shed at the Orange Grove Road property. Almost two years earlier, Dad had taken a job in the bush at Merrygoen, as the station mechanic on a big sheep and wheat property, house supplied, on a two-year contract. Our house had been rented for two years to the Pearson family, and the early arrival back of Dad, Mum and Jennifer, carrying only what they could fit into a small ute, for reasons never revealed, did not prompt the Pearsons to cut short the lease. So, they stayed in the house, and we moved into the shed. Dad had a small caravan. I got that, so I had space to work on lesson preparation and so on.

"Remember, I told you about Mum and Beryl Pearson becoming friends and working together at Cable Makers in Liverpool?"

'Yes, go on.'

"Well, it could not have been long after that before Mum found herself pregnant. A change of life baby. Excited at the prospect of a new sibling, I dubbed the foetus Algy as in:

'Algy met a bear, the bear met Algy.

The bear grew bulgy, the bulge was Algy.'

"Mum made the best of her life in the shed with the new baby coming but was able to move back into the house just before my sister Dianne was born, her only post-Exclusive Brethren child, and the only one untouched by its cruel influence.

"Dianne doesn't recognise the father her siblings describe. She says she had 'a different father' from the one we knew.

"He was a real father to her... and by the time she was eight, she was living with Mum and Dad on her own."

'So, the other girls left home early?'

"Yes, I sometimes wonder about that, and they stayed married to men who were authoritarian, attitudes probably inherited from their Russian and Greek fathers. Both marriages worked 'until death do us part', despite one sister's husband's constant and indiscreet affairs. She stayed with him until he died. I still don't know why."

'Did they marry to escape him, do you think? And then owed their husbands?'

"Yes, that makes sense. Each pretty much married the first man she went out with, I think. Eleanor had a few to choose from. She was striking. Very beautiful. At least two of my mates were after her, but she chose the Russian, and he wouldn't allow her to have children."

"Hello! Anybody home?"

'Hello, Ford.'

"What are the signs for? "This is a child-free house" and "Children not welcome here". Aren't you going to ask us in?"

'No, we decided not to allow children into this house.'

"You mean I just drove a thousand kilometres to show you my baby and you won't let us in?"

'Not with the baby.'

I'm numb. No anger, just shift to automatic. It's their reality, and they're entitled to make their rules.

"Okay. Maybe I'll see you at Mum's."

"Eleanor and Dmitri even went so far as to ban all children from their home. When Sally and I visited when Matt was a baby, we were blocked from bringing him into the house. I thought it was weird but then, I always thought the Russian was a bit weird."

'You always refer to him as the Russian. Why's that?'

"He seemed to have attitudes that were foreign to me. But that's ancient history, and I don't want to hurt them. We get along fine now. Well, we always did, and now that they are older, even better... we're all survivors."

'Okay. You said that Vera's family and yours did not get on. What happened?'

"Not the whole family, just her mother. I suspect she had higher hopes for her daughter. She was very bright and could have gone on with her education if she had not had children early. But it was Elvira's verdict after the Spanish Inquisition she put Mum through that set the tone for any family interaction. As I said earlier, she had declared my family to be white trash, so after that I felt that I was always on trial."

'Yes, that was a bit harsh.'

"A bit harsh? That came after I had spent the entire six weeks of the Christmas holidays rebuilding her kitchen, with a false ceiling that included a hood over the stove with fume extractor. I built new cupboards and doors from scratch and replaced the house's old galvanised-iron water pipes and painted it all, so I did expect some recognition. Oh, but to be young again and not know that such attempts to gain acceptance merely reveal neediness and attract contempt."

'Wisdom is rarely visited upon the young.'

"Indeed. However, at the time we were engaged, she probably presumed the worst and as a Catholic, who boasted that she never used contraception, she would have been terrified of an unwanted pregnancy and the shame that would bring.

"Then, probably knowing more of her daughter's sexual history than I did, she agreed to the marriage if I 'found somewhere to live'.

"Back then, in August 1958, accommodation in Sydney was impossible. Searches for a flat had to begin before daylight with the Sydney Morning Herald classified, to arrive on doorsteps as early as we could without upsetting landlords.

"Large rooms in old houses had been roughly divided into two rooms with used packing case plywood. In one room, I saw just such an arrangement, with a divider that created two rooms, but stopped just short of the ceiling so there was no need to install a second ceiling light."

'Sounds a bit like now!'

"No, as bad as it is now, I can't imagine anyone renting a room for what was almost the whole of a first-year primary teacher's salary. My salary, as a second-year primary teacher was less than ten pounds a week and that was about the going price for a basic two-bedroom flat in the suburbs if you could find one.

"However, as I mentioned another time, I did find a room in a house in Haldon Street, Lakemba. Five pounds per week bought a single bedroom with use of kitchen and if notice was given, use of the dining room. The house was owned by a not-long-retired driver for Joe Cahill, then the current NSW state premier.

"Our landlord bore an uncanny resemblance to the great man himself. The likeness was so strong I wondered if he was a brother. Nepotism was alive and well before the establishment of ICAC."

'What was he like to live with?'

"He was a cranky old bugger. He insisted we not flush the toilet unless the deposit was more substantial than mere urine and whinged if the toilet paper decreased its diameter too quickly whether we provided it or not.

"Looking at my old diaries of that time, the reason we could afford the room was the average of three gigs a week with John Speight, most at Elim, a huge federation home in Croydon that operated as a wedding reception house. It paid each of us four guineas per wedding in cash.

"John was probably the best organiser of anyone I ever knew. We played all the appropriate songs and kept that job for years. We continued playing there until he married and moved to Newport, and I took a job in Newcastle.

"John instigated the Manly Jazz Festival and mentored hundreds of young musicians over forty years. One of the stages is named in his honour."

'What did John think of your situation?'

'Are you all right? You look a bit stressed.'
We are setting up for a wedding gig at Elim.
"I got married today"'
'You're having me on. Why aren't you off on a honeymoon?'
"Mate! I'm broke after paying her college fees and I need the money for tonight to pay the damned rent!"

"We were married in a registry office, had a party at her mother's house in the afternoon, and then went off to our room at Lakemba. Finances were so tight that I played a gig on my wedding night. John couldn't believe it and looking back, neither can I.

"But I was broke and needed the money, and if I tell the truth, it also revealed my paranoia. All my professional life, I moved mountains to never miss a gig, believing that one missed booking might lose me future jobs and brand me as unreliable, a death sentence in the entertainment industry, where, if you are late, the show starts without you.

"The worst feeling I ever had in music was walking into a gig and finding the band already playing, with a gap on the stage where I should have been.

"It might also have revealed the nature of the relationship. I think we were both desperate. I needed to resolve my sexual drought, and she wanted to escape from her parents, so the deal was done."

'You mentioned in another session that you weren't a virgin when you married.'

"No, my virginity didn't quite make it to the vows. Engagement finally relaxed my inhibitions, and I remember the first time. She looked so young, her body beautiful and smooth as she guided me. Entry was easy, and it was soon over and in the wonder of my feelings of release, I failed to fully register how tense and unyielding her body was, stiff and unmoving, her eyes averted."

'You say she guided you. What do you mean by that?'

"Well, she seemed to know what to do. I knew what went where but was unsure how to go about it."

'I see. But you said she didn't enjoy sex with you?'

"I've got the condoms, so you won't get pregnant."

'Your parents might come home.'

"No, they're away for the whole weekend and nobody else ever comes here." We sit on the lounge, we kiss, and I peel off her clothes until she is in her underwear. She removes the last of her clothes and turns away.

'You'll hate my breasts.'

"You have a lovely body."

'My breasts are too small.'

"I'll have to see them sometime. (laugh) We'll be married in a couple of months."

'Promise you won't laugh.'

"Somebody said "more than a handful or a mouthful is a waste.""

'(laughs) I'm having treatment to make them bigger. Mum has perfect breasts!'

"I hadn't noticed. In fact, I hadn't noticed yours much. You've got great legs, great skin, great smile. Three out of four ain't bad and anyway, it's your personality I'm in love with. Don't worry about it!"

'Okay. Happy now? Put the condom on. Come on, I'll lie here on the carpet. What are you looking at?'

"I'm looking at your vagina."

'Well, stop it and get on with it. Come on!'

It was easy, didn't take long.

'Happy now?'

"Deliriously, but you didn't get much out of that."

'That's okay, help me up.'

"As they say, (laugh) good sex is good and bad sex is good too!"

'(laugh) Maybe, but was there a time you felt she enjoyed it?'

"I tried to make it good for her. I tried being subtle and cuddling for a long time, and I loved that, then I tried just touching erogenous zones I had read about."

'Was she responsive to that?'

'What are you holding me there for?'

"When I snuggle up to your back my hand just likes the feel of your breasts."

'Well get it off. You only want one thing. That's all you ever want. You don't love me. You only want sex!'

"No, I really like to cuddle you, and of course, you turn me on. I love you!"

'No, you don't. You're a sex maniac, and I have a headache!'

I've heard it all before. I turn over and eventually sleep.

"She accused me of being a sex maniac. She told me her doctor said sex every two months was normal."

'(laughs) Her doctor said that?'

"(laugh) I doubt it. No, having thought about it a bit, I think the conversation went like this: She says: 'I only want sex about every couple of months. Is that normal?' The doctor answers: 'Of course, whatever you're comfortable with.'"

'So, was sex rationed to bi-monthly?'

I come home after the gig. She is asleep. I try not to wake her and face away. I can feel her warmth and am aroused. This is not just about her, but the ballet, the topless dancers, the whole show is sex-charged, and I can't help it. I need release. I roll over and put my arm over her, hoping for a response. There is none. Maybe tomorrow. I roll back and wait for sleep.

"I think it was even less than that at times. There was a feeling that maybe she was right. The shame from school was never far away. My advances were rebuffed so constantly that I avoided bringing it up or starting anything for months at a time. Eventually, I think I stopped being the instigator and waited for her to start something, and as I've said, I masturbated when I felt I needed to."

'Did you masturbate with her?'

"(laugh) No. It was always a very private and shameful thing to do. It wasn't until recently that I remembered the incident where she touched my penis and I stopped her. She was never interested in touching me after that, and I never joined the dots. I wondered if my stopping her had a long-term effect."

'What did you wonder?'

"I wondered if that was the start of her coldness towards me. Maybe she took that as my final word. It was a shock!"

'The realisation?'

"Yes, and the suspicion that had that not happened, our marriage might have worked, and she would still be alive."

'That is drawing a very long bow. I suspect that was only one of a very long list of factors that influenced your marriage breakdown. But why do you think you stopped her?'

"There was probably not much I wanted more, but I was so cut off then from my feelings. I was still frightened to offend."

'Offend? Who were you frightened of offending?'

"Oh, God, I suppose. But I was always too frightened to let myself go."

'And that changed?'

"No, not really. Maybe I don't worry so much now, but up until recently I desperately needed to satisfy my partner before myself and there was the niggle that it was still not quite acceptable behaviour."

'You mean the whole sexual act thing?'

"Yes. The whole thing still had a sin-guilt component. Except for masturbation, which still brings shame, despite a GP telling me, during my time with Mum when I didn't have a sexual partner, that I should masturbate regularly 'to keep the pipes working'.

"I'm pretty much over the guilt, but it still really depends on the woman. I need permission to not feel guilt and that has happened relatively recently."

'So, your current partner gives you that permission?'

"Oh yes, she does, and I guess that's one big reason why I'm so attached. It is the first time I have fully felt confident that I'm good enough. Her attitude has taken away the need to perform. She orgasms quickly, sometimes more than once and is vocal about it."

'Is there any component of this relationship that is transactional?'

We meet, and she is as I thought she would be. We have Skyped, so I know her voice and her face, and I like her laughter lines and her openness. She seems non-judgemental. Physically she is small and neat.

We arrange to meet, and I order coffee for me and tea for her in Fast and Fresh at South Nowra, where we take up our conversation from where we last spoke.

I hadn't been well, and she was giving me a medical interview. I know she is a doctor and am reassured that she is taking an interest, and then she talks about her type 1 diabetes and how she really needs someone in the house with her to keep an eye out for hypos.

Is she telling me that she wants me for a medical monitor? If so, I don't feel the usual tug of being needed so I can trade help for sex.

There is no opportunity here to be clever and impress and really, I am the one who needs help. We keep talking until the tea and coffee are long gone, and then talk some more. She is clearly interested. I feel I must tell her about the herpes.

"Yes, on the face of it. But my feelings were different this time. She is a type 1 diabetic who needs a house buddy in case of emergencies and, although I didn't think it at the time, I needed to get off the boat."

'The boat? Were you still living on the boat?'

"Yes, I lived on it for over ten years."

'Let's come back to that later. Tell me more about this new partner and transactional sex.'

"That's it. I didn't have the usual need to trade my skills and love for sex. She didn't need anything really, but the difference was that I felt it didn't matter."

'But you had felt that it did matter in the past.'

"It's not something I realised was happening, but thinking back, there must be subliminal messaging that attracts co-dependent people to each other."

'There is, and clearly you were receptive to it. You needed to provide a service over and above the usual to deserve sex. I don't usually make such statements at this stage, but you have self-identified as a co-dependent sex-addict.'

"Sex addict?"

'Yes. You don't feel complete without it and to get it you have been quite self-destructive.'

"I got lucky a couple of times, but you are right. I did reject women because they didn't have a problem that I thought I could fix, so there was no quid quo pro."

'I'm interested in the boat years, and we can explore that later. Tell me what happened with the doctor?'

"I was looking at her with my brain rather than my heart or my dick and found her attractive, but I didn't feel I would suffer a great loss if she turned me down, so I told her about my herpes. I said: 'I must tell you something and it might be a game changer. I have genital herpes.' I waited for this neat and tidy person to run, but she smiled and said, 'Me too'."

'Did you always forewarn potential lovers about your herpes?'

"Hello, I'm glad I got you early."

'Why, what's up?'

"I need to tell you something important. I carry the genital herpes virus. Sorry, I forgot to tell you last night because, I guess, I haven't had lesions for ages. Sorry."

'Shit! After what we got up to last night... what can I do?'

"Go to a doctor right now, this morning, and get antivirals. They

work best in the first forty-eight hours, I believe, but obviously, the earlier the better. Again, I am sorry."

'Well, at least you told me. Bye.'

She hangs up before I can repeat the 'sorry'.

"No. Well, yes, I always did and early, before there was much attachment, but the lesions came and went, and the more time that passed, the rarer they became. So there was one time, when a friend and I had dinner on the boat and then we had sex, but I hadn't had lesions for months and forgot to tell her then, but did the following morning when I realised I hadn't said anything."

'I bet she wasn't happy.'

"No, and I didn't expect her to be. I was very sorry I had not told her but advised her to get medical help immediately, because there are preventative treatments available in the first couple of days, and she did that."

'Did the sexual relationship continue?'

"No. I was disappointed but not surprised, and she did tell a few friends, so a couple of people I was close to acted a bit strangely for a while.

"(smile) She never spoke to me again. Although it was unintentional, it was a betrayal of sorts and it caused me to be super careful to never let that happen again, which it didn't."

'Was your doctor friend the first one to admit to you they had it?'

"Yes. The relief I felt surprised me, and it lifted my interest to another level."

'So, that was the start of a new relationship?'

"Yes, but it had to wait for a few weeks before I could spend any physical time with her because I had my yacht moored near Gosford and I would need to arrange for a mooring in Batemans Bay, where she lived."

'You knew you could get a mooring there?'

The coach pulls into Batemans Bay for lunch, and we all head for cafés. I get a pie and coffee, then wander along the waterfront. There are yachts here as big as Heavy Metal on swing moorings. I ring Maritime and get a quote: five hundred a year rent for the space, and it might cost about a thousand to have a mooring dropped, compared to eight hundred every month at Booker Bay. I tuck that away for later and continue my trip to Queensland to visit Helen.

"Yes. Nearing the end of my time nursing Mum in Eden, I took the occasional few days off to visit Helen, a new friend in Mudjimba. At Batemans Bay, on the way through and out of interest, I checked on mooring cost because I knew I couldn't afford to stay where I was."

'All right, let's come back to Helen later. How was sex with the doctor?'

"Let's say she didn't use it to manipulate me, so the pressure came off the whole thing. It became a non-issue... very relaxed."

'Seems like you found peace in that area of your life?'

"Yes, I was, and am, blessed."

'I would agree, but you did create the relationship and for the right reasons. Your needs were being met without you sacrificing your time and wealth. Now, can we go back to your wife, Vera?"

"Yes, I was married twice. Vera was my first wife."

'Right. So, with her you needed to perform. You were desperate to satisfy her. What did you do?'

"Just about everything in the manuals."

'But she was never satisfied?'

"No, not by me."

'But she was by others?'

Two black African students are sitting at the next table at the pub in Armidale, talking in English.

'Come join us!' Vera calls to them.

I'm not sure this is a good idea. She is pissed. Barbara is pissed too and single again.

'We're going back to the house for dinner. Like to come?'

We've finished dinner and I'm smoking. Where is Vera? She and one of the black dudes have been gone a while.

I have a bad feeling and find them in the hallway, kissing passionately.

"You'd better go home."

David walks in.

'Are you going to kill him, Dad?'

"You've been watching too many bad movies. Go to bed." *And to her,* "And you'd better go to bed too."

Shit! It's three a.m. and she still isn't home. Call Loretta.

"Sorry to get you up, but Vera isn't home yet and I'm getting worried. Is she there?"

'Fuck! I don't know, she left hours ago. She must have had an accident. She was pretty pissed!'

"I guessed that. Okay, I'll backtrack and see if I can find her. She might just be asleep in the car. Okay, bye!"

"What the fuck are you doing still here? I thought you'd had an accident. You scared the shit out of me. And you, mate, you'd better get going!"

'Leave me alone. We're just talking. Fuck off!'

"Well, you're talking partner just left, so we'll leave your car here and you can come home and sleep it off. Come on."

"I don't really know. I found her in a few compromising situations, and some of my friends had said things, but I didn't really know she was actually having sex with others until she infected me with herpes."

'How did you know it was her? You had no other sexual partner then?'

"No. Not that I hadn't had other partners before then, and except for luck, it could have been me that infected her. But I hadn't had sex except once or twice with her for many months, and in any case, it was the doctor who gave the game away."

'He told you she had herpes?'

"Not exactly. I went to see him because I had a rash and a sore. He didn't even look properly, didn't take a swab or refer me to pathology. He just pronounced it to be 'herpes simplex penisatum' and recommended we both be treated together to put a stop to 'the ping-pong effect'."

'But it's incurable.'

"Yes, but even he didn't seem to know that then. But he must have diagnosed it in her some time before, or he couldn't have been so sure."

'I see, and she didn't tell you?'

"No, she didn't then, and it was years before she said anything. I had been gone from her house for two years by the time she did."

'What did she say? How did she tell you and why? Why so much later?'

Sunday night after the gig. The kids are in the car, probably asleep by now. We are having coffee before I start the two-hour drive home to the farm. She is a bit drunk, but not unusually so, and being pleasant. Really drunk and abusive would come later, but I liked her at this stage of inebriation. She was funny and sexy, but I knew not to trust that mood and was keen to get going.

At the door. She opens it and stands aside to let me through. She lets her hand drop to brush my penis on the way past.

'We could have another baby, you know.'

I stare. I can't believe she doesn't get it. It took all my resolve to take David away from his drugs and her alcohol. I was trying to save our heroin-addicted son. Our daughter had chosen to live with me to put some distance between her and her mother's dependency, abusive temper tantrums and despair.

"Thanks, love, but I think I'll pass on that now. We can talk about it later. I have to get home."

'I'm sorry I gave you herpes.'

"Okay."

"She just apologised. Simple as that. 'Sorry I gave you herpes'."

'Did you get treatment? What did you do for sex?'

"Didn't have sex, even with her. I was referred to a virologist and he tried injections of smallpox inoculation, and it helped a bit, but I mainly sunbaked nude to get UV on the sore and abstained."

'Sore? Doesn't sound like herpes if it was a sore. Blisters and rash, short-lived lesions, but not a sore. Are you sure it was herpes?'

"Yes, I was eventually tested, and I have the antibodies, but the sore was a secondary infection that the doctor eventually fixed in three days with antibiotics."

'How long after the original diagnosis was that?'

"Maybe six months, a long time."

'And you were lying around in the sun, in the nude because you heard that UV kills the herpes virus.'

"Yes, something like that."

'(laughs) Maybe you're lucky not to have melanoma penisatum!'

"(laugh) Yes, but I do have a freckle."

'A freckle! No don't show me! (laughs).'

'The herpes thing seems to have been a watershed in your life. What changed after that?'

"Nothing for a while. I was busy on the farm, trying to create an income, growing rockmelons and watermelons for the Newcastle markets. I had Julia at Wollombi school and David at Cessnock High, then along came Sally."

'Your second wife. We will get to her, but I would like to explore what happened at the school. Greenacre?'

"Yes, my time at Greenacre was transformative in many ways and was the start of the end of my marriage to Vera."

'In what ways was it transformative?'

Ken, the principal, asks me to swap periods with other teachers so I can take their classes for music. I'm flattered and start the following week with three other classes, but then I find my own class restive upon my return, and I am not sure what they have covered of my planned lessons and suspect it is not as much as I would have liked.

"I started doing music lessons for other classes, but when I realised that my class was suffering from lack of continuity, I devised a way out. The school had a Grundig tape recorder, so I recorded lessons on tape. I presented the first lesson myself, then provided the teachers with more lessons on tape.

"Then Paul Manning asked me to think about writing a musical play with him. He called the play *The Clock of Lonk*. We started on it, then the Eva thing happened, and I dropped the idea for ten years. When Compact Cassette tapes turned up, I had the ideal medium to continue the musical play idea."

'That seems an interesting subject for another day.'

"Okay, and its commercialisation came from a chance meeting at Sally's new school at Paxton in the Hunter Valley."

'We haven't talked about Sally yet, so maybe we can start there next time?'

"Okay."

I nod, pick up my sunnies and leave.

Marriage and other rides of my life
A roller coaster.
Appearances.
All happy.

Concentrate on the laughter.
See only joy,
buy a ticket.

One way, no return,
no worries.
Safety in numbers.

Watching ahead.
At the gate,
smiles, excitement, easy.

Nearby, others leaving.
'Been there, done that'.
Fake laughter, disappointment.

No, not me,
I'll be okay.
The queue moves.

Pressure.
Abandon caution, take the step.
Seat for two.

Sharing with a stranger.
Bumping bodies on the way to the high,
differences refreshing.

Overcompensating,
repeating the mantras.
Hoping for satisfaction.

Pregnant pause.
Seat belts tighten,
brakes off.

Control gone.
Noise, excitement, fear,
We drop.

Pressure of twists and turns
Ups and downs, grinding together.
Hurting, threatened sanity.

Then for some, lost ego.
Too much,
And we jump.

On the outside again.
Looking in at laughter,
crying and living.

We toss a coin,
and buy another ticket.

Session 11

I'm at the door, wondering how much I should say about Sally. She was the love of my life, despite everything that happened since she left. I think I understand what motivated her and perhaps why she did what she did. In any case, I always loved her right to the end.

I find myself in the room, and Loren is looking at me. She hands me a coffee, and I sit.

"Thanks. Sorry, I was thinking of Sally and must admit I was considering what I should or shouldn't say because I am aware that our children and hers might read this. I am only now beginning to understand her and don't want to be unfair."

She smiles, sips her coffee, watching me over the rim of the cup. She nods, then puts her coffee down.

'That's always something we are very sensitive to when dealing with emotionally charged issues like marriage failure, particularly how it affects the children. But this is your time to look at those relationships, why they worked or didn't, and from that you learn, you understand yourself better and I hope you can forgive yourself for hurt you caused and forgive those that hurt you.

'In the end, I believe most people try to do the best they can. But as you already know, after talking about your father, his efforts to mould you the way he thought was best was ultimately about him, not you. It was not only cruel and against nature, but ultimately failed to make you the perfect little Brethren he needed to satisfy what he believed God wanted from him.

'The Brethren fairy tale was constantly being challenged by what you were observing in the real world. To punish you for merely reporting what you saw was gaslighting. That led to a mistrust in your own observations and judgement and has led you to lose self-esteem to a dangerous level where you had suicidal thoughts.

'That is not normal. But you are still here, and the truth is the truth. How people handle that is their business. Would you agree?'

I agree in principle but, and here I go, trying to please everyone again. What happened from my point of view is not how anyone else would see it and, in this situation, there is no opportunity to interrogate most of the others, so it is inevitable that some will see it all differently.

"Yes, but whatever I say, someone else will have another opinion, so I had better stick to the facts I can verify. How's that?"

'(laughs) How can you verify an emotion? This is at the heart of what we are doing here. 'When you told me about the presumption of homosexuality at school, you revealed the most shameful event of your life, and that was almost all about perception and emotion, almost all about someone else's perception and emotion. But now you realise, after most of a lifetime tainted by those perceptions, that they were based on perceptions that you accepted as fact until you eventually realised that they were anything but.'

"Yes, but now I can see that it was not what it was presumed to be, so I can reveal it."

'Who have you told apart from me? Did you tell Vera? Sally?'

"No, I told Steve, my college friend, then I explained it to Mum when she was maybe seventy-five, then recently, I told Jo."

'We will come to Jo eventually, and I also want to explore David's behaviour and Vera's death. But for now, can you tell me how you met Sally.'

Herbie rings me at the farm. He wants me to play in a jazz trio at his daughter's bat mitzvah. I say I will book him a band, but not play so I can be there as a guest. I arrive and am given a beer, then Herbie introduces me to a tallish young woman wearing a loose cotton frock, lovely smile and eyes hazel like Mum's.

'I'm so glad you could come,' she says, taking my hand and holding it just a second longer than is customary. She starts with questions right away, so she collects a white wine, and we sit away from the crowd. We talk as time flies by, and suddenly I see that the party is starting to break up, so I say my farewells to Herbie and my muso mates and head out. She follows, and we kiss before I get into the ute and head home to Wollombi.

"I think I was set up. A bit of matchmaking courtesy of my old mate Herbie Marks. She did some team teaching with Herbie at Earlwood Infants, where she was 'Mrs Tidy'. I asked her about the name, and she said it was a professional name, like 'B Neat', 'B Tidy' as seen on sample work in school displays."

'And was it?'

"(laugh) No, it turned out that she was married to an Alan Tidy, who was a manager at Honda, but that was not revealed for some time."

'The plot thickens, so what happened then?'

"Just after the bat mitzvah party, I had four sessions over two days at EMI to record backing tracks for a Ted Egan album with Herbie, so I turned up at the studio and Sally was there. She sat beside me all that morning, so we had lunch together, then she left, I guessed to go back to school.

"Next day, I brought with me *The Australian* newspaper for the cryptic crossword to fill in the time between takes, but she was there again and set herself up beside me on a stool. I didn't know how to interpret her interest and picked up the crossword. Then, as had never happened before and has never happened since, I knocked off the cryptic in about ten minutes."

'I bet she was impressed!'

"(laugh) She might have been impressed, but I was astonished. Anyway, in the breaks we talked about what I did at Wollombi."

'What did she ask you about?'

She is wearing a blouse and jeans that show off her figure. I'm not really looking, but I can't help but notice.

'How many acres do you have there?'

"A hundred, but the title is complicated, in fact I'm squatting on about a third of it, but up there, it is considered mine and I have applied for title over it."

'Is there a house?' I nod. 'What's it like?'

We talk about what I do there, and she seems interested in all of it.

Ted is getting through a slab of Fosters, adding percussion with the cardboard case, so by the end of the day, his percussion sounds hollower than it did in the morning. I remember Vera's Uncle Ernie downing a bottle of gin before breakfast every morning to keep his addiction at bay and wonder if Ted has the same problem. Like Uncle Ernie, he showed no signs of being the slightest bit drunk.

"She asked for details about the property, and I told her pretty much everything there was to know, including my phone number there, Wollombi 24."

'So, it was a wind-up phone?'

"(Laugh) Yes, and as rumour has it, a source of entertainment for the family who ran the post office and operated the exchange."

'Entertainment?'

"Yes, I think I caught them at it once. That was much later, when I was the fire brigade captain and needed them to ring some people urgently. When I got no immediate attention at the counter, I lifted the flap and went to the doorway to the exchange, and there was almost the whole family, sharing headphones and trying not to laugh as they were apparently listening in on a conversation."

'Did they say anything?'

"No, they were clearly embarrassed, but I backed out and they pretended it never happened."

'(laughs) I bet they were embarrassed. You could have reported that, you know.'

"Probably, but what would happen to my relationship with them? I had an arrangement that in the case of a fire, I would head out with the fire truck, and the PO would ring my members on a list I had provided so they could join me at the fire."

'I see, so did Sally use your wind-up number?'

I have just settled down with a book and glass of red. It is school holiday time, so Julia and David are down with Vera. When the phone rings, I look at my watch and see it is almost ten.

"Hello?"

'Hi, it's Sally. How are you?'

The conversation goes on for three minutes and an operator cuts in.

'Are you extending?'

She is, and I can hear the coins dropping. I look at my watch again and see that our exchange should have closed, and can imagine them listening in.

"How much money are you prepared to spend on this call?" I ask.

'I've got ten dollars' worth of twenties. (laughs) That might not be enough.'

"Ten dollars is more than enough to pay for petrol to come here and back, so why don't you hang up now and come and visit me for the day some time?"

There is a pause for a few seconds, then she agrees, asks for directions, and hangs up.

I go to bed, then just after midnight, the dog barking wakes me, and I can see light on the blind. A car is coming up the driveway.

"Yes, she rang just on closing time for the PO exchange, so I suggested, rather than spend the money on trunk calls, she should visit me some day. I was not suggesting she come right away, but within two hours she was there and after a glass of red and a half hour chat, she was in bed with me."

'Wow! And you were okay with that?'

"Not one hundred per cent, and I thought the herpes would scare her off, but no, she was not fazed by that and just followed me into the bedroom. I say she never left, but she did for two weeks in early January.

"After being at Wollombi for a couple of weeks, during which she accompanied me to Sydney for my Saturday-Sunday gigs. Then out of the blue, so told me she was married and needed a couple of weeks to sort that out and would be back."

'So, she hadn't told you she was married?'

"Not until she went off to 'sort that out'. When I took her in the ute to Sydney to pick up her stuff, I met Alan there and my impression was that he was as surprised by events as I was. But by that time, she was fully integrated into my life and had formed relationships with David and Julia, whom she treated like a younger sister."

'How old was Sally then?'

"She told me she was twenty-three, which worried me a bit. I was thirty-nine, but she seemed older in her attitudes. She was very attractive, competent in anything she did and seemed to think I was exactly what she wanted. She was a delightful package, and I was falling in love with her."

'So, she wasn't twenty-three?'

"No. A few months later, at her next birthday, I wished her a happy twenty-fourth and she said that was her twenty-third. I asked her why she said she was a year older, and she said that she was afraid that might put me off. She was right. It might have, but by then I was fully committed to the relationship."

'How was she with David?'

We are driving into Cessnock and David is looking out the window at the clouds and spouting stream of consciousness about colours and shapes. Sally is talking to him, and when we get home, she tells me he has been eating gold top or blue meanie mushrooms. I despair that the move out of Sydney that was mainly to get him away from the drug scene has made no difference. They are sitting together in deep conversation. I can guess they are talking about drugs, and I'm relieved that she is taking an interest and seems on the same page.

"She seemed to take the role of counsellor, but she soon realised that he was seriously addicted."

'How did you discover his addiction?'

I have time to fill after a morning gig, so I call in to Canterbury High and ask to see the deputy head. I ask him how David is progressing, and he informs me that David left school six months earlier. I point out that David has just turned fourteen and ask why I was not informed. He claimed that David told him he was already fifteen, so he just let him go.

That afternoon, David arrives home in his school uniform with his school bag, and I ask him a few questions about his day and what he is studying. He becomes suspicious and then asks me what it's all about, so I tell him about my visit to his school.

"I visited his school where he should have been in year nine and discovered that he had left six months earlier."

'Weren't you told?'

"No, and I found that extraordinary. That afternoon I confronted him with it, and he told me he spent his days doing drugs and dealing drugs around Earlwood."

'What did you do then?'

Vera has been out, so as soon as she is home, I tell her what David said. She says: 'You just don't understand us, do you?' I say I don't, and I take them to St George Hospital Drug unit to see what can be done about his heroin use.

We wait for an hour or so, then he is taken to talk to a psychiatrist. He is with him for some time, then the doctor, who looks like he is a patient, dressed for gardening, with a shock of curly grey hair, scruffy beard and thick specs tells us that David will come off heroin when he is ready to and not before. I am flabbergasted at this and leave, believing that I should be taking responsibility and doing something.

"We took him to a drug clinic in the hospital and the psychiatrist said that he just wanted to feel 'out of it' and would stop when he was ready to. But then I decided I needed to do more and questioned him about why he did it. He said it felt great and it was brain food. I then asked about his dealer."

'Did he tell you?'

Dad, it's brain food. You should try it.' I ask him where he gets it. He says one of his school mates has an uncle who is the sergeant at our local police station, and it comes from there. I am angry. I front up to the police station and ask to see the inspector.

"Yes, he named a police officer, and naïve me, I told the inspector of police at our local station. He assured me he would look into it."

'And did he?'

I come home early and go downstairs to the office. The toilet had a chair jammed under the doorknob, so I remove it and look in. David is there, slumped against the wall, barely breathing. I call an ambulance and drag him onto the office floor in case I need to do CPR. The ambos arrive and rush him off to hospital. I leave a note for Vera and follow. I arrive to be told he had had a serious overdose of heroin, but they think he will be okay.

"It was a weekend, so Mary wasn't in the office. I found David locked in the downstairs toilet, having overdosed on heroin. He told me later that two cops had come to the house, injected him and locked him in."

'Did you believe him?'

"Well, I suppose it was possible that he set up the scene, and also possible that he could have injected himself, got rid of the kit, then manipulated the chair to lock himself in. That would have been difficult, and why would he make up the story about the cops? So yes, I did believe him, and as soon as he came out of hospital, I bundled him off to Wollombi."

'Did you take it further?'

"No. I know in the movies, the crooked cops are called out and the goodies prevail, but I wasn't prepared to expose him to any more danger, and I was clearly out of my depth."

'Is it possible that David said that so you would drop it, as you did?'

"I hadn't thought of that. I guess it's possible, but he was always open with me."

'You didn't know about the heroin or the dealing or that he had left school.'

"Yes, that's right, but when I asked him about it, he told me."

'Right, so tell me about what happened when you left with him. How did Vera take that?'

I make the decision to move David to Wollombi, and I tell Vera. I ask her if she wants to come, and she mumbles something about being 'too far from facilities'. I don't suspect then, but do later, that she needs to be close to her three prescribing doctors to access all the prescription drugs she is taking. We pack David's clothes, drum kit and schoolbooks into the ute. It is after my Sunday gig, so it is past eight.

We are about to leave when Julia comes out with her school bag and declares that she is 'coming too'.

I am not comfortable, knowing how fragile Vera is, and tell her I would rather she stay, but she is adamant, so we get a few more of her clothes and squeeze her in.

Next morning, Monday, I call Mary, my office manager to ask about

Vera and she says she hasn't seen her and that her car wasn't there. I ask her to check the garage. Her car is there, so I call an ambulance, and she is taken to Canterbury Hospital.

"Remember, I had that business with an office in the basement of the house, with Mary Cockley as manager. I rang her the next day to check on Vera. She had overdosed again, but the intervention was in time, so she recovered."

'Did you come to the hospital?'

"No, and this was a hard thing to do. I told the nurse who rang me I would not be visiting Vera. She said I was a bit hard, but I suspected that my refusal to overtly take responsibility for her might stop her manipulating me with her overdosing."

'What do you think now?'

"Well, she didn't overdose for another twenty-five years or so. She married a man with three daughters who were around Julia's age, but I got the impression from what Vera said that Julia wasn't happy there, but Julia disputes this and said it was after that, when Vera went to live with Ron Martin that Julia was not accepted by him and wasn't happy. Vera married once more after that, and as far as I know, did not overdose again until she was eventually successful. She died in the early hours of the morning after my birthday."

'Was that intentional?'

David rings me and sounds worried. He tells me that his mother has been at the pub, offering ten thousand dollars for someone to shoot me. I laugh, but he insists that I need to take precautions, so I make sure the doors are locked at night and the dog is in with me, but otherwise am not overly concerned.

"I don't know but toward the end, she seemed to become fixated on me and it was said that she tried to have me shot."

'That sounds serious.'

"I guess so, but I imagined her, quite drunk, talking to random men at the pub where she was known, trying to find a hitman. David must have been there, because he was the one who told me. But I couldn't imagine anyone taking her seriously. I wasn't really worried, but I did lock the doors at night."

'Did she do drugs with David?'

Vera calls me. It is late, and the exchange is closed, but they put the call through. She is very drunk and is demanding I do something about David. David has turned up at her door, out of it, demanding money. She is scared, so I advise her to ring the police, but she can't bring herself to do that.

Her relationship with David is a loving one, but dangerous. She does understand his addiction, but David being around when she is depressed leads to them both drinking and taking drugs to a dangerous level. They both seem to give each other permission to get plastered, and there is nothing I can do for either of them.

"I don't think so. But they did drink together. On the night she died, she had drunk a bottle of vodka and taken some opiates, so she was certainly taking risks.

"David frightened her sometimes and she would call me late at night for help. But I was two hours away, and by then, I had another family, so all I could do was tell her to call the police."

'Did she?'

"No, she never did. But he did straighten up enough to take a job playing on the *Turkmenia*, a Russian cruise liner, with Peter

Northcote's band. He met Sharon there, and they married aboard. The ship put on the wedding, gratis, the captain conducted the service, and the Russian band played. It was lovely and we all had such hopes that David's worst days were behind him."

'I remember Peter Northcote. David must have been pretty good to work with Peter.'

I come into the office, and I can hear singing and a guitar in David's practice room.

Peter and David are sitting on the floor. David is singing phrases to Peter, who is repeating David's phrases on his guitar.

"They were school mates. Peter lived in the street behind us and came over often. That is the tragedy. David was exceptional but never realised how good he was. He always felt that he needed a drug to support him.

"Will Dower, my bandleader at the time, was a top studio drummer when David started playing with Peter. He was very impressed with David, and I remember Will listening to him play, then asking him to play a lick slower so Will could see what he was doing.

"David's sense of time was as good as Warren Daly's and maybe he was more creative. I played a few gigs with him, and it was a delight, but the drugs were his undoing always."

'Did he have a falling out with Peter?'

"Yes, apparently Peter booked Dave for a recording session, and he arrived stoned. That was the last straw for Peter. He sent David home and never spoke to him again."

'I'd like to ask you about Warren Daly later, but how did David's marriage work out?'

I visit them in their flat over the shops in Earlwood. They want to buy a car, and I advise them to borrow through a bank rather than the finance company attached to the car yard. I take them to the bank and find that despite all that income, they have no savings. David is earning well, and Sharon is working at an illegal casino as a croupier, bringing home five hundred a week, cash in hand, a substantial amount at the time.

The bank manager refuses the loan because they have no evidence of saving. There is no plan to save for a house. All of it goes on eating out three meals a day – just like it was on the ship – on clothes, and entertainment.

"They were earning big money, but saving nothing, spending it all as they went. On the *Turkmenia*, three meals a day were provided, but now they were on their own. Neither Sharon nor David cooked. They wanted a car but couldn't get finance from a bank because they had no history of saving.

"Then Sharon became pregnant, and they were relying on David's income, which was nowhere near what Sharon was bringing home.

"I imagine he was scared shitless by this. But he kept it together until the baby was toddling, then he got back on the heroin. Sharon was having none of it, so she packed up the baby and flew back to England where she could be supported by her mother, Jean."

'How do you think his drug problems started?'

We are pretty chuffed that an established band, Judge Jeffries, made up of young men in their twenties, would want David, just turned thirteen, to join their band. I don't have an opportunity to hear them, but Vera takes him to gigs. He is with them for some months and there are no red flags for me, until he is sprung for skipping school. He is convinced that heroin is good for him and doesn't see it as a problem. He is out of the band about then, and I wonder if his heroin use started with them and continued until his addiction became too hot to handle.

"He was too young to be mixing with older musicians unsupervised. I had no qualms about allowing him to be in the band and didn't for a moment suspect they might be introducing him to drugs that would steal much of his life. I can't be sure, but I suspect that he was given a taste of dope and heroin while he was in that band. They were adults and aware of the dangers, but he was just a kid, so if what I suspect is true, they were really responsible for his addiction. Of course, he had probably inherited an addictive personality through his mother and grandfather, so the genetic trace was there."

'How about your family? Were addictive traits evident there?'

There was never any alcohol at Coromandel, nor at Baker Street or at Booralla Road. There was the famous brandy jar, but that stayed unopened for years at a time. Wine was passed around at the Meetings, but they took only a sip.

Christmas at Eric and Normas in Springwood, and Dad drinks a beer shandy then goes into his drunken routine, falling about and slurring his speech. I don't know why he is being so silly and find it bizarre.

"There was no alcohol in any of the Brethren homes that I was aware of, but I wondered much later in life if they were actually riddled with addicts who avoided activating their addictions by never drinking or smoking. The sip of sweet sherry on Sunday mornings was as close to temptation as most of them came.

"There was one Shirtcliffe family member who we were told liked a drink, so apparently he was the sacrificial lamb sent to the bottle shop to replenish the supply of sweet sherry when needed."

'(laughs) So, was he allowed into the service?'

"(laugh) Yes, and he also smoked a pipe, not one of the worst sins, but frowned upon nevertheless, so he sat by the door, in the extreme outer circle that consisted of just the one chair."

'So, take me back to Wollombi and David there.'

David comes home stoned. He doesn't hesitate to tell me that a mob of bikies at a pub in Cessnock are dealing. I can only limit that by making sure my money is secure, and he seems to be settling in at school. Then I come home to find him in bed with a neighbour who is about twenty. He is still only fifteen and supposed to be at school. I send her home and give him a lecture on rules of the house and insist that he must attend school every day, but I soon get a call from the school.

He has been arrested. I go in, and the police say they found cannabis seeds in his school bag. I find him at the police lock-up in an outdoor cell and wait with him there. He is taken in a cage on the back of a police ute to Worimi Youth Centre at Broadmeadow, where he will be for three weeks while he is assessed.

The court agrees that David needs rehabilitation rather than incarceration.

"He continued to use drugs, bought from bikies at a pub in Cessnock and he found mushrooms – 'gold tops' and 'blue meanies' – somewhere and used those. He was determined to be 'out of it'. Then he was arrested for cannabis possession, so was ordered to go into rehab."

'How did that go?'

I make the necessary calls and drive him to Odyssey House near

Campbelltown. He seems happy to be going into rehab and we chat pleasantly on the two-and-a-half-hour drive. He says his goodbyes, so I leave. When I arrive home, I ring. They say he left right after I did.

I don't hear from him for a couple of years, but he does visit his mother, and I find she has been topping up his benefits by twenty dollars a week. He sometimes stays with Vera for periods of time, when she is separated or divorced, but he doesn't get on with her third husband, Olof.

He gets in while they are not home and cuts his arm, writing on the walls in blood that he 'will haunt them all'. She comes home and gets him to hospital just in time to save him.

"He agreed to go to Odyssey House, but he stayed just long enough to know I was on my way home, then he disappeared into the drug scene in Sydney for a couple of years. He visited Vera and sometimes stayed for a week or two, but that wasn't helping either of them.

"When she married for the third time, the man she married tried to intervene, but expected me to take control of the situation from 150 kilometres away."

'Did he come home again?'

"Yes, he was always welcome to come to me if he wasn't using and did from time to time until when I lived on the boat and couldn't cope. I handed him over to the Salvos in 2003 and from then on, I only saw him at cafés in Sydney where he was homeless. I would buy him a meal and a coffee and show him photos of the family, that sort of thing."

'That was after his mother died, so tell me what happened there.'

"That was after his successful appeal and release, but by then what was left of his share of Vera's estate was gone, so he lived on the streets."

'Okay, tell me more about Vera's death. What was David's involvement, and yours?'

It is the day after my birthday when I get a call from the police to say that Vera is dead. Later we learn that she had a blood alcohol level of .41, which they say was enough to kill her. I drive down to the house to find David there with Julia's friend Peter. David is very drunk and drinking more. He is being quite loud. Someone must have called the police, because they turn up to talk to David. He tells them his mother has just died and he needs to drink. I assure them that we will be there, and they leave.

Vera's downstairs tenant arrives and offers condolences to David, who assures him that because David now 'owns the house', he can continue to rent the downstairs rooms.

"My knowledge of what happened came from Julia and the police. Apparently, at the bar she drank only tea. But he was demanding that she buy him more drinks until she bought a bottle of vodka and took him home. After she got home, she drank with him, and even rang a late-night talk-back show, where she had quite a long chat, apparently."

'So, she was relatively sober at that point?'

We have had guests for dinner, and we drink two bottles of red between the four of us, then move to the lounge and drink more. I have stopped drinking because I have an early call next day, but she keeps drinking. I know she has had a lot of wine, but it doesn't show. They leave, but as soon as the door closes, she collapses, and I carry her up to bed.

"I have never met anyone else, male or female, who could drink to oblivion, but up to that point, hold a conversation with no signs of having drunk anything. No slurring, no loss of train of thought. In fact, when she was in that state, she was the funniest."

The party at Vera's cousin Norma's is fun. Her guests are interesting, mostly her friends are from uni and are younger than us. We are sitting with a young, bearded man with a North Shore accent who suddenly declares that the 'party is boring'.

"At a party, after she had had a few, there was a pompous young bloke who said he was bored, so she told him that if he wanted better entertainment he should 'go home and have a wank'. Remember, this is 1959, so saying things like that was not quite done. But the others at the table thought it was hilarious, and he left. I was proud of her."

'Take me to the court case when David was convicted for "assisting a suicide".'

Justice O'Keefe, John O'Keefe's brother, is presiding. David has been assigned a public solicitor and barrister. He pleads "not guilty", and the trial begins.

It is clear to me that Justice O'Keefe is keen for a conviction. Vera's doctor is asked what he gave her for pain, and he says: 'Morphine, I mean paracetamol'. It could be a slip of the tongue, but maybe he had given her morphine. David's barrister then explores the 'doctor's bag' and what that held, pointing out that pharmacy records show that he had replenished his supply of morphine on the day after treating Vera for severe head pain.

Justice O'Keefe orders David's barrister to cease that line of questioning.

After the evidence had been given, O'Keefe spends a whole day basically convincing the jury that David is guilty, at one point saying that David 'had looked shifty' when answering questions. His summing-up is long, rambling and clearly designed to assure a guilty verdict, which he gets.

"I think Justice O'Keefe was keen for a guilty verdict so his name would be cited in future legal precedents. His summing-up virtually told the jury what to think, even drawing attention to David's demeanour, indicating it was that of a guilty man. He was sentenced to, I think six years, and taken away."

'Do you think he gave her morphine?'

"I don't know. I have no doubt that if he had money, he could find any drug he wanted, so he could have had some. And, if he did, he would have found it nigh on impossible to refuse her if she asked him for it."

'Where was he sent to jail? Could you visit?'

"At first, he was in Silverwater, and I could catch the train from Newcastle to visit him, which I did about once a month. Then he was moved to Goulburn, where I continued to visit him monthly and drop $50 into his account for cigarettes, etc. When he was moved to Junee, that put him beyond where I could drive to see him, so we wrote and had the occasional phone call. Then the appeal came up.

"I was still living on my boat at the marina after my partner Dianne left me, but it was before I moved the boat to Lake Macquarie."

'How did the appeal go?'

We file in and there are three judges at the bench. David is in the dock and the two same barristers are there. After the announcements and introductions, plus a few thoughts, the chief justice turns to the prosecution and says: 'You never did have a case, did you?'

"No, Your Honour, we didn't," he answers, and then the judge turns to David and says: 'Appeal upheld. Not guilty', and they all walk out. It is over in ten minutes.

"The chief justice said a few things about errors of procedure and then declared that there never was a credible case to prosecute David, and he was free."

'I bet you were pleased.'

"Of course. But what happened then surprised me. Everyone left the room, so David and I were the only ones there. He walked over, and I hugged him, then we left. We drove out to Silverwater to collect his belongings that had been taken from him two years earlier, then to Newcastle and the boat at the marina."

'What was wrong with that?'

"As far as I know, nobody was told I would be there, with transport and the wherewithal to take care of David. When they walked out, it was late in the day and he didn't have even his wallet, money, credit card, nothing. That was all at Silverwater. If I hadn't been there with my car, God knows what he would have done.

"I thought it was appalling, but at the time, I was just glad he was out."

'Did he sue?'

"We never thought of that. When he was arrested, he was in a stable relationship and had a lot of computer equipment that he had used to set up a recording studio in his bedroom. The set-up was first class. He also had money in the bank and, although he was still drinking, he was otherwise clean, and who knows where his life would have led?"

'So, what did he do then?'

It is after midnight, and he is sitting at the galley table, nodding. He won't go to bed, and I know he has been smoking aboard. Because of the danger of fire, I can't leave him there alone, so I stay up, trying to read or write. Then it is daylight, and I can't sleep, but he does until I drive him to the hospital for his methadone.

I know from the smell that he has been missing the bowl when urinating and that is bad news for the steel hulled yacht. I will need to dismantle the head and treat rust that I know will be there. He expresses a desire to help make the boat 'schmick', but I have no available money, and his drinking leaves him unable to do much.

"He was on methadone and drinking, so he never slept at night, seemingly half out of it with 'the nods', so I couldn't sleep. After a few days, I went to the Matthew Talbot centre to talk to a counsellor. Within minutes I was crying with fatigue and stress, so she sent someone to collect David and bring him there.

"At that time, Dianne had frozen my funds, and my assets were too high to qualify for the pension. With no income, except the occasional music gig, I was struggling. Then one of my friends on the marina was losing her berth, so I made the decision to relocate to Lake Macquarie. There, I put the yacht on a mooring at the Toronto Sailing Club, then run by Tony Purkiss, a sailing friend from Newcastle, and rented out my marina berth. That was a good move. I was out of Dianne's space and was able to do some one-handed sailing around the lake, which was great practice in a safe environment.

"Then I met Robyn Single, who had a soft spot for musicians, I think."

'How did that happen?'

"A mutual friend suggested that we meet, which we did. We became friends, then she offered me a bed when I wanted to be ashore.

"It was in her house that I started to write *Cull*, my first novel. I would get up at four, and write until she appeared, then we often went to the yacht."

'How long were you at Robyn's?'

"It must have been about two years all up, but I spent a lot of time on the yacht. Basically, it was over the period when the property settlement was dragging on.

"As soon as that was settled, and because I no longer had enough to buy a house, I put the remaining cash into shares, managed by a broker, and we set off on a voyage to the Whitsundays. Robyn had two gay friends, both in their forties, who came as crew.

"We left early 2006, day sailing and anchoring or tying up at marinas at night, depending on our need for a laundry or fuel."

'How did the crew handle the sailing?'

"(laugh) One was an ex-navy man, so he was fine, but his partner, who was at one time a male model, a redhead whom I would describe as 'pretty', did not take to it at all. They were really nice guys and both in great physical shape, but the model spent much of his time aboard wrapped in a blanket looking miserable. So, when we reached Ballina, they left us, and it was just me and Robyn.

"Coming past the Gold Coast, I noticed that the salt-water pump, that was essential for engine cooling, was leaking, so we came through the Seaway into Southport to stop and check it out.

"I took it apart and found that its axle bearings had collapsed, and it is a wonder that the pump was working at all. A dinghy ride took me to a chandler where we pored over parts books, but the pump was so old that there was no mention of that model. However, we reckoned the makers would not have changed everything and went looking for bits that might fit.

"We found bearings the right size from one model of the pump and seals the right size from another and eventually had enough parts for me to replace all the faulty parts.

"Meanwhile, the yacht beside us sank one night in about ten metres of water. We went to bed beside a yacht and woke looking at the top of a mast. So, using the dinghy, we towed our yacht to a safer anchorage in Marine Stadium, known locally as Bum's Bay, where we stayed for a couple of weeks.

"Robyn went back to Newcastle to attend to a family matter for a week, while I completed the rebuild of the pump.

"From there we motored through the Nerang River delta into Moreton Bay, and that wasn't without incident, with a couple of groundings and careful negotiating of pathways under power lines that were probably higher than they looked.

"We spent the early part of one night near Jacob's Well aground but got off on the high tide and anchored. We spent two more nights in Moreton Bay, then headed into Mooloolaba where we spent a couple of days at the marina and had visits from my sisters Dianne and Eleanor and my brother-in-law Dmitri."

'Did you get to the Whitsundays?'

"We spent nearly a month in Bundaberg, where I needed to repaint the hull. There we met Ngaire Thomas who wrote an exposé of the Exclusive Brethren called *Behind Closed Doors*.

"She was parked beside the boatyard in her motor home. Robyn made the connection by introducing herself through the fence, then went around to see her. Over the next few weeks and numerous cups of tea, we spent a fair bit of time discussing our experiences with the sect.

"After she wrote the book, she feared for her life in New Zealand and was moving around, currently at the marina visiting a son who ran the chandlery."

'I suppose you meet interesting people in boats.'

"Yes. A few days into the stay there a bloke rode into the boatyard on a motorbike, and it was Greg, a one-eyed prawn man from Newcastle who had retired with his wife Katy to Bargara.

"They had us around for dinner, and he told me then how Dianne had spread a rumour that I was having an affair with Katy, so we cleared the air on that one.

"Then there was one couple who had a yacht on a hard stand near us who came every weekend to spend time on the yacht on dry land. The yacht had not touched water for years, and they were probably too old to go to sea anyway.

"Another bloke there was doing up a fibreglass hull and spent his nights playing the international money market.

"It rained a lot, and we couldn't paint every day, so we did the tour of the Bundaberg rum distillery and there discovered the origin of the term 'dunderhead'."

'Do tell!'

"(laugh) Dunder is the useless residue that rises to the top of the first stage of fermentation. So, a dunderhead is all froth and bubble and utterly without value.

"We left the Burnett River in a southerly gale and rode the seas up to Baffle Creek.

"On the first morning at Baffle Creek, we had a tap on the hull, and it was the census lady in a speedboat who left the forms then came back later to collect them."

'(laughs) There's no hidin' from the gumment!'

"(laugh) Indeed. And so, we day-sailed up to the Whitsundays and spent a couple of months there."

'What happened to David in the end?'

I have anchored the yacht in Cowan Creek, and I am with Helen, visiting her son at Cottage Point when Matt rings to tell me that David has died. He has no details, so I ring Julia, who does, and we meet at the police station in Day Street, Sydney, where detectives tell us that he died from injuries sustained when he was assaulted in George Street and that they have the assailant in custody.

He is refused bail and tried, and we are in the courtroom every day.

CCTV footage shows David sitting on a doorstep with a woman and then the accused kicking him in the head. A psychiatrist gives evidence that the accused has a mental illness and was under the influence of methamphetamine. He was hallucinating, accusing David of stealing his money.

"David had been homeless, despite several attempts by the Salvos to house him. We spoke regularly by phone and whenever I came to Sydney, and as I said earlier, would meet him for coffee and a burger, when I would show him photos of his girls and his grandson Joshua in England. "Unfortunately, he was in the wrong place at the wrong time and drew the attention of a man who was severely affected by drugs. He kicked David in the head several times, causing him to sustain a brain bleed, and he died."

'Didn't he receive medical help?'

"Yes. What happened came out in court. He appeared to be drunk, which he apparently wasn't. Symptom of a brain bleed can be similar to intoxication, and they were busy. So, he was left to 'sober up'. He then went across the road to a park for a smoke and died there, to be found by walkers the next day."

'That is so sad. Next time, I would like to hear what happened at Greenacre school that caused you to leave. I hope that's less traumatic.'

"You won't get your wish there. It was devastating."

She nods and says nothing as I pick up my sunnies and stand. Reliving David's death has left me feeling down.

Session 12

I enter the room, and she is not there. I sit, hear footsteps approaching and she is in the doorway, carrying two coffees. She is wearing a white silk blouse and navy pedal pushers. They suit her. She kicks the door closed and places one coffee on the desk.

'Running a bit late today. Sorry about that. (laughs) I know how you are with punctuality.'

I reach for a coffee and take the usual chair, she sits, crosses her legs, picks up her notebook and reads silently as I speak.

"Only for me. I don't worry about other people being a bit late, now that I am no longer a bandleader. Like I used to say to my musicians who expressed contempt for tone-deaf committee members who were often our bosses: 'They might not know much about music, but they can all read a clock'."

'So true. Now, you mentioned that you had an affair with one of your staff members at... Greenacre school. How did that happen?'

"Mmm. This is where life became so much more complicated."

'For you or her?'

"For me, I think. I doubt she suffered any consequences, unless we include the loss of me as her lover. It did go on long enough for me to see myself as her lover, and she did make it clear that I mattered to her. It started innocently enough on the surface, and I walked into it with open eyes.

"She had joined the staff when Darcy, the other fourth grade teacher retired, so we shared a grade. She was the only female in the staff room. There were a couple of single younger men, but I was closest to her age, maybe eight or ten years younger. I was twenty-nine, but I was more conditioned by the real world than most teachers. I had been a part-time professional musician since John's band started playing the CYO dances at Enfield Catholic Church Hall in 1956."

'But you were still at college then.'

"Yes, I rode the bike down one weekend a month with the guitar in one pannier bag and the amp in the other."

'Did I hear you right? It was a Catholic Youth dance? (laughs) What did your father say about that?'

I know he will be waiting up. That must take some determination. He is usually in bed at nine and up at five, but I open the door and there he is. He has put on the scowl and the cranky voice.

'Have you been playing the Devil's music?'

"No, Dad, just music to dance to, you know, songs from the radio, Strauss waltzes, that sort of thing."

He stands aside. I pass into the house as he speaks to my back. 'If you're playing the Devil's music you can't stay in this house.'

"He asked if I was playing the Devil's music. I assured him that I wasn't, and I mentioned Strauss, I think that got me by."

'He didn't ask you about the CYO?'

"He didn't ask. If he had, I would have denied it, lied to him."

'Did you often lie to him?'

'What happened to the spokes?'"

"I fell against a stump, and they snapped."

'Looks like they were filed through to me!'

Shit! Here they are!

'Hello, is the lad all right?'

'Who?'

'The lad who was giving my son a ride... doubling him on his bike. Taking him home.'

'You mean Ford? He's all right. What happened?'

'Oh! Didn't he tell you? He was giving Kevin a lift on the bike and Kev's foot got caught in the wheel spokes... between the wheel and the frame... a bloke in a truck filed the spokes through to get the leg out. We just came over to make sure he was all right and the bike could be fixed, that's all.'

"From very early on, I got into the habit of lying about everything."

'Everything? Surely not everything!'

"Just about everything. Truth never protected me from Dad's strappings, so I lied, and it became such a habit that I did it automatically much of the time."

'Was that only when you were threatened, or at other times?'

"(laugh) I don't really know why it was, but I made up stories instead of answering questions. Answers were framed by my need to not seem ignorant or even to avoid criticism. I remember a couple of times when I wrote scathing letters after hearing or reading a negative comment that was not really aimed at me anyway. Later, I regretted having revealed such a thin skin and became more careful."

'Do you think you were more careful, or did you become less sensitive?'

"Careful, I think. I'm still really hurt by criticism. (laugh) I'm meant to be perfect and less than that is shameful."

'But you have hinted at acts in adulthood that you are ashamed about, but your moral compass didn't stop you.'

"Yes. Funny thing about that. When the Brethren straitjacket was removed, so was their set of rules, and I never really replaced them with another full set. What developed were deeply embedded inhibitions left over from the Brethren, but otherwise, I guess I have always been compassionate, so that has been a guide. And then there's the 'do unto others' mantra that I seem to have pretty much used in circumstances where I wasn't sure of what to do. But with the lying, I need to be always watchful."

'How about now?'

"(laugh) No, and this isn't a lie, I decided fifty years ago that truth is the only way I can avoid trapping myself, so now I'm a menace with the truth. Really. It's as if I'm making up for lost opportunities to share. But having said that, as I said, I need to be always aware that a story might replace the truth at any time."

'Why do you want a transfer? We're very happy with what you're doing here. We really value your work. Can I help?'

Vera has told him about Eva. I can't stay here. It will kill her career and mine!

"No, but thanks Ken, I just have to get out of here... my wife isn't well and there will be more trouble if I stay. I have to go, but thanks."

'So, you were never really frank with anyone, never trusted anyone with the truth? Who tried to communicate with you before Greg?'

"Many people, and I did trust some. My boss at Greenacre school. He tried, but I felt too much shame. I had just spent almost a week at the hospital with Vera after her first overdose and felt that it was my responsibility to fix. I didn't know how to do that, so I just wanted to run."

'How did you get into the relationship with... Eva at the school?'

'You're pretty good at fixing things, I hear.'

We are sitting in the staff room drinking instant coffee and she has taken the chair opposite. She is new to the school. A little older than me, slim, dyed blonde hair, happy disposition, European accent.

"What do you want fixed?"

'It's on your way home, and I can't really afford a mechanic. It's the washing machine.'

I look at her again and wonder what is really going on, but I feel a stirring of excitement and ask her where she lives.

'You can follow me home this afternoon and have a look. Do you have time?'

Cosmic Sparring
We dance around each other
like planets in orbit,
Pulled and held by a gravity
We don't understand.
But we do know
That when we touch,
It will be the end
of innocence.

"We worked together on the curriculum, that sort of thing, then one day she asked me to pop into her place on the way home to look at her washing machine."

'(laughs) A good opening line! Were you attracted to her?'

"Not much at first. She was older than me, had two teenage daughters but was a widow and outgoing. And she smelled nice. I liked her well enough."

'So why did you go?'

"If you had asked me then, I would have said it would be mean not to take a look at her washing machine, but now I can say I needed to be needed. Like with Dad. I was always useful, good at fixing things, so that became my basis for self-worth. Unless I can be of use, I am not attracted."

'Attracted or attractive?'

"Um... I never saw it as both then, but now it's clear that I needed to be useful to be attracted and attractive. It was subconscious. But I can see that just being me was not enough to justify a female wanting sex with me. I was never attracted for long to any woman who seemed to be okay – self-contained. Like it was with the others, it seemed that I needed something to trade for sex."

'So, you went, and what happened?'

"I fixed the machine. It had a loose wire in a switch. Ten minutes and it was going."

'Do you think she set that up, to get you there?'

"No, I don't think she knew what was behind the switches, but in any case, I never suspected anything. I didn't ask myself the question. I was looking inwards at my own feelings and did feel excitement, some element of danger, but also presumed it was just me and my sex-starved state."

'Don't touch me there! You only want one thing. I've got a headache, and I forgot to take the pill.'

"But, as soon as I walked through the door, I felt I was in dangerous territory. It was exciting, but on the surface, very proper. I behaved impeccably (laugh)."

'Did you want to not behave impeccably?'

Looking down from the stage. She's dancing with her tits almost bouncing out. Christ, I need a fuck. How long is it now? Must be a month. Two months? I won't let her humiliate me. I will not start it.

It is such a bad feeling when she always has a headache, and I know she's lying. My own wife. Before marriage, full on. After marriage, almost nothing.

'All you ever want is one thing! You're a sex addict! My doctor says once in a couple of months is normal!'

She's right. I should be able to do without. That and wanking too!

This one is old enough to be my mother, but I'd fuck her! Shit! What has become of me!

"Yes and no. I wanted sex but had no way to get from how I felt to getting it. I had to wait for her to make the first move."

'Maybe she already had.'

"(laugh) Maybe. But I needed more than that, and I think she understood how I was because she kept me there long after I had fixed the machine. She could have been laying the groundwork for another visit because she made coffee and wanted to talk.

"She told me about her young life as a Jew in Austria, her husband's death, a lot of intimate details, and I was happy to listen. Remember this was less than twenty years after the end of the war. I was in a state of heightened awareness and wanted to see where she was leading.

"Her teenage daughters came home from school, and they seemed to be, well, not negative toward me."

'So, how did it get from there to sharing a bed?'

"I left without making any arrangements, but of course, next day we were back in the staff room and talking over coffee. At one point we were alone, and I was looking out the window at the kids in the playground. She joined me there and leaned against me, so I turned and kissed her."

'So, your affair started then. Did it remain a secret?'

"(laugh) No. One of the younger guys walked in on us kissing. He backed out quickly but there was no mistaking what he had seen. He must have talked, because my best friend on staff, Paul, knew."

'What was the next step?'

"She asked about my gigs and suggested that I might like to call in on the way home for a coffee. Of course I did, but we didn't drink coffee. There was a single bed in a spare room. She led me there and stripped off."

'What time was this?'

"Oh, probably one in the morning."

'So, you had sex in the single bed, then went home?'

"Yes, that's about it. After a few times, she gave me a front door key so I didn't need to knock, which she said might wake the girls."

'How did it end?'

"Ah yes. I was booked for a Saturday night gig in Wollongong so I told Vera I would stay overnight but had arranged with Eva to be at her place about 2 a.m. She had the girls stay somewhere else, so we could spend the rest of the night together and the Sunday morning."

'And you were sprung?'

"I had bought myself a Citroën car. It was the same model as Joan's in Bathurst, so it was conspicuous."

'Was that reliving a romantic past?'

"No doubt. But what I didn't know was that Eva's ex-boyfriend lived near her and had noted my car parked out front of her house and was able to get my identity from the plates, I guess."

'Can you do that?'

"Well, clearly he could, because he contacted Vera and passed on his suspicions just in time for our Saturday-night, Sunday-morning arrangement. She rang Ken, my bandleader, on the Sunday morning and because I hadn't told him of the arrangement, he dumped me in it."

'Oops!'

"Right. I arrived home before lunch to find her unconscious, with empty drug containers in the bathroom. I rang the ambulance and rode with her to Liverpool Hospital."

'But she survived.'

"Yes, and I felt so guilty that I was almost catatonic. Her mother moved into the house to mind the children, and I stayed in the hospital for about three days. I didn't eat or sleep much. I didn't know what to do and just kept apologising and promising that I was there for her. I have never felt more miserable in my life."

'How do you feel about that now?'

She just lies there, skin grey, unmoving, the respirator moving with her breathing. Again, sex has brought me to another point of absolute shame. Her mother has taken over the house and says she had a good mind to stick a knife into my chest while I'm asleep, and I believe her. Then I am ill. I see Dr Sproule, and he writes a script for antibiotics, asks me what I intend to do. I say I have 'woken up to myself' and he gives me a funny look that I don't understand until forty years later.

"Back then, I was devastated that I could have done anything to cause her to want to end her life. Now, I see it as the ultimate weapon in the armoury of the co-dependent. On many occasions following her recovery, she would make demands while shaking a pill bottle. The message was clear and for many years it worked.

"To keep someone under control by threatening to take your own life if they don't conform is at least pathetic, but I now see it as extreme passive aggression. It expresses a desperation that you are losing control, and control is more important to you than life itself.

"I also felt that society would judge me and presume the pill-taker was the 'innocent' one. What do you think about that?"

'Did your friends give you a hard time?'

'You should have moved in with the Austrian!'

"What do you mean?"

'Vera's a stupid bitch. She's not worth the sacrifice of your career. And she's been fucking anything with a pulse!'

"No, I can't leave her, she needs me, and the kids…"

"Eva said I could move in with her, but I was too deep in shame to consider that an option. Some of my friends wondered why I stayed on. Most did not express an opinion, but none of my friends gave me a hard time.

"Nobody in my immediate family had ever divorced, so it was a new concept for me on a visceral level. I was too overwhelmed with negative emotion to think straight, not that I had any respect for any of my own thoughts."

'That's interesting. Did you think you were dumb?'

"I had no respect for my own judgement. It came as a surprise relatively recently that throughout my life, some of the people I talked to had listened and used my ideas."

'Was that because of your father's attitude do you think?'

"I'm sure of it. He put down everything I attempted, but strangely, he sometimes took my advice and that didn't always end well."

'I'll come back to your father later but am interested in what happened after she came out of hospital. Did you go back to playing happy families?'

"No, she went to Brisbane to stay with her aunt Amelia for a few months and that was hard for me."

'I bet. You mentioned that your boss at school, and I presume that was the headmaster, was keen for you to stay, but you asked to be transferred?'

"That's right. Ken had given me a free hand to try some new techniques in math, which I loved and achieved amazing results, and of course, there was the music."

'Tell me why it became impossible for you to stay in the school where you were successful and appreciated.'

I am not expecting the inspector, but he comes in while we are doing some mental arithmetic. The kids are doubling numbers. I stop them at a 1,024 and then we treble numbers and are still going when he sees my guitar leaning against the wall.

'What do you use that for?'

We stop counting and the kids watch him. They want to go on with the threes a bit longer. They know what they are doing is special and they have exam results to back it up.

I pick it up and run a finger over the open strings. It is in tune.

"We sing songs and practise pitching notes, the guitar is a reference."

He looks down his nose, literally, and pronounces: 'I don't regard that as a suitable instrument for teaching children.'

I had heard that he sang in a choir.

"I believe you sing in a choir, Mr Crago. Would you like to sing

something for the boys before you go?"

'Do you know "Drink to Me Only with Thine Eyes"?'

I sling the guitar strap over my shoulder. "What key?"

'E flat.' I can see in his eyes that he thinks he has me beaten, so I play a 1-6-2-5 arpeggio intro, and he sings. He sings well.

Into the last few bars, I rit, and then over his last note I play a 4-1, the plagal cadence. The boys clap enthusiastically, and he leaves without a further word.

"The inspector was not keen on me. I don't know why, but he tried to undermine me in several ways."

'Why would he do that?'

Ken asks me if I would like to run an Inservice course on music and the use of guitar in the classroom. I am chuffed to be doing this and spend countless hours producing Gestetner stencils of music and chord diagrams. About eight of our own staff attend the first session, then a couple of nuns turn up and it grows to be a roomful.

We include some 'music maths', a variation on the use of standard numerals that I have been developing with my own class. A copy of my notes goes to the inspector.

A few weeks after we have completed the guitar course, Crago calls a staff meeting, where he proceeds to give our teachers a lesson on music in the classroom.

"I have no idea why he did that. He went so far as claiming some of the ideas I had included in my course as his own. For instance, I would draw musical notes on the blackboard and create mathematical equations; quaver plus dotted crotchet equals a minim."

'What did you say?'

"I found it difficult to believe he would do that, and felt helpless to comment, but a few of the teachers pointed out that what he was presenting was all in the notes I had given them, and they knew he had received copies. He claimed it was coincidence. But there was more.

"Vera had rung the school and told Ken I was having an affair with Eva. In those days, that could have led to both of us being dismissed, so I went onto the permanent casual staff, which means she had no idea where I would be on any given day."

'So, she was in Brisbane, and you were home alone in Cabramatta?'

"Not all the time. After a couple of months, the summer vacation arrived, and Vera's eldest cousin was sent to keep an eye on me. She was also a teacher and the wrong person to send."

'Why's that?'

We are in the lounge room. Christmas holidays are here, and I have Miles on the turntable. We are into our second bottle of red. I don't have any motives, ulterior or otherwise. She moves closer and lets her hand slip down to rest on my penis. Is she testing me out? If so, the test is a bit hard, pun intended.

She is pretty, intelligent, voluptuous and here, and I am sex-starved and miserable. I am aware of the irony. 'The fox sent to mind the chooks', and I decide to let the fox in. We go to bed, and it is pretty messy. We are really too drunk to be doing this. But we do actually sleep together that night.

In the morning, she is contrite, and by lunchtime she has phoned Vera and told her.

"I claim she seduced me. I could have knocked her back, and there was some poetic justice in it after all. But, unknown to me at the time, she told Vera. Why, I will never know, and she was ordered back to Brisbane.

"We were both on vacation, so we drove up in the Citroën. It was a nice drive up and when we arrived, it was like the three of us were on holiday together.

"We went to clubs and pubs, danced and drank then, when she was ready, Vera decided she needed to be home, and as I hadn't actually left the marriage, she was willing to give it a go, but the sex didn't improve."

'In the end I know it didn't work out, but how was it in the beginning?'

"Vera seemed happy to be going home, and I was beginning to feel there was hope. But for the last few hundred kilometres the car was running roughly, and by the time we got home, it was burning oil and could hardly pull itself up the driveway and into the carport."

'Did you find the problem?'

There is nothing for it but to pull the engine apart and have a look. I take off the head and find the combustion chambers are coated with what looks like black diamond crystals. I taste it, and it is sugar. I drain the petrol tank and out comes a pile of at least half a kilo. God knows how much was put in there. I ask Vera, and she says Eva's boyfriend did it.

"Eva's ex and Vera conspired to wreck my car engine by putting sugar in the tank."

'So, sugar in the tank really does work?'

"Not as quickly as you see in the movies, but two thousand kilometres later and the whole engine was stuffed. Bores, bearings, every moving part has been scoured and torn by sugar crystals."

'Would you agree that doing that was an own goal?'

"I thought it was pretty kamikaze, considering it was the car I used for work, so now I had to take her VW, leaving her with no transport. But maybe, although I never told her about Joan in Bathurst, she might have made the connection that the Citroën was more than just a car to me."

'Nostalgia.'

Dad comes with me for a look. It is parked at a slope that shows its lines to advantage and I know I must have it. The vendor has polished it and dressed the leather, so it gleams and smells great. Driving it home, I am back with Joan in Bathurst, and I fight back tears of regret. Maybe this is not such a good idea.

"Yes, nostalgia. But I did really like the design, and this car was the 'commercial' model that had a rear hatch door and, in its original configuration, a third row of seats, so it had heaps of space to transport instruments. It had belonged to the French ambassador when it was new, but I discovered when I got it home that a previous owner must have had sheep. The guy who sold it to me had prettied it up but had not done a good job of cleaning it. There were sheep droppings under the carpets and under the seats. The smell when I inspected it must have been sprayed on."

'But otherwise, it was what you expected?'

Within weeks, the suspension starts to rattle, the steering feels loose. The whole car, except for the engine, feels worn out. I jack it up to find cardboard in all the worn parts and sawdust in the transmission. I am dismayed, but probably can't prove that it was the vendor, so I start reconditioning.

"A lot of the car's suspension had been padded with cardboard, so it felt tight for a week or two, then I needed to do extensive repairs."

'So, the vendor did that? Seems like a lot of trouble. Why not fix it properly?'

"I asked myself the same question. Parts were available, I found they were not difficult to find, and bought through Nouméa, were not expensive. Anyway, I reconditioned the gear box, fixed all the suspension and steering, and it went very well.

"I was doing two Sunday gigs, one in Wollongong and another in Unanderra, south of Wollongong, playing bass in Ken Bennett's band. To save on transport costs, I met the sax player, Pat Harrington, in Liverpool every Sunday and drove him down. He brought three saxes, a clarinet and a flute, and with my bass and amp, they fitted neatly into the space between the seats where the original third set of seats had folded out of the floor. They had been removed, I was told, to accommodate the ambassador's long legs."

'Was this the same gig where you said you would stay over?'

"No, that was before this one started. Back then I played only guitar."

'So, why did you change to bass?'

It is Monday morning, and Ken is at the door. I usually see him in the afternoon when he comes to sleep for the night.

"Hi Ken, what's happening?"

He steps aside to reveal a bass guitar case and a hefty amp. He lifts them through the door.

'Thursday night, Manly Warringah, you're playing bass for me. Get there at seven.'

"But I've never played bass. I can't..." *But he has already gone. I shut the door and look at the instrument.*

I had played Fender six-string bass guitar at Channel 7 in the Johnny O'Keefe Show, filling in for Lennie Hutchinson, but those charts are all written in treble clef. This is a four-string bass, and the charts will be in bass clef. That is another world. I sweat.

"Ken Bennett was a brilliant musician, but like most of us back then, he needed a day job. He was working for a car finance company repossessing cars so, although he lived in Maroubra, he was often working in Green Valley, unkindly dubbed 'Dodge City' because all the homes were built by the Housing Commission and most residents were low income and many overextended their ability to pay for a car.

"He was a mate I had done a lot of work with. Anyway, he dumped a bass and amp on me one Monday morning with instructions to learn to play it for a show on the following Thursday night."

'Could you do it? Did you do it?'

"I have a lot of respect for Ken and didn't think he would want to make himself look bad by having an incompetent bass player in the band, so I thought, 'If he thinks I can do it, I probably can'. I spent the next few days practising and then, very nervously turned up at the gig.

"I had copied hundreds and written quite a few band charts in the past and knew what bass parts looked like. I had been a fan of Ray Brown since I first heard him on the album at Joan's in Bathurst and was aware of what he did, but to play on a gig? To say the least, I was anxious."

'I bet you were. So how did it go?'

We do the talk-through, and I am relieved to see that all the parts have chord symbols, so I don't need to read bass clef. Des Egan is on drums, so I don't need to worry about time keeping.

When I pick up the bass, Des gives me a funny look but says nothing. The acts are all stars of TV which adds to the tension, but before I can worry too much, Ken counts off, and we are away.

"The first act went for about twenty minutes and then the compere was there telling a story. Des, the drummer leans over and says: 'How long have you been playing bass?' I look at my watch, laugh and say: 'Twenty minutes.'

"He joins in the laughter and says I have 'found my instrument'. There were even a few compliments from the acts.

"At the end of the night, Ken gave me a folder of Lallys to practise and announced that I was now permanently in his band, playing bass."

'What are Lallys?'

"Some said that Jimmy Lally was a cover-all name for a group of English arrangers who produced flexible and easy-to-read dance band arrangements, starting in the fifties, or he might have been a real person. In any case, they were cheap and basic, and they came out following the release of new songs, so bands could keep up to date at little cost. In fact, I remember in my really early days in bands, some bands got free copies to popularise new songs.

"Anyway, the bass parts were written out as notes in bass clef. So, for practice, they were useful, and in Ken's band, we did play many of them, particularly for the old-time dances."

'So that marked a change of direction for you?'

Ken wants the bass and amp back, so I buy a second-hand bass for twenty dollars and find that my record player amp, bought from George Golla along with a stack of guitar records, coupled with a double twelve-inch speaker box is a nice sound. Then Ken uses me in the Harris Coffee and Tea ad, and people start asking: 'Who is the bass player?'

"Yes. I was a competent guitar player, but as John Speight said, I would never be a George Golla, and the change to bass came at the right time. Plenty of acoustic bass players made the change to electric, but when they did, what they had been getting away with, that is, mysterious thumps in the bottom end, was suddenly clear to hear. I didn't play guitar seriously again for over fifty years."

'I'd like to hear about that, but let's get back to you in... (looks at notes) Greenacre and you have told the principal that you want to go on the permanent casual list. How did that work out?'

I turn up at Glebe Primary with my guitar and am shown to a big room in an almost empty, double-storey block where I am soon joined by forty or so fourth-grade boys. I ask them to get out a workbook and take them through some of my Newmath puzzles, and they love them. I am here for three weeks and am soon immersed in the fun of watching young minds play with concepts and numbers. We write down stories, sing rounds and have fun. A couple of times the principal pokes his head in and once or twice stays for a few minutes.

"It was rewarding, and it kept me busy. I made an impression in one school where the principal asked me if I would like a permanent position, but I was afraid of what Vera might do to poison that well, and it was a long commute, so I kept moving until some months later, I was offered a job as a music teacher at a high school close by. Things had cooled down at home, and it seemed we might patch up the relationship, so I took the job, but that was a mistake."

'Why's that?'

I have no idea what I should be doing, so I bring in some Beatles records and we analyse the backing, working out the form, time signatures and the keys. I don't think that is going to cut it, but next time the class seems to have grown. I bring in a tape recorder and we start to record our own backing track, and by the third week, there are not enough seats for the number that turn up and I am aware that I have some of the other teacher's students.

I visit the deputy principal. He is aware that kids from the other class have been attending my classes and asks why I think that is.

I don't want to poach her students but know that my experience in professional music has allowed me to bring some of that to the classroom. I am emotionally very unstable. In fact, I should not have been working in a classroom. When the deputy asks me what's going on, I say that I don't know what she had been offering but suggest that maybe the other teacher's material might be a bit dated. I look up and she is standing there. I am so embarrassed that I resign on the spot. I tell the deputy that I am about to start full-time university, which I had been thinking might be a way forward.

"Firstly, it was a high school, and I didn't know the curriculum and I now think I was in a mental health crisis, going through the motions, following the prompts, but not in control of anything. I was still able to take the role of teacher, the role of musician and the role of husband and father to the extent that was permitted. I was offered no advice, and being me, I was too afraid to admit I was struggling and ask for help."

'I have no doubt you were in a mental health crisis, and you badly needed help, but tell me, was seeking advice always a problem for you?'

I'll meet you at Central under the clock. Seven o'clock, Saturday, okay?
"Okay, Lindsay."
'We can see a movie.'
"Good idea."
He won't notice if I don't go. Can't be bothered. He won't wait long.
"I always seemed to think I was invisible."

'Invisible?'

"Yes. Invisible. If I spoke in a group, I felt that nobody listened. It was as if I never spoke. When I left a group, I just left. Never said goodbye to anyone, just left. I felt as if I wasn't there for anyone, so in the end, I was always uncomfortable unless I had someone with me..."

'Backup.'

"Yes, backup. That's why I liked being with Vera. She always set the pace. A few drinks and she was funny and outrageous sometimes."

'Did she ever embarrass you?'

'You want to go home! You want to fucking go home! Well, I don't. I'm just starting to enjoy myself you control freak, so fuck off!'

"I'm tired, I've been working all day and tonight, and I can hardly keep my eyes open. I just have to go to bed. Come on... you've had enough to drink. Let's go."

'Enough to drink! Don't you tell me when I've had enough to fuckin' drink! Fuck off home! You never take me out, so go on, fuck off!'

"No, I'm not usually embarrassed by things other people do or say, even though I would never do or say them. I just go numb and wait."

'Do you still do that?'

"Yes, and that applies to things that go wrong, like the floods that wiped out crops or the diseases that caused me to abandon certain lines of produce that could have been profitable had I taken advice."

'So, this invisibility for you means that you don't feel that you are important enough for someone else to invest in you?'

"Yes, something like that. And now I think back on many times in my life when advice might have not only saved me time but could have saved some projects that I abandoned way before I should have. Some could have become lucrative.

"The people who could have helped me were there, but I felt that to ask showed ignorance, or weakness, and that was shameful. I learnt early not to ask Dad for anything."

'When you asked him for help or advice, what did he do?'

"I stopped asking for help from him as a small child. It seemed that he was always too busy to give me time, unless it was his idea, or he could show off. Questions from me irritated him. It was just his attitude to anything I was doing.

"It applied to the other kids too, but it was me who bore the brunt of it. We have a family joke... Whenever Bill or I come across each other doing anything we always say, sarcastically, 'And what do you think you're doing!' It was never a question, it was a put down, like we were sure to stuff up without him being there to supervise."

'So, he insisted on supervising?'

'What do you think you're doing there?'
"It's a picture for homework."
'What's it supposed to be?'
"I'm supposed to paint a picture that shows 'temptation'. It's for scripture."
'So, what's that you've done so far? Doesn't look like temptation to me. Get another bit of paper.'
"It's a kid thinking of stealing some fruit from a tree. Something like that."
'All right, give me the brush and watch.'
'Did you do this painting yourself?'
"Yes, sir."
'No help from an adult?'
"No, sir, all by myself."
'Amazing!'

"No, he didn't supervise, he usually took over completely. He just did it. An early example that stands out is when he took over a project when I was maybe ten. I was told to paint a scene that showed 'temptation' for scripture homework. He took over and painted a very threatening scene, complete with Satan, pointy ears and tail, looking over a fence, watching what could have been me stealing an apple from a tree."

'Very biblical.'

"(laugh) Yes, but I insisted I painted it myself. It would have been clear to any adult that it was the work of an adult who was also a pretty good artist."

'That was when you were a child. Did it stop when you were an adult?'

"No, he kept it up until I called him out on it. But it caused me to think I couldn't draw well, and it wasn't until I was middle-aged that I tried drawing for the covers of my play scripts and found they were pretty good."

'How did you call him out on it?'

It has been raining for days and we notice a wet stain seeping across the lounge room carpet in the new house. The wall had been coated with pitch on the outside, but clearly that isn't enough to keep this water out. Next day I start to excavate along the outside of the wall. Mostly, the digging is easy because it's backfill. I've decided to create a metre-wide gap between the house and the soil and add a drain along the bottom of the gap.

A metre down, I find a lump of concrete stuck to the wall that was excess and dumped when the floors were poured. I hire a jackhammer and have removed about three-quarters of a ton, when Dad turns up. I look up.

Hands on hips, he is grinning. 'What do you think you're doing?' he asks, and the sarcasm is there. The failure of the wall to keep out water is really his problem, and he is trying to shame me again.

"We had been in the Orange Grove Road house for a while when the lounge room flooded during heavy rain, ruining the carpet. The house was built into the side of the hill and water came through the wall, so I dug the hill away to insert a drain beside the foundations. It worked."

'So, what did your father do?'

"(laugh) "What did he do? As usual, he turned up and did his sarcastic line 'What do you think you're doing', but he got me at the wrong time. He had taken over the building project, and I'm not saying it was totally his fault, but there were mistakes made that left the building's integrity compromised and the massive cost overrun left me with an unimaginable debt.

"The arguments Vera and I had over that did not help our marriage. In any case, my response, unusually, was anger, and I said: 'This should be your problem, so get down here and help or bugger off!'"

'What did he say to that?'

"Nothing. He just left without a word."

'Did he ever come back to help?'

"(laugh) No, and I didn't want him to. I was able to dig down below the foundation, put in the terracotta drain, support the soil with a wall of Besser blocks laid on their sides to allow water through and cover the top with concrete pavers. It looked professional in the end, but Dad never came for a look."

'Was he afraid that a compliment might weaken his influence? What do you think stopped him from recognising your achievements?'

Mum and I are chatting. She would be about eighty-two or three. We are in her apartment in Nullica Lodge in Eden, and we have been talking about Dad and how hard he found it to encourage his children. Mum says Dad loved the babies but felt threatened by grown-up children.

She tells me that he once attended a Daly-Wilson concert at the Sydney Town Hall to watch me play, but never told me he would be there or said anything afterward.

"You know, in a way, he did. He wanted to be involved in the solar passive house, so much so that he kept pushing me to spend more to make it special. Out of the blue, when I was fifteen, and still a soprano, he organised with my school music teacher, Ken Brown, to have me recorded at EMI when he worked there. Of course, he kept control of the material, so I sang only songs he approved of.

"He trusted me to rewire that truck. I laid the five thousand tiles on the new house in Orange Grove Road. Then there was the contract ploughing that I did to bring in cash for years in my teens. We often worked together when my contribution was important, but I cannot remember any time when he encouraged me overtly."

'But it seems you had the confidence to go ahead and do stuff, be entrepreneurial?'

"It is still a wonder to me that I did anything off my own bat. But since early childhood I had ideas and tried them out. Now, I think I must have done those things when he wasn't around.

"I am now sure that if he had been there, he would have stopped me. Most of the early inventive things I did were during the war, then after I left home. So maybe that's it. Of course, later in my life he was out of the picture, physically if not totally emotionally.

"When we were ready to build a house, we had a plan and a budget. We had planned to dig into the hill for a garage and put a project home over that. The 'Beverley Home' did not have a garage, but the shape of the site made the addition of a garage easy."

'Your father and you?'

"No, my wife and me. We had saved enough and with a bank loan of 2,500 pounds we could do it, but Dad butted in and said we would do better if we built it ourselves."

'And did you build it yourselves?'

"I did the design, but digging out the foundations was the limit of my physical involvement. I had been fiddling with an idea for a passive solar house for some time, working out the orientation, eaves overhang, window size, direction and angles of the sun through the seasons, that sort of thing.

"The calculations and sketches were done on the shared dining room table, so he knew what I had been thinking. Anyway, he reckoned he could build the solar house for the price of the project home, so we agreed that he should manage it.

"I had already started the digging, so we finished that. But from then on, he took over everything to do with the construction. He got the brickies and in no time, walls were up, and it was his project!"

'Was it a good outcome?'

"No. To me, it was a disaster. The house was as we planned almost... The suspended floors had been designed by ARC, the concrete company, but the concreters didn't understand the plans or didn't look and missed a vital part of the reinforcement design that used cantilevered sections to balance other suspended sections. The steel reinforcing was not correctly placed so there was no cantilever effect, and that ruined the integrity of the building. Floors cracked, and I needed to prop one floor up with steel verticals.

"It should have been pulled down and the floors re-done, but Dad was the builder, typically with no insurance, so we just had to fix what we could and leave it at that."

'Were you worried it might collapse?'

"I still worry it might collapse, but sixty years later, it hasn't changed. Really, there was no chance it would collapse. The cracks were superficial, but I was upset that it had gone wrong. It was not perfect and that reflected on me.

"I have been back to look at the house twice. I just knocked on the door and asked if I could look through the house I built, and it was okay. We were confident it would stay up, but the mistakes spoiled my joy in the design and put huge pressure on the marriage."

'How did it do that?'

'He made the estimates. He stuffed up. It's his problem!'

"No, he did ask me if I wanted copper guttering, if I wanted Klip-Lok roofing, if I wanted cork flooring and so on. He never talked about cost, but that's what it cost. He spent the money."

'But more than double the price? He hit you with a bill for 7,500 pounds. He should pay it, not us!'

"No, he paid the money out and we have to pay it back or we sell up and start again."

'No way! I'm not losing my house because he stuffed up. He can afford it. He should give us the house for nothing, the mean old bastard! You tell him to go jump!'

Numb again. Can't do anything. Just have to work harder.

"Vera always said Dad should be held responsible for the cost overruns. In fact, she always said he should have given us the house for nothing. I insisted that he should be paid back, even if he was responsible for the overruns, because he had spent the money and he had given me the block of land."

'That was generous of him, wasn't it?'

"Yes, I thought it was. I didn't ever expect him to give me anything. I chose one of the cheapest, but it suited me."

'Why the cheapest? Why do you say it suited you?'

"Oh, the site looked over the golf course, and like I said, it also offered an easy way to add a garage to an off-the-rack home. But I have always been afraid to ask for anything. He took requests as a challenge and usually refused automatically. Any kindnesses had to be his idea. He offered. We didn't ask."

'But he went through with the gift of the block of land, didn't he?'

'You can plough this bloke's paddock... take the disc harrows on the back and you can do the whole cultivation job for him. Twenty-five bob an hour and you keep the five bob.'

"Yes, he did, and maybe it was in recognition for all the years I brought home cash, driving the tractor out to farms, contract ploughing. When he was building a house there was no income until the end of the job. I was paid five shillings an hour and I saved most of it... bought a new push bike. One hundred and twenty-five pounds. That's five hundred hours of driving for the bike alone."

'How old were you when you started the contracting?'

"I had just turned fourteen and I was a small kid for my age. The old farmers used to ask for the 'little kid on the big tractor'."

'But you must have been good at it.'

Dad is bogged at Bob Perno's farm. He climbs down, scratching his head, so I climb up and drive it out. They are amazed and my reputation spreads.

'He's good!' says Perno. Dad just stares.

"Yes, I was good at it, but the plough Dad had fitted to the tractor was particularly suited to the type of farming around us. I'm not sure why Dad chose that type of plough, but it was soon in demand."

'What made it so special?'

The Egyptian's accent makes him difficult to understand, but I think he wants what his neighbour wants, and that is to turn the soil to twelve inches deep. I do that and follow up with the disc harrows and by the end of the day, the paddock looks flat and ready for planting, but I know he will be growing early tomatoes, and needs raised beds. Next day, I arrive on my bike, and he has started the huge task of throwing up beds with a shovel. I take off one disc and demonstrate that I can shape his beds with the other disc in no time.

He catches on right away, so before I ride my bike home, his five acres is well on the way to being prepared for tomato plants.

"The cultivator used most widely around there at the time was the Howard DH 22 rotary hoe, but many of the market gardeners grew tomatoes for the Christmas market and preferred the soil to be dug deeper than is possible with the rotary hoe. There was also the problem that rotary hoes generally leave the soil susceptible to erosion."

'How's that?'

"They leave the soil with very fine tilth but under that is a flat pan of harder soil, so if the rain is heavy enough, the pan stops water from seeping through and it runs along the hard pan, gouging gulleys and carrying topsoil away. My plough left the base rough and the structure of the soil less prone to erosion. And I could shape their beds for them with the plough. They liked that."

'You talked about driving to the farms. Did you have a licence?'

I have just finished a job on the creek flats at the end of Bowden Street, Cabramatta, and am almost home. A cop on a Harley and sidecar pulls me over. I expect the worst.

I can sense Dad watching from the house and hope he stays there. The cop parks the bike, and I climb down. He stands for a moment looking at the tractor, then turns to me. 'Have you got a licence for this thing, son?'

"No, I haven't."

'Then why are you driving on the road?'

I look up at the house, and nothing is moving. "Dad's away, Mum doesn't drive, so someone has to take it for service."

He looks at the tractor again and I can see discs, shining with very recent use, with a few clods of fresh dirt around the plough frame, and I know he should be able to see that I have been ploughing today.

Whether he thinks that or not, he goes to the sidecar and comes back with a pad and pencil. 'What's your name, son?'

I tell him my name and address. He folds up the pad and looks again at the tractor. He must know what I have been doing, but just nods and says:

'Better get you a licence for it then, hadn't we?'

He throws his leg over the bike and before he kicks it over, he gives me a hard look. 'And no driving before you get the licence. Okay?'

I just nod and watch him ride away down the hill.

"I had been driving it for maybe a year and a half before I was sprung, but in those days, we saw a cop maybe once a year and there was no specialist Highway Patrol. Traffic was light too because petrol rationing was still in force and stayed that way for another few years. I was almost home from a job when the local police sergeant pulled me over just as I was about to turn into our driveway, and after quizzing me for a bit, all he said was that he 'better get me a licence'.

"A few weeks later a dapper little man in a suit turned up and gave me a driving test."

'(laughs) And you passed?'

"(laugh) Look, if I had more sense, I wouldn't have shown him every trick I could do, including 360 skid turns backwards, using the turning brakes with him standing on the drawbar, probably scared shitless. Anyway, a licence arrived a few weeks later in the mail and just after I turned fifteen, I was legal."

'A lot of trust to place in a fifteen-year-old.'

We have been blowing up stumps. Dad bought a wooded crate of gelignite, a roll of fuse and a box of percussion caps at a clearance sale and we have great fun inserting the charges under stumps, lighting the fuses and running to hide behind trees, fingers in our ears. But before the stumps are all out, and when the box of gelignite is still half full, we are out of fuse and almost out of caps.

He sends me off to Murray Brothers in Parramatta with a note and a signed cheque. I ride my bike to Cabramatta Station, train to Parramatta, which requires a change of trains at Granville, then walk down to the store. I hand over the note and the cheque. An old bloke reads the note, then disappears into the innards of the store, to emerge with a hessian sack. He hands over the sack and says: 'The docket's inside.' And off I go to retrace my steps home.

"You know, this still amazes me. About then, we were blowing out stumps on the Orange Grove Road farm and Dad sent me to Parramatta to buy fuse and detonator caps. Imagine what would happen now if a spotty-faced youth in bare feet turned up at your store to buy fuse and detonator caps? (laugh) You'd have a SWAT team there in minutes."

'(Incredulous) They didn't give them to you?'

"(laugh) Yes, and typical of me, despite Dad telling me not to touch any of it, in the train I opened one of the two detonator boxes to see inside. The boxes were beautifully made from pine, dove-tailed joints at the ends and had a sliding lid."

'We know that the defiance is a rection to abuse, but despite the theory, it still amazes me that you defied your father after all the beltings.'

"I don't remember any beltings after we moved to Orange Grove Road, which coincided with me going to high school, driving the tractor, and doing most of the work on the farm, including servicing and fixing the machinery.

"But in any case, it had been years since they were a factor in my behaviour. I just did as I thought fit, or wanted to do, regardless of his direction.

"I remember shortly after I rewired the Chev truck, he needed a crack in a mudguard welded, so he towed it with me steering, to a welder. On the way home, he told me not to start the engine to climb the hill to our driveway.

"I really wanted to drive it, so I started the motor, applying just enough power to make it easier to tow. All went well until we were crossing the deep gutter into the driveway. The Dodge stopped dead, and I ran into the corner of the tray, shattering a headlamp glass. I turned the engine off, and I still don't know if he knew I had been driving it up the hill."

'How did you feel?'

"Sorry. Embarrassed. But at another time he might just as easily have unhooked it at the bottom of the hill and told me to drive it up. I knew how arbitrary his decisions concerning me were, so I eventually made decisions without asking him, and as in that case, in defiance of him like I did when I was playing (laugh) the Devil's music."

'Did you ever drive the truck on the road before you had a licence?'

We are in the shed at Coromandel, and I'm looking for something for Owen. I see a packing case full of wheels, a two-stroke motor in bits and more, lots of parts and pipes. "What's all this stuff in the box?"

'That's the Wog. Edgar sent it up for me to fix. Do you want to have a go?'

It takes me about two days, and I have it together, minus the exhaust pipe. It is a bit finicky to fit and I am impatient to see if it will run. I kick the starter, and it goes after a couple of tries. It is loud, with a high-pitched cackle coming from the exhaust port. I stop it and eventually fit the exhaust pipe. For the rest of the week, I ride it around the farm; up to the gate for the mail and newspaper, over to the back orchard for oranges, anything as an excuse to ride it.

"No, I didn't drive the trucks before I had a licence, except around the farm. But Wal's dad, Edgar, bought a Waratah motorcycle in 1935, and it was used as family transport by him and his Turnbull brothers-in-law for many years. Edgar had it when it stopped going, so it was shipped to Owen in a box in around 1950, to be repaired.

"Owen gave me the job of fixing it, which I did and rode it around the farm until it was time for me to go home, then Owen did something that was quite naughty and said that if I rode it home, I could keep it. It wasn't registered, and I had no licence.

"What I did have was knowledge of the back roads south and west of Liverpool, where I had been with the tractor, and an understanding that rules about licences were to be ignored if the circumstances warranted. This was one of those circumstances, so off I went, arriving home in one piece and undetected."

'What did your parents say?'

"I don't know if they had given up on me by then, but Mum said nothing. I was smart enough to know not to ride it on the road. I had the tractor licence and feared that any infringement would take that away. So, the bike stayed in the shed until I got a bike licence on Wally's BSA 250, on the first day I was legally allowed to do so."

'I want to take you back a bit. After you moved to Orange Grove Road, you say the beltings stopped?'

"No, I can't remember a belting from Dad after I went to high school and that more or less coincided with me driving the new tractor and bringing home cash. The tractor made me an honorary adult as I took on adult tasks and things improved at home, but I was caned at school."

'Did you think you deserved to be caned at high school?'

"No, I didn't do anything naughty. (laugh) I was never really ready for the level of education I was exposed to at high school. Having been a primary school teacher myself, I can see how that could have happened, when it happened.

"I started school at the outbreak of the Second World War. Most young male teachers joined the services as officers, so for almost six years we were taught by older teachers, recruited from retirement, and unkindly called 'retreads'. I remember discipline being lax as was the lesson material, so our education suffered somewhat. I must have missed out on some subjects, particularly maths, because when I started high school there were two young maths teachers who brought long canes with them to punish ignorance.

"It was 1948, and I guess they were fresh out of college and felt insecure. They caned boys for not knowing stuff, or even for not understanding their mathematical language. They talked about products and quotients, that sort of thing. These were terms I doubt my country schoolteachers knew, much less taught!"

'But you went well at college?'

"College was relatively easy and so was uni, after I resigned the second time and started a degree in Science."

'How did you support yourself at uni? Was Vera working then?'

I have paid my first year's fees and am wondering how I will make enough to live on, when I get a call from drummer, Ivan Kenez. I have never heard of him, but he makes me an interesting offer.

"No, as I mentioned before, Vera was unable to work after she quit at Cabramatta West. Julia was about two, and things had settled down at home, despite the rationed sex. I threw myself into the uni work to compensate.

"But Cabramatta was still a long way out of town, and I was becoming a bit desperate, doing copying for Channel 7, and any gigs I could get. I was looking at an insurmountable set of problems when a guy I had never heard of rang me and offered me a gig on bass in a jazz trio, five to nine weekdays in the Keller Room at the Menzies Hotel at ninety dollars a week, a fair rate of pay.

"That fitted what I was doing more than I could have hoped. I had two lectures I needed to cut to start the gig at five, but I had mates at uni by then, who shared notes and caught me up on missed lectures over coffee the next day."

'You said you found uni relatively easy. So, you not only coped, but did well in that first year?'

$2(x+y)=2x+2y$??? Write it down, all of it. Write, write, write! I ring Ray Delangre.

"Hi, Ray, can I meet you at the club and buy you a beer?"

'Oh, hello, what's happening?'

"First maths lecture. Might as well been in Swahili!"
'(laughs) Okay, what time?'

"I might have mentioned meeting Ray Delangre, who was a student at college when I arrived. He played clarinet in John Speight's band at college and Tony Ferness's band in Sydney after college. He was doing an arts-maths degree part time, I think through Armidale Uni. Then sometime around 1960, he announced that he was giving up music to concentrate on getting his degree, which he did.

"Jump ahead to about 1967 and he was living near Strathfield and that was on my way home. At the first maths lecture, I understood almost none of it. The starting point would have been matriculation level general maths, which I'd never been taught, didn't understood or had forgotten.

"Ray kindly met me at Wests Leagues Club several times and helped me understand my lecture notes. After a few of his tutorials, I got it. From then on, I surprised myself by being quite intuitive with the calculus and mathematics in general, getting distinctions and then high distinctions in my maths assignments."

'That's impressive, so why didn't you go on with that?'

I arrive home at 10:30 and she is asleep. I set the alarm for 7, make tea and go into the third bedroom, which I use as a study, and open my notes. Can't wait to tackle the maths assignment, so put aside the other subjects. Take a sip of the tea and pick up a pen and start. I try one avenue and that is a dead end. Try another and can see the way through. I'm excited and follow the logic for two pages until I have the solution. It seems like no time, but it's midnight, and tomorrow is a full day. I pack up the notes and drink the tea, now cold.

"I could see that there would not be enough money for the whole of second year, so I applied for a scholarship. With the gig and the two hours a day driving, plus home duties, I didn't really give the other subjects their due time. So, in the exams, I did very well in maths but gained only pass marks in everything else. But I enrolled for second year subjects. I couldn't help myself and took on a second year of pure maths."

'You didn't get the scholarship?'

"No. I managed to pay my way through the first two terms and did well at maths. I was hoping that the maths success would have been enough, but there was no scholarship and then serendipity stepped in again."

'(smiles) I sense a turn for the better. Can we look at that another day?'

"Of course." I stand. "This is a good part of my story where my financial situation takes off, but the marriage is in real trouble."

'(laughs) I'm tempted to ask the question, but we must stop.'

I leave smiling, remembering some of the good times. Can't wait to talk about them.

Session 13

I have with me the Daly-Wilson album with Kerrie Biddell on a USB drive and hand it to her as I sit. She passes me a coffee.

'What's this?'
"(laugh) All in good time. As I said before, serendipity strikes again."
'(laughs) Okay, so tell me about serendipity.'

Playing guitar for some dude who is recording his compositions. It is a mid-sized band and on bass is John Bartlett. John comes over in a break and asks me if I would like to play bass with Will Dower at South Sydney Seniors club. He tells me the deal and says the base pay is $130 for a rehearsal on Wednesdays, then Friday and Saturday nights, and two concerts on Sunday. By any standards that is really good money, so he arranges for me to replace him.

I have agreed to do The Seekers tour of Australia with their opening act, Pepe Jaramillo, who is a star in Mexico and has a new recording out. I do the first weekend with Will, and I tell him I have a contract to do The Seekers tour and will be away for a month. He is okay with that, so I come back a month later and stay with the band until Will leaves to be MD for Sandy Scott.

"I'd like to start with what happened in Will Dower's band that ultimately led to that." I point to the memory stick.

The sound system at Souths Seniors in 1968 is typical of clubs of the time. A 20-watt AWA amp with a volume control and two-tone knobs, driving banks of 4X6 speakers mounted around the walls. It is tinny and harsh. I invite Will to come with me to Newcastle to see what the Bill Bates band does – a dedicated sound system with operator. Will says he sees the point without the need to go to Newcastle and asks the band members to put in $120 each to buy a system. All except Kel agree, so we buy a Freedman system with two speaker bins, three Shure mikes and a tape echo.

"I suggested to Will that we buy our own sound system because the club system was so dreadful. He agreed, so we all – except for one band member who wouldn't contribute – bought a good sound system. Straight away, the crowd grew until at every performance, there was a queue waiting to get into the room.

"Then Ricky May joined the band. Again, serendipity intervened, and we enjoyed another quantum leap in popularity.

"Don Thompson, our trombone player had a habit of listening to *Voice of America* with a tape recorder wired in so he could record the latest music from America. One night they played the *Spinning Wheel* album from Blood, Sweat and Tears and then *Chicago Transit Authority* by the band of the same name, so we had that music two years before the albums could be released in Australia."

'Why two years?'

"(laugh) Well, the Musicians' Union, in its wisdom, had managed to have imports of British and American albums delayed for two years after their release at home, purportedly to allow Australian musicians time to catch up. But all it did was keep us in the dark for two years."

'So, you had that music early and I guess that put you ahead of the locals.'

"Not only that, but Don and Les Dempsey, both great arrangers, wrote all the bass parts out in notation, so I got to read that stuff and that's where the magic happened."

'So, this is you on here?'

"Yes, but not with Will. I got a call from Warren Daly who asked me to fill in for their regular bass player who he said was off sick, so I attended and was given a book of charts that include some boogaloo, like I had been reading in Will's band. So, I had a wonderful afternoon playing with the great Daly-Wilson Big Band."

I'm totally immersed in the music. I have never played anything like this and am thrilled to have such great musicians around me. I turn the last page of the last chart and look over at Warren. "If he's ever sick again, I'd love to fill in for him anytime."

'I think his illness is terminal, would you like to be a regular in the band?'

"They must have liked what I did, because I was offered the chair permanently and so began years with the band, touring, concerts and recording. That is the second recording we did, which features all Australian compositions, mostly also featuring the genius of Kerrie Biddell.

"If it hadn't been for Don and his tape recorder, I wouldn't have been able to read those charts at sight and that opened a whole new career in recording."

'So, you got more work from that?'

"I always say that Will's band was the best band I have ever played in, but it was the Daly-Wilson Band that got me known and led to a busy recording career and money, which was the point of becoming a full-time musician in the first place."

'I remember you said that. But you didn't stay with Daly-Wilson. What happened there?'

Warren turns up at my house and wants to talk. We jump into my Alfa and adjourn to the pub. He tells me they are planning a big tour and will be out of town for some months and will pay $100 per week. I can't make ends meet on that, with the mortgage, and Vera sick all the time, so I knock it back and they take John Hellman.

"They had signed up for a long tour and I couldn't keep up my financial commitments on the money they offered, so I resigned. (laugh) The tour was extended to include London, Las Vegas and Moscow. If I had known that, I would have borrowed the money to go.

"Anyway, I had just been replaced on the *Naked Vicar Show* by a younger bass player, so maybe Warren was glad I pulled out when I did, and I was having so much trouble with my hearing that I knew I was nearing the end of my first-class music career."

'What happened to your hearing?'

We have been married about a year and just moved into the new house. I am lying on my right side, and Vera is behind me. She is talking and I lift my head to hear her, then drop it again while I answer. She notices and asks why I am lifting my head, and I say I can't hear her otherwise. She turns on the light and grabs my watch to test my hearing. I can't hear a thing from my left ear. We decide it must be wax, and I make an appointment to see my GP.

He finds no wax and sends me to a specialist in Macquarie Street where the diagnosis is 'otosclerosis'.

"I was diagnosed with otosclerosis in one ear when I was twenty-five, with a prognosis of total hearing loss inevitable. I was advised by the specialist to think about my career paths and make other plans. There were treatments available, but none were compatible with teaching or music."

'How awful.'

"That came just after I had the bill for the house from Dad, and Vera was pregnant, so the timing could not have been worse."

'So that is when you decided to resign?'

School is back at Green Valley Primary, and I have the same class. We no sooner get settled in than an Asian Flu hits the school. I am always a bit run-down, doing as many gigs as I can at night while teaching full time in a school of migrant children, and I get the flu. It knocks me flat, but I keep playing the gigs and after two weeks am back at school just in time for a second wave of flu to come through, and I get that too.

"I got two bouts of flu within six weeks, so they cut me back to half pay. I objected and explained that I caught the flu from the children and maybe should be entitled to compo. "They still refused, so instead of going to the Teachers Federation for support, I resigned."

'I bet that hit the bottom line!'

"Not really. I had been knocking back daytime gigs, any two of which would exceed my teacher's pay, so I was better off almost right away. Then I was offered a full-time position playing guitar in the ABC Dance Band with Jim Gussey."

'So, you landed on your feet there!'

I arrive at Jim Gussey's office just before ten for the formal interview. I know I am not yet ready, but I have done several fill-ins, so he knows my ability. With this job I am determined to work at it to improve. I am told that Mr Gussey will see me shortly, and I wait. Then a short, slightly stooped man in a scruffy grey suit goes through the waiting room straight into Gussey's office and I wait almost an hour more.

"No, (laugh) or maybe I did, because Gussey must have had a phone call from Roy Plummer, a guitarist he had worked with in the UK. While I waited to be called in to do the interview, Roy arrived, and I was told the job had been filled."

'How disappointing.'

"Well, yes, but there was a rule then that if you worked for the ABC, you were forbidden to work for anyone else."

'Was that enforced?'

"(laugh) No. I worked with many of them on recording sessions that were not ABC and when I was working for Ken Bennett setting up recording sessions, I often booked ABC players and even scheduled some sessions to coincide with their availability. But not being tied to the ABC let me mature a bit in less demanding bands."

Australia Day 2012
(For my friend, Jimmy Little, the gentle activist)

Into the bay the tall ships came.
Brave, desperate, driven.
God given arrogance
hidden behind social graces,
a veneer
of civilisation.

Men, custodians of forty, fifty,
sixty thousand years of culture.
Older, wiser,
watched them come
to a land where none knew
coal and iron slept.

'A land for a people,
A people for a land!'
It started then, this short history
written by victors
as it always is,
Biame's people,
dispossessed, demonised,
shot by Christians.

This must be the year when The Apology
wrought in guilt, delivered in hope
should be judged.
Man to man,
woman to woman,
as we really embrace
our common humanity.

'Did you record with many famous people?'

"(laugh) Hundreds, but that was mainly later in my career. The first big hit I played on was Jimmy Little's 'Royal Telephone', which is in the National Archives, but I was struggling and a bit amazed that I was being booked. At about that time, I did a fair bit of recording at Festival in their studio at Pyrmont.

"It was on old weatherboard house, where they had set up the rooms so the musicians were separated. We listened to the other musicians spread around the house through small speaker boxes and the hallway was set up as an echo chamber with a speaker at one end and a microphone at the other.

"We recorded a Delltones album there, and one famous singer, who will remain nameless, took over sixty takes to get in tune. Of course, they now use computers to bring wayward voices into pitch, but back then, what you sang came out on the recording."

'What happened with the hearing?'

It is a long operation, and I'm worried. Nothing is guaranteed, and it costs a lot. I can't hear a thing from the ear until the follow-up, when he takes out all the padding. I don't notice much until we are walking back along Macquarie St towards St James Station, and I notice that I can hear the wind.

"I kept in touch with the specialist, who had originally offered me a fenestration procedure, in which the ear drum and bones are removed, a hole drilled into the cochlea and a skin graft stretched over the aperture to act like a secondary tympanum. We decided against that, because its side effects included middle ear infections and it could not be exposed to water, which ruled out swimming.

"He also suggested there might be a better option in the near future, so he called me in 1962 and performed a procedure called 'stapes mobilisation', which worked, so I had good hearing back in both ears."

'Great news.'

"Yes, but it was temporary. I got about three years out of it, then I was back to being deaf again and that coincided with a drop in gigs for me, so I was struggling financially. I was still making more than I would as a teacher, but it was not enough to pay the mortgage and the bills.

"At about that time, Vera's medications were soaking up about a quarter of my earnings. That was before the Pharmaceutical Benefits Scheme."

'Wow! That must have been hard to finance.'

"Yes, it was. The reason I kept a record of her medication use was that it was tax deductable."

'You mentioned Newcastle. What happened there?'

I get a call from Trevor Mitchell. He wants to visit me at home with his boss to talk about a permanent gig there. I agree, and they turn up. Vera is out and I am at home with David, who is only a few weeks old. They talk about us moving to Newcastle and arrange for me to meet them there next week.

In Newcastle, they take me to see a couple of clubs where they work and to lunch at a club where there is an amazing smorgasbord. The pay is thirty-five pounds per week after tax for the regular gigs, plus any extras that come along from time to time. I agree to give it a go for a year before I would be willing to move permanently.

"I took a job there with Bill Bates, who I had never heard of. But he was the Mr Music of Newcastle at the time. We rehearsed on Wednesday afternoons, had a live radio show on 2HD on Thursday morning, a cabaret on Friday and Saturday nights at Tattersalls Club, then two backing gigs on Sunday at Adamstown RSL, then Toronto RSL in the evening, so I was back home by midnight on Sunday."

'So, you were away from Wednesday until Sunday night?'

"Usually I came home after the Thursday radio show then back up for the Friday cabaret."

'A lot of travelling.'

"Well, yes, but I was looking at other possibilities Newcastle had to offer apart from the work with that band and still intended to move there eventually. Houses right in town were half the price of Sydney, so there was the prospect of getting out of debt."

'So, why didn't you move?'

"Vera didn't want to go. Her family were all in Sydney, and I understood that, but I also had reservations of my own. The band was a very professional outfit, but if they lost one gig, the money would cease to be so attractive."

'It did finish up eventually, so what happened?'

I board with Trevor when I stay in Newcastle, so we have a lot of time to talk. He wants to know when I might decide to make the move permanent, and I voice my doubts about my prospects. I say that I would need to widen my employment mix, and that leads us to talk about recording jingles for radio.

I have been doing studio recordings of jingles for some years, so I suggest with his production skills and my composing, we could start making jingles for Newcastle radio stations.

We go to see Twink (Twinkle Story) at 2HD in Broadmeadow and see that they have a sound studio, left over from the days when they did radio plays live on the premises. She was keen to partner us in the venture and looked forward to us starting.

"Trevor and I had decided to expand into jingle production at 2HD, which the manager, Twink Story, was keen to do. We had a ready-made market of 2HD sponsors, so we decided to go ahead.

"Maybe Twink told Bill, but in any case, he bailed me up on the Saturday night and demanded to know what I was doing 'behind his back'.

"I told him of the plan to write jingles and then use the band to record them at 2HD. He was angry.

"'You don't do anything in this town without my permission. You're my guitar player, so you only play for me!', he said.

"I pointed out that as I saw it, I did every gig he booked me for, so in that sense I was 'his', but outside those gigs, my time was my own, and I was keen to expand my income into a new venture.

"He asked me if I was still going ahead with the jingle idea. I said I was, so he said: 'Then you're fired!'

"(laugh) We had just taken delivery of new jackets that had been tailor-made to fit us, and we were all to pay twenty-five pounds for the coats. I took off my coat and handed it to him and said: 'I hope your new player fits into this.'

"'I expect you to do New Year's Eve before you leave.'

"'No, Bill, I've been fired so after I finish tonight, I'm gone.'"

'Wow! So that was it for Newcastle.'

"Not quite. After I moved to Wollombi, almost fifteen years later, I was offered gigs in Newcastle.

"By that time, Bill Bates had been gone from the scene for some time and Trevor had a management position with Wormald Brothers, the fire extinguisher people. That was after I had been playing bass for some years in the Sydney studio scene and after Daly-Wilson, so I was fairly well known by then. But I must tell you about Julia's birth."

'Okay, go ahead.'

I'm not comfortable leaving Vera at home with the birth so close, so I talk to the doctor, and he agrees to admit her to King George VI in case she goes into labour while I'm in Newcastle.

I ask Bill to cancel the rehearsal, so I turn up Thursday morning for the radio show. After that, I ring the hospital and ask after Vera. They say: 'no change' so I spend the afternoon and Friday morning with Trevor planning the jingle venture, then on Friday afternoon I ring again and am told there is 'no change'.

I ask for more detail but am told they are not at liberty to say anything else. On Saturday morning, I ring again to be told there was 'no change', and no, I am not permitted to speak with her, so I drive to Sydney to see for myself and find that the baby was born the day before.

"Vera is in hospital because the birth is imminent, and I will be away. I call the hospital many times and am told each time there has been no change, so I ask: 'No change from what?'

They refuse to tell me more, so when Saturday comes, I drive down early only to find that Julia was born the day before.

"Vera is angry with me, so the atmosphere is not good when Dan junior arrives, but his good humour helps calm things down. Then in comes Vera's mother and Dan senior, dressed in their Sunday best, to tell us they have just been married.

"Because she was Catholic, she couldn't remarry until her first husband died. I knew all that, having been told by Vera, so I was aware that her parents had not been married when her mother had her family. But I guess that Dan junior did not know, because his reaction was most interesting. He was clearly upset and blurted out: 'Then what does that make me?'"

'What did he mean?'

"Of all the children, he was the only one to go to a Catholic high school, so he was taught that, when he died, he would go to Limbo, not Heaven, if his parents weren't married when he was conceived."

'So, were you forgiven?'

"(laugh) Not really. I don't know what else I could have done. I rang often, but there was, it seemed to me, a deep antipathy toward fathers. At David's birth I was cooped up in a waiting room on my own, listening to the screams and moans coming from the birthing suites. When I was told anything, it was as if I had been a naughty boy to get this poor girl into this situation.'

'It's different now.'

Sally and I make it clear to Dr Pitsch that we want me to be there for the birth, and he agrees. She is due to go into labour at any time, and I am at the club. We are opening the second spot for the act, and we are into the Crunchy Granola Suite. The band is cooking, and I am enjoying a rare chance to play guitar, when the piano and keyboard bass stops. I look over in time to see Bill Murray keel over, falling off the dais and onto the stage floor.

The curtains close. I drop the guitar and run over. He is not breathing and there is no pulse.

He has a chunky watch on the arm I can reach as I try for a pulse, so I slip it off and hand it to Bill's son, Frank, and begin pumping his heart. I do about twenty pumps, then hold his nose and fill his lungs and pump again. Colour begins to return to his face. I keep pumping, then the club's first-aid people arrive with oxygen and a mask.

They start the oxygen and hold the mask loosely over his face, but he is not breathing, so none is getting in. I shout that they need to hold the mask on tighter and force it in. They tell me to 'shut up and get out of the way', so I do. Then the ambulance arrives, and they pronounce him dead.

It haunts me that I know he was getting air while I was doing the CPR, and I was sure the first-aid guys were wrong to not force the oxygen in. But I said nothing to anyone because in the end he was dead, and everyone involved thought they were doing the right thing.

"Yes. On the night before Matthew was born, I was working, and our piano player, our bandleader, died on stage of a huge heart attack. I did CPR on him, but he couldn't be saved and died there in front of us. The rest of the show was cancelled, and we were taken to the boardroom and given whatever drinks we wanted. I don't think I have ever drunk so much scotch.

"Anyway, I arrived home pretty pissed at about 5 a.m. Sally met me the door, and I cried. Bill Murray had been a good friend and boss, and we all loved him. I went to bed, then it seemed like no time, but it was probably about 9 a.m., that Sally woke me to say her water had broken and we needed to get to the hospital.

"(laugh) I told her to relax, it would be hours yet and made her a cup of tea and me a strong coffee. We finally got going around ten for the drive to Cessnock, and Sally started to moan and ask me to hurry. I told her again that there was plenty of time, but did hurry a little, a bit more sober.

"We arrived at the Maternity Ward and were shown to a bed. We waited a while, me holding her hand and rubbing her back, which had started to ache, then a nurse came along with shaving gear, had a look, then called out to the others that they were needed now!"

'So, you were allowed to stay for the birth?'

Sally is handed a mask and told to use it for the pain. She takes a few puffs, then becomes quite giggly. A nurse notices and advises her to 'go easy' on the nitrous oxide and that someone will be along soon to shave her. Fifteen minutes later, a nurse arrives with shaving gear, takes one look and calls out for the team to 'come now'.

I am holding Sal's hand and suddenly there is a scrum of nurses busy at the business end, when a square-looking grey lady orders me out. 'No fathers allowed in the birthing area!' she shouts. I look at her, and she repeats, 'Out.'

I stand and face her. "We asked Dr Pitsch if I could stay, and he agreed I could."

'Well, Dr Pitsch is not here, so out!'

I look over at another door and see a tall, bearded man appear, a stethoscope around his neck and holding what I guess are forceps. He says nothing, so I ignore her.

Sister is turning an unhealthy shade of purple as she yells: 'Get out now!'

I say: "I'll go when the police arrive," *and walk over to stand beside the doctor.*

I'm not in the way, but I can see what is happening and am in awe. The head shows, then after a couple of pushes, he is out. He looks like a white rubber doll. Then he opens his mouth and lets out a loud squark and his skin turns pink. The nurse cuts the cord, wraps him in a towel and hands him to me.

"(laugh) Almost not. Sister Salmon, apparently notorious in the medical profession as a bit of a harridan, ordered me out."

'So, you weren't there for the birth?'

"I don't know if I was still a bit pissed from the night before, but I stood my ground and told her I'd stay until the police arrive. She left in high dudgeon, and the police did not arrive, so I was there for the birth, and I can recommend it to any father-to-be.

"I was holding this new little human, crying my eyes out with relief and joy. For the first time, being a parent felt like I was in a real partnership with the mother."

'So, it was a quick birth?'

"Yes, very quick for a first apparently. Between the water breaking and the birth would have been five hours, but most of that time there was nothing happening."

'Were there repercussions? You refusing to leave?'

"We had friends that had bought the property across the road, and Jenny, who was a nurse on the board of the hospital, said they discussed my presence there and decided to change policy and allow fathers in for the birth, unless there was an unusual intervention required, like a C-section."

'That was a great result. Was Matthew a planned pregnancy?'

I have just moved a one-ton boulder to be part of a rockery near the front door. It is hot and Sal has brought me out a beer. We are sitting on the newly placed rock when she leans in and whispers: 'I want to have your babies.' She then holds herself against me, waiting for my reaction.

I hadn't thought that far ahead but am immediately filled with love for this woman who seems to have given up a lot to be with me.

I squeeze her and whisper back: 'When do we start?'

"(laugh) Yes, he was. She wanted children, so when she decided she was ready, she asked me, and I agreed. I had so much confidence in her abilities to do anything, that I was totally sure that it was the right thing to do for both of us."

'What did you do about the herpes?'

"(laugh) I had been using condoms, so I just cut the little bit off the end."

'Did she fall pregnant easily?'

She is dressed to go out, so I ask what she has planned for the day.

'I've seen Dr Pitsch, and he recommends that I have a procedure. He diagnosed salpingitis.' I have no idea what that means but drive her into Newcastle for day surgery and home the same day. Within a couple of

weeks, we are trying again for a baby, and she soon announces that she is pregnant and sets about preparing for the arrival.

I am trying to make the farm productive and have a dam built so I can grow more crops, but it is becoming clear that this lovely, picturesque property can never be a viable farm.

It is a hard decision to leave because we are well embedded in the community. People call in to see us and stay for dinner regularly. I'm now the fire captain, so am responsible for the equipment and keeping up the membership, and I have moved jobs to be in the band at the Long Jetty RSL and that pays well, so the farm is a secondary income, and we stay.

"No. She needed a procedure to open her tubes apparently, but once that was done, she was pregnant almost immediately."

'What was the problem with her tubes?'

"The diagnosis was salpingitis, but at the time I had no idea what that meant, and Sally didn't offer any more information."

'It's usually caused by an STD, you know. Probably gonorrhoea.'

"Yes, I know that now, and I suspect she got that when she was working as a call girl for a while."

'So, she told you?'

"When she arrived, she had $2 in her bank account and the Honda Civic. But when we collected her stuff from where she had been living with Alan, she brought back a case of very expensive port wine and an Afghan Hound. I asked her about the wine, and she told me it was a present from a girlfriend, a call girl, who she 'helped out' from time to time. So, I knew about that within a month of her turning up at Wollombi."

Loren is looking at me, her expression a grim smile.

'You realise what you did there, don't you?'

"(laugh) Yes, I do now, but at the time, I just felt it endeared her to me even more."

'Exactly, so in your mind, the deal was done. You save her, and she rewards you with sex.'

"She was always available sexually, although she rarely initiated it, except when she wanted to become pregnant. But I always felt comfortable with her sexual history."

'Do you think now that she saw it the same way you subconsciously did, as a deal?'

We decide that the Wollombi property will never be a viable farm, and my hearing is deteriorating further, so we decide to look for a more suitable farm. This coincides with increased interest in Wollombi as a holiday home destination, so I sell the property in several tranches, and in the end make a healthy profit, so we are cashed up.

We look around Wyong, because that is near the gig at Long Jetty and inspect several properties, but none has a good water supply. The proprietor of Crossley RE takes us out to Dooralong, fifteen kilometres north-west of Wyong, and we stop in front of a fifty-five acre property.

The house looks okay, relatively modern and there is plenty of water in a large wetland. But from the road I can't see much land that can be cultivated, so we decline. We go to a different agent, and he takes us straight to the same property. We tell him we have seen it with Crossley, and he asks: 'Have you seen down the back?'

"Maybe, but I also owned a house. Sally once told me that she was unhappy with Alan because he was 'going nowhere'. They couldn't seem to save money, and he wasn't interested in buying property. (laugh) She always said she wanted a two-storey house with a portico and a circular driveway.

"She didn't get that with me, but she did with Rodney."

'Who's Rodney?'

"Rodney Cavalier. When she met him, she was a vice president of the NSW P & C Association and I think he was then, or had been the Minister of Education, so they met at educational do's."

'So, you think she saw Rodney as a better prospect and moved on as she had done with Alan?'

"Yes, that's how I see it now, and I started to get an idea of her thinking before Rodney came along. I won't say she used people, because she was offering an attractive package and certainly worked hard to help her partner in whatever they did.

"But her choice of partners, at least after me, seemed to be dependent on their wealth."

'How did you know about her target partners, if I can use that term?'

Sally tells me she has been invited to dinner in Sydney by 'Mr Penney'. He is in Sydney from Darwin for a P & C conference, and she would like me to come. We have a pleasant dinner with a man who I saw as a typical successful businessman 'with good capon lined'. She asks me what I think of him, and I say I don't have an opinion after such a short meeting, but he seems pleasant enough.

Within a few months, we drive up to Townsville to visit Julia and to meet granddaughter Ashleigh, almost a year old. We are there only a couple of days when Sally announces that she is going to Darwin to attend a conference, so off she goes.

I get daily phone calls, so all seems well until she comes back, and I meet her at the airport. There she tells me she has been offered a job in Darwin, so I say: "Okay, I wouldn't mind a change, so when do we go?"

She keeps walking and says, quite coldly: 'You're not invited.'

"She took me to meet a man from Darwin, who offered her a job. I was prepared to move to Darwin, confident that I could find music work, but she had not planned on taking me.

"The point of taking me to meet him, I felt, was that she wanted my approval in some way. "The same thing happened with Rodney. She took me to meet him in his home in Gladesville and we talked about computers, which I was just getting into. Later, she told me she intended to move in with him in Merrylands, which she did. I also thought that her breast cancer was a factor in her wanting to secure a wealthier future."

'So, she had breast cancer?'

"Yes. Jess was about eighteen months old, so it was a few years before the Darwin episode, and she was still being breastfed. Sally had been trying to wean her because she had some breast pain.

"Jess wasn't having it, and would not take a bottle, so we got some stuff called Thumby, I think, and smeared that on a nipple. I tried it first (laugh). No, not on the nipple. It left the mouth furry as happens when one eats an unripe persimmon. Anyway, Jess took one suck, then backed off, demanding a bottle."

'Was the breastfeeding masking the cancer?'

"Yes. Once she stopped nursing, we noticed blood oozing from her left nipple and went to the doctor. It was a very invasive type of cancer that required a radical mastectomy and some chemo, which Sally seemed to tolerate well.

"It was then that Sal's sister Sue, who holds a PhD in Medicine, suggested to me that another pregnancy could well trigger cancer in the other breast, so I had a vasectomy right away."

'Did you discuss that with Sally?'

"No, unfortunately."

'Why unfortunately?'

I'm still sore from the vasectomy and Sally is pushing me to have sex. As soon as I can, I respond and she is uncharacteristically frantic for me to ejaculate and after a few times, I realise she wants another baby and is hoping some sperm cells are still 'in the pipeline'.

"She wanted more children, danger or not, and maybe that was a factor in her wanting to move on. If we had discussed it, maybe I would have done a bit of research, and she could have had another child or two. She was a great mum, so I would have been fine with it."

'So, she had more children?'

In the motel at Emerald on the way home from Townsville. I am still angry after the Darwin rejection and can barely speak to Sally. She takes off her top and is trying to seduce me with the children in the same room. Matt asks what is going on, so she stops, but I wonder what is going through her mind. We arrive home, and she is trying to make our lives as normal as possible. Then she announces that she is pregnant. It is too long after the vasectomy to be mine, so I ask her if it's Penney's.

"I think it was in Darwin that she became pregnant. But apparently when she told him, he rejected her, and the Darwin deal was off. A part of me was sympathetic, thinking that the cancer had made her desperate and led her to look elsewhere to be inseminated. So, I offered to forget all that and be a father to the child. In fact, our relationship seemed to be so good that I would welcome the child."

'Here you go again!'

"(laugh) Yes, I still felt love for her and wanted her in my life, but she had it aborted. Her plan to move on was still alive. I soon knew that, with more liaisons following in quick succession, and that became harder and harder to take.

"We had a wealthy neighbour who she befriended and had a brief affair with, then a teacher at a school where she was a casual, the guy who taught us karate, who was the odd man out because as far as I knew, he didn't have money or prospects.

"It was after the rejection by Penney that I did the rebirthing."

'Did that help?'

Sally introduces me to an older woman, a teacher at Wyong High who facilitates rebirthing. We meet in a group of half a dozen people who pay fifty dollars each for the session. It is my turn, and I lie on the mattress. She is sitting on the floor beside me, instructing me to 'Breathe deeply and out, breathe deeply and out'. This is not totally new. I know how to meditate, and this feels similar, but then I slip deeper into what seems to separate mind and body and then I can feel it. I am burning and yelling for Mum. I am calling out in panic, but there is a part of me, like my adult, watching and knowing I am safe.

"Yes. I think I regressed right back to the time I was scalded. When I came out of it, I had lost an underlying fear. The weirdest part of that was that I had to relearn some driving techniques."

'Why was that?'

"I was always a fast driver, and I am sure I scared the daylights out of some passengers, but after the rebirthing, I realised that I had been setting the speed through curves and so on by the level of anxiety I felt. Suddenly the anxiety had gone, so I found myself driving too fast for the conditions and had to change the way I judged what was a safe speed through thoughtfulness."

'Did you also drive slower, generally?'

"Yes, I did. The thrill of being on the edge had gone, so yes. Hadn't thought of that."

'I suspected that would be the case. Did you have more rebirthing sessions?'

"One more, but it was not as dramatic or effective as the first time. It was there, while we ate lunch, that Sally told them that I had agreed to take on the new baby as my own, and they expressed delight, but later I wondered what they thought Sally was up to."

'Did Sally do the rebirthing too? What were her reactions?'

"I watched her, and she clearly had some dramatic events to process, but she didn't disclose her analysis, if she had formed one. After the second time, we never went again and Sally changed her mind about the foetus."

'Did she become pregnant to Rodney?'

"Yes, they had two children. The first one I feel quite close to, the second one is still a bit of a mystery to me. I was still living next door to Nan, Sal's mother, when Milly was born, so as a child, Sally's daughter visited me when she came to visit Nan."

'Did you ever visit the two-storey house with the circular drive and the portico?'

"(laugh) Yes, many times. I knew she had persuaded Rodney to buy it. I was in Nan's place one day and saw on the table the listing for the house they moved into in Bowral, for $475,000. It was on an acreage, which suited Sally, who had a green thumb, like her mother."

'How did you feel about the house and her new life?'

"I felt miserable, but I saw it as inevitable and knew that I needed to give her my blessing to maintain a relationship for the kids' sake. When I realised that my time with Sally was over, I helped her move her stuff. I was always made welcome, and at Sally's funeral, I was asked to 'say a few words'.

"I get on well with Rodney, and I am sure there is mutual respect. That meant that none of the family celebrations were ever awkward. I always appreciated that."

'Did the cancer come back?'

Julia organises a big eightieth birthday bash for me over three days in November in Kangaroo Valley and hires a whole resort. I hadn't seen Sally since the previous Christmas, so we are dancing and catching up on the news when she says: 'I've got Alzheimer's, you know.'

I can't believe it and say so, but at Christmas at Jess's, a little over a year later, I do notice that she doesn't remember things. But we talk about our time at Wollombi and then Dooralong, and she enjoys that.

By the next Christmas, she needs help to eat, and I am profoundly saddened to see this feisty woman, who I still say was the love of my life, falling apart before our eyes.

"Alzheimer's. She would have been about sixty-two when it was first noticed, so very young, and I sometimes wonder if the chemo played a part in that.

"But she kept up her speaking engagements for the P & C Association, talking up public education, until she just couldn't do it anymore and I must say, she always seemed happy, even in her dementia, unlike others I have seen where the anger comes out."

'That seems like a good time to leave it. Next time, I will ask you about *The Clock of Lonk*.'

I smile and stand. She turns to me and says she thinks I'm finally getting into the anatomy of co-dependence. I am not quite so sure, but I nod and leave.

Session 14

She is reading notes as I enter, then looks up, indicates the coffee and closes her folder. I sit and face her.

"You were asking about *The Clock of Lonk*."
'Yes, did you go on with that? The play with Paul?'

I meet Terry Lee, Sally's boss at Paxton School, and his wife, Helen. Sally has had the pregnancy confirmed and is radiant. She is also aware of the power of her body. We are on the school veranda, and Terry is trying not to look at her breasts, but they are hard to miss, pressing against her blouse and clearly not protected by a bra. She once said she didn't need a bra, but usually wore one.

In a way, I was enjoying Terry's discomfort. He had once asked in jest if I was her father and that hit a bit close to home. But I get to know Terry and we become friends, so I offer to write an anthem for the school and do.

I record the backing on one side of a C 30 tape using the guitar, and sing the song on the other. That went well, so I wrote a musical play for the Paxton kids and was teaching it to them when a salesman for KC Electronics walks in.

"After the fuss with Eva, then uni, and then trying to secure some sort of future as the deaf person that I expected to be, Paul and I met rarely, so *The Clock of Lonk* was forgotten. "However, when Matt was just a toddler, Sally brought home a children's book, *Where the Wild Things Are*, by Maurice Sendak.

"I read that and used the general ideas as the storyline of a play I called *David and the Monsters*, recorded as I had planned, and was trying out a mock-up of the music at Sallys school when I bumped into Bill Burns and explained the two-sided tape idea to him."

'Who is or was Bill Burns?'

"Bill was in the year ahead of me at Bathurst College and he was at the school selling audio tape teaching aids. I told him of an idea to produce musical plays for schools. The new idea I had was to record the backing music for the songs in a musical on one side of the C tape and the backing plus singing on the other side.

"The idea grew from my work at Greenacre where I recorded lessons for other teachers, but this was next generation. Now any teacher, regardless of musical ability, could present a musical play.

"They could read the script as usual, playing the songs with lyrics to the kids at the appropriate times, and then when the kids knew the songs, turn the tape over to use for later rehearsals and to back performances."

'Was he interested?'

"Right away. He asked if I had a play ready. I had, so we worked out a contract where I would pay for the recording and receive twenty per cent of the sale price."

'Did it go ahead?'

"Yes, we took the mock-up to show Ken Bailey, who was the main man in KC Electronics, the company that produced the audio material. At the later recording session, we used pro musos and three senior students from Cessnock High plus Julia, to sing the individual songs and together for the choruses. We recorded the backing at Jam Sound in Gosford.

"That cost me $2,000, but the end result was as good as I expected. KC had the books printed and they went out as a kit, advertised along with their other offerings."

'How did it go?'

"It went well. It sold five hundred copies in NSW and Victoria. My share of the royalties brought me in about $2,000, so I broke even. But I had proved the concept, and we were talking about doing six more, with Australian themes for the American market."

'That must have been exciting.'

"(laugh) Yes, it was for five minutes. I had written the libretto for one play, based on an Aboriginal myth, called *Mungoon-Gali and the Poison Stick* when I got the message that KC Electronics was winding up, so that was the end of that. I knew there was a market out there for musical plays in that format, but I was overtaken by the need to move farms and prepare to be totally deaf so, not having a plan to advance the taped play idea, I put it on the back burner to attend to more pressing matters.

"Then something happened with Sally which changed our focus. She had planned to go back to work after the birth when Matt was a year old, then she had a health scare."

'What went wrong?'

The growth out of her back is worrying. It is as if a thumb is pushing through her skin on her lower back. Dr Pitsch excises it and sends it away for analysis. The verdict is melanoma, and she is six months pregnant with Matt. We see a specialist in Sydney who discusses the possibility of termination, and Sally is against that, so he suggests she go on with the birth but right after, have extensive surgery to remove her lymph nodes from her back and groin. She would be laid up in hospital for maybe two months. She chooses that option, and we go ahead as planned.

"Six months into her pregnancy, Sally had a growth removed. It was diagnosed as a melanoma. She chose to go ahead with the pregnancy and have radical surgery right after, that would have been disfiguring and long-lasting. But she wanted that baby, so we tried to forget about what was coming."

'How awful.'

"Yes. Then we got a call from the Sydney specialist, who asked us to come in. We expected more bad news, but he said that he was never completely happy with the diagnosis of melanoma and had sent a sample to a colleague in the US who said he was almost certain that it was a Spitz naevus."

'I've never heard of that. Is it a type of melanoma?'

"No. He examined the site of the growth and seemed happy with what he saw, then told us that it is quite rare for Spitz naevus to occur in adults and that is what fooled them on the original diagnosis. There is usually pigment in the tissue, like in a melanoma, but in a Spitz naevus it is not the melanin-producing cells that are out of control. It is benign and often falls off as the body ages."

'Sounds like all went well after that?'

Nan wants to come to see the baby and is on the phone asking which is the closest railway station. I answer 'Maitland', which it is. Gosford rail is almost as close and infinitely more convenient. However, Maitland it is, and I meet the train. Nan is excited to have a grandchild, and it shows. This is her first visit, so she has never seen the house.

Right across the road from our lovely old home is a derelict house of peeling timber with a rusty roof. There is no front door. The veranda is sagging at one end, and the railing dangles from the two remaining uprights.

Over the whole mess, a vine grows, which is probably what is holding the wreckage together. We are coming up to our driveway and I say: "Almost there," and drive up to the derelict pile of wreckage. I stop and look at her face. She is trying really hard to keep herself under control.

Then I laugh and back out, stopping at the lead-lighted front door of our impressive 1916 house, built by a publican, with big rooms lined with tongue and groove Oregon, red cedar doors, windows, architraves and skirtings. There is a veranda around three sides, so I have knocked a doorway into the western side and made that part of the veranda into a walk-in wardrobe.

"Following Bill Murray's death, I took the job of bandleader at Long Jetty RSL, and that was going along well, up to a point. Life became idyllic in a way. Matt was an easy baby who slept well. Sally breastfed him for the whole year, and he thrived. She read to him from birth, and he soon became a little chatterbox. He also walked early, so he needed watching.

"We had plenty of money coming in, despite Sally not having paid maternity leave, as was the case back then. We had some friends, Stephen and Catherine Pile, who had a similar aged girl. That couple were closer to Sally's age, so we had a nice social life with bright friends and a newly revived tennis club.

"Then not long past Matt's birthday, we were shocked to see that Sally had a mass in her abdomen."

'So, the cancer thing was back?'

"We were afraid of that, so we went to Dr Pitsch, and he had a feel around. He was soon grinning and asked, 'Did you think breastfeeding prevented pregnancy?' Sally said she did, and he laughed.

'It might make it less likely, but I can tell you that what you have in there is a three-month-old foetus.'

"Our reaction was one of disbelief and relief. We were not planning another one quite so soon, but it proved to be lucky because Sally was later diagnosed with breast cancer, and I would have been unwilling to risk her life with another pregnancy."

'When was that?'

"It came two years later, so a lot happened in between, including selling most of the property and buying in Dooralong, so we were busy going through the process of relocating and developing a new farm."

'(laughs) Yes, just as well we don't know what's around the corner sometimes. Let's leave that for another time. What was happening with David and Julia?'

David has come back to Wollombi, and Sally seems okay with that and again talks to him as a counsellor. I give him some responsibilities, hoping he will 'get into' farm work and no longer want to be 'out of it'.

I ask him to check the oil in the ute. He comes to where I am fencing and says there wasn't enough oil. I know there was an almost full twenty-litre drum and go to check. We get to the ute, where he lifts the oil filler cap on the rocker-box cover and points in: 'See, it's not up to the top.'

I'm flabbergasted that over all the years I have done my own repairs and services, he has never noticed me use a dipstick to check the oil levels. We drain the oil from the engine and fill it to the top dipstick mark. He apologises, and I am sure he is genuinely sorry.

Then, a few days later I ask him to fuel up the tractor. We are pulling out dead trees to cut up for firewood, so he is driving and snigging the logs to the house, while I am cutting them into blocks for the stove.

After a couple of hours, he says the tractor is not going well. I have a look and can smell petrol. He has filled the tank with the wrong fuel and in the process, ruined the high-pressure pump.

"I tried to integrate David into the farm routines, but within three days he had gone close to wrecking the ute motor, put petrol in the diesel tractor and ruined its high-pressure pump.

No sooner had I fixed that at great expense than he parked the tractor up the hill from the house and failed to secure the handbrake or leave it parked in gear.

"He came to me at the house in time to see the tractor picking up speed, heading straight for the carport side of the veranda. It hit with a huge crash, the front of the tractor ploughing straight through the carport wall. Then the anti-roll bar on the tractor hit the beam at the top of the carport, and the tractor reared up onto its back wheels, then crashed down to fracture the bolster that supports the front axle and the engine mounts. If it had continued through the carport, it would have ended up in Julia's bedroom, and of course, there was always the danger of fire."

'What did Sally have to say about that?'

"Not much. She left it to me. He must have been stoned when he parked the tractor, but I'm not sure about other times, so I asked him what he intended to do. Was he prepared to clean up his act or did we need to ban him from using any machinery?

"He admitted that what he did had cost me heaps and the tractor crash endangered the lives of people in the house, but he was not prepared to stop the drugs, so he left to stay with Vera. Sally had finally had enough and so had I."

'And Julia?'

"Julia was doing well at school and had a great group of friends at Cessnock High. They came out to the farm often and she sometimes stayed over at theirs. Sally and Julia were more like sisters than stepmother and daughter.

"Years later, when I once remarked that Juila was a good cook, she said that she learnt that from Sally. I understood that the good relationship lasted until Jessica was about six months old, but Julia disputes that and claims it started when Matt was small. I believe Juila, but I was not aware of a problem at that time."

'We have jumped a bit here, (laughs) as we do, and that's okay, but tell me about Jessica's arrival on the planet. I bet she was even quicker than Matthew.'

Saturday night and we have just played the chaser to end the floorshow when a waiter comes on stage to hand me a note. It says that Sally has gone into labour. I look up and see Ian Whittaker walk in. I call him into the band room and ask if he has his bass with him. He does, so I take off for Cessnock. I am within a few kilometres of the hospital and the car's oil light comes on.

I have no idea why, but fear that to continue driving might ruin the engine, which I've just installed and is new. I can't afford another one, so I leave the car and try to thumb a ride and for quite a while, nobody stops.

I must look strange in my beige short-sleeved safari suit out here in the bush, but eventually a taxi stops, and I get to the hospital expecting to have missed the birth. I rush in to find Sally having a cup of tea looking serene and comfortable.

Soon she begins to push again, but after a few tries, it all stops again. This goes on all through the night and well into the next day, but the midwives don't seem concerned.

Then, at about two in the afternoon, her labour pains come back in earnest and the team arrives. She is pushing and there is a lot of discussion, then there is worry. The top of Jess's head is visible, but she isn't moving. Somone is muttering that they are losing her, and I can see that all is not well.

Then one of the midwives slips her hand in beside the head and feels around. This is hurting Sally, but there is nothing I can do, so I watch, heart in mouth, and then suddenly, as the hand is withdrawn, she is out and wailing. She is passed to me, covered in slime and blood, and then I see the clock. I have just enough time to get to the Sunday afternoon gig if the car is okay, so I get a lift to the car and check the oil. It looks good, so I start it, and the oil light stays off.

"No, against all expectations, her birth did not happen until about three the next afternoon. Apparently, the baby had moved her arm to be over her shoulder, so that was holding her back. But a midwife guessed or recognised the problem and pulled her arm back by her side, and she was then born within seconds.

"I rang my mate and drummer, Jim McBeath, to tell him I would be there for the Sunday afternoon concert. So, unwashed, unshaven and sleep deprived, I arrived at work just as the band was about to start, to a standing ovation from the audience."

'So, they were both okay to come home with you after all that?'

I visit every day, and they are both fine, but there is a heatwave. The hospital is not prepared to let them leave for the house, which is uninsulated, has an iron roof and is stiflingly hot. Nan, Sally's mother, is at the house to help and is looking after Matt and Julia. She goes into town and returns with an air conditioner. I measure its outside dimensions and with the chainsaw, cut a hole right through the weatherboard cladding and the tongue and groove lining. The saw enters from the outside because from there I can see where the wall joists are and can place it in between them.

When the weatherboards fall away, I see there, within centimetres of the right-hand cut, wires dangling. I have cut into the space where the electrician had brought wiring from the ceiling to the meter box. I say nothing to Nan, but the near disaster leaves me a bit shaken.

"We were in the middle of a heatwave that was expected to last for the rest of January, so Nan bought an air conditioner, and I installed it, so within hours we had one cool room to bring her home to."

'How did you get on with Sally's mother?'

We have been together now for about three months. Sally seems happy with her new job in Paxton School, and we are still commuting to Sydney for my Saturday and Sunday evening gigs with Kel's band. I do wonder about her family. She seems unwilling to talk about them, but then she suggests that we visit her parents in Dundas. I remember as a teenager going with Dad to the new Housing Commission houses in Dundas to clean paint from window glass prior to them being rented to low-income families.

Dad's main job was fixer-upper for the building company. After the tenants had been in for about six weeks, Dad would call in to fix any faults that had revealed themselves, so I know the area well, although I have not been back for over twenty years. We arrive at the front door, and she is welcomed in with a hug from Nan, then they stare at me, bewildered.

"Sally eventually got around to introducing me to her family. We arrived on a Friday evening, apparently unannounced because when the door opened, they were expecting to see Alan Tidy. So, there I was, this older bloke that they knew nothing about, not having been told that Sally had moved to Wollombi and changed schools.

"I must say, they recovered quickly, and we stayed for dinner and then the night. The two younger teenage daughters went to friends' houses to stay. Sal's next sister, Sue, was overseas. I got along with Nan right away, and after they retired, they moved into the house beside my farmhouse at Dooralong. But I never seemed to get to know Bob, Sally's father."

'Why was that do you think?'

The youngest daughter must have upset him because he lashes out and slaps her face in front of all of us. I say nothing, but he knows I'm watching. He tells her to go to her room, and she does. Both younger girls are attractive, but Sally is the stand-out beauty and, considering Sally's dabble in prostitution, I wonder about their history with their father.

They moved in next door to the Dooralong farm but Bob didn't see the point in buying a lawn mower when he can help himself to mine. I rarely use it, but he spends a lot of each day riding it up and down his couple of acres of immaculate lawn. I'm always busy on the farm and am a bit dismayed when he comes over to tell me the lawnmower has broken down.

I fix it, and he takes it again.

I come to realise that he is using me like a servant. This repeats until I have had enough. He tells me it needs fixing, so I tell him I am too busy now and I leave it in the middle of his paddock.

It sits there for almost two weeks, during which time I see him walk over to it, look toward my shed, then go back inside, until what I expected happens, and a new mower arrives. It is bigger and better than mine.

I get mine back and within fifteen minutes have it going again and mow my rarely touched grass.

Julia arrives from Townsville with her two infants, fleeing her abusive husband. Nan offers a temporary home for them, so they sleep there. If the girls, aged one and four, slump on the settee, Bob angrily tells them to 'sit up straight'.

"My girls described him as 'creepy'. One night, travelling in my ute, which had a bench front seat, Bob was beside the passenger door and Jess was in the middle. I noticed Bob's hand resting on Jess's thigh, and I felt ill. I didn't say anything because to do so would have embarrassed Jess and exposed her to an idea that she was not ready for.

"We were close to home, so she was soon away from him.

"I was careful from then on to never leave him and her alone together. It could have been less than I feared, but I never really trusted him after I saw him slap his daughter Julie across the face in front of me.

"He always seemed to think he was the smartest person in the room and often asked me scientific conundrums. I was able to answer them, which clearly surprised him. And it annoyed me that he always expected me to drop what I was doing and help him if he needed it."

'What happened to him in the end?'

"He developed prostate cancer but had left it too late for effective treatment, and it metastasised into his bones, so his life became all about misery and pain.

"Nan, who had been a nurse, cared for him at home, keeping him comfortable with morphine until there came a day when he went to sleep and didn't wake up."

'Did you ever contemplate an affair while you were with Sally?'

"No, I never did. In fact, the only partner I deceived with an affair was Vera. I never thought of straying again. With Sally, and with the others, now that I think about it, the deal was honoured, you might say. I had enough sex to satisfy me, and I was content with the relationships. I now wonder sometimes if the human deal, up to the modern era, was: 'I give you security, you give me sex'."

'Did you think that women don't enjoy sex for its own sake?'

"Whoo. At one time I thought that, probably a left over from the Brethren. And I'm not sure I ever really lost that attitude completely until recently, thus the need to offer more than just being a friend and sexual partner."

'Did you ever express that to anyone? Did you discuss it with any partner?'

We are parked in Ron Martin's Combi-camper in the lane outside Chequers back door. I am sounding off about how sex is overrated because it can reduce a man to being a beggar in the bedroom. We decide, after drinking half a flagon of red wine, that music and other creative pursuits are the only reliable roads to satisfaction.

Ron is telling me how he threatened a romantic rival with a shotgun, then proceeds to show me his arsenal. He brings out a large hunting knife, the shotgun, a Luger pistol and a .22 rifle with suppressor.

I am a bit sceptical about the effectiveness of a suppressor, so he offers to show me.

"No, not with a partner, but I did with a mate. For a short time, I led a band that was put together to back Gary Shearston, called the Sharks. It was a quartet with me on guitar, Loretta Lawson on piano, Laurie Watkins on drums and Ron Martin on bass. It was a pretty hot jazz group, but Gary really didn't need a dedicated band, so we did very few gigs.

"Then, in about 1964, Ron and I were in the Chequers late band, so in the early hours, Ron and I found ourselves drinking wine in his VW camper in the lane behind Chequers and we agreed that sex was overrated.

"But he was in love with Loretta and told me how he had threatened a fellow bass player who showed interest in her, with a shotgun. The words he used were: 'I said to him, "If you don't back off, I'll blow your shit bag clean out!"'

Part of the arsenal he carried in his Combi was a silenced .22. He demonstrated it by putting the barrel up a kerbside drain that disappeared in the direction of the Chequers kitchen and fired it.

"(laugh) What we didn't know was that the confines of the drainpipe cancelled out the effects of the suppressor. There was an almighty bang, followed by women screaming and footsteps hurrying toward Chequers open back door."

'My goodness! What did you do?'

"We jumped into the Combi and disappeared in a cloud of blue smoke."

'(laughs) Sometimes I wonder if you're making things up!'

"No, I swear that's all true. I couldn't make that up."

'Okay, so you said that you thought Sally's relationship with Julia was good until Jess came along. What happened there?'

I walk in the door from the farm and can hear the baby crying. I go toward the baby and see Julia bending over the cot to lift her out. Then Sally comes through from the kitchen and her face is red with anger. She screams at Julia to put the baby down. 'She's not your baby! Get to your room!' Julia runs out crying, and Sally picks up the baby. I watch Julia leave, then turn to Sally.

"What happened? She's only trying to help."

"When Matt was a baby, Julia was like a second mother. She took a lot of pressure off Sally by soothing him when he was upset, giving him a bottle while Sally cooked, that kind of thing.

"She was always cooperative and a really easy teenager, so I was flabbergasted to see Sally round on her when she went to pick up Jess. She screamed at Julia that Jess wasn't her baby, and to leave her alone. Of course, Julia was devastated."

'Was that the only time Sally did that... showed bursts of extreme anger?'

We are at the checkout at the store in Cessnock. I'm standing behind Sally, holding the trolley, while she is lifting the groceries onto the conveyor belt. Suddenly Sally yells at the check-out girl about some price being too high. She is giving the poor girl a loud dressing-down. The girl has moved back as far as she can, and she is terrified.

"Once in a shop, she verbally attacked a check-out girl over the price of a grocery item. She was screaming and out of control. I stepped in front of Sally and told the girl it was okay. I told her that I understood that pricing was not something she had control over and apologised."

'What was Sally doing then?'

"As soon as I stepped in, she stopped yelling and then when I looked back at her, she had calmed down, continuing as if nothing had happened. I asked her what prompted the outburst, and she just stared at me, speechless."

'You realise that the price was not the problem. The anger was due to surface anyway, but you say it happened only twice in the fifteen years you were together?'

"Yes, just the two times I witnessed. I am sure there were more when I was not present, but after her outburst at Julia, Sally was adamant that Julia could not stay with us in the same house.

"Julia was devastated, and I was torn between protecting Julia and supporting Sally and our new family. I visited the psychologist I had consulted over David, and he said that Julia might be better off with her mother for now."

'What did the psychologist say about Sally's behaviour?'

'Mate, you put two unrelated women in the same house, and you will see sparks fly. Your dilemma is that you're now responsible for two infant children, and you aren't about to tell Sally to go, but Julia does have a mother who will probably welcome her. You have no choice.'

"Nothing specific, but I didn't think to tell him about the incident at the shop. He advised me to send Julia to live with her mother. Vera indicated that Julia wasn't happy in the Williams household, with three daughters more or less Julia's age to compete with, and I got the impression that Dick, Vera's husband, did play favourites. However, Julia says that she was reasonably happy with the Williams family and it was when Vera moved to be with Ron Martin that Julia suffered the discrimination."

'Sally was clearly expressing a suppressed anger there that had little to do with grocery prices or Julia picking up the baby. Did you mention to anyone your misgivings about Bob and inappropriate touching?'

"Yes, I asked Nan if Bob was ever inappropriate with Sally, and she was a bit offended, but said no, she hadn't seen anything."

'I guess we'll never know, unless one of the other girls says something.'

"The other girls are all interesting people. Two of them were careful to choose a man with wealth or excellent prospects and were pretty blatant about it. One made it work very well, but in any case, she was highly qualified and found work in areas that were specialised and, I guess, lucrative, but I'd rather not say too much about that."

'Are you afraid you might hurt some feelings.'

"Yes, there's that, but it's none of my business and except that it might show a pattern, which I think it does, I can't see it being of much value with Sally and Bob both dead."

'Fair enough.'

She closes her notebook and stands. She takes my coffee cup that I realise I haven't finished drinking and smiles. I stand, slip on my sunnies and turn toward the door.

'We strayed a long way from *The Clock of Lonk*, so I'd like to take you back there next time. Okay?'

Session 15

I see my coffee waiting and pick it up as she turns from her screen and motions for me to sit.

Today is her wool day, but it is colder. Turtleneck loose jumper and woollen skirt. Nice.

'So, you had success with your first play, *David and the Monsters*, but the production company folded, so did you go on with it elsewhere?'

"As I said, we were moving to the new farm, so I was busy with other things. But I restarted it later for the Dooralong school."

'How did that happen?'

Sally and I are delighted to find that there is a school within walking distance of our new farm, and although Matt is only just four, we attend a P & C meeting to meet the teacher and parents. The meeting is mid-year, and we are deciding if we will send him at age four and a half or wait until he is five and a half.

We arrive to find quite a gathering and soon learn that pupil numbers are down to eight and the school will close at the end of that year. Small schools are comparatively well-equipped, so there are a couple of other school principals there to scoop up any equipment that might come with the pupils. We learn that the teacher has been in this school since graduation and is due to retire in two years but seems to have become lazy.

One of the parents holds up what looks like a blank sheet of paper and wants to know what it is.

The teacher examines it and says it is maths homework.

The parent points out that the print is so faint that she cannot make out all the numbers.

His reply? 'The Fordigraph stencils are pretty worn out, but if you expect me to make new stencils within two years of retiring, you're crazy.'

I stifle a giggle, but there is worse to come. He has been advising parents of the older children to send them to Wyong for their last two years, because 'they can offer more experiences, like team sports'.

Of course, a side effect of this is that the older children take their younger siblings with them on the bus, so there are potentially three or four times the number of pupils available if they can be coaxed back.

Sally says the teacher 'has to go'. She ascertains that he has two years of unclaimed sick leave and has never taken long service leave, so he is entitled to resign at any time. She starts lobbying her contacts to force him into early retirement.

I try to think of ways to keep the school open. I suggest the school needs something dramatic to make the school more attractive.

He is angry at that, and suggests that if 'you're so smart, you do something', so I suggest we stage a musical play for Arbor Day, which I recall was in August of that year.

"The school was about to close from lack of pupils, so I wrote a musical play called *Arbor Day in the Watagans*.

'Watagans?'

"The Watagan mountains rose just behind the school and defined the western side of the Dooralong Valley. Most of it is a state forest, although at that time, there was a sawmill in the forest that gave employment to many of the locals, (laugh) including Brother Francis. Do you mind if I digress and tell you a story about Brother?"

'No, was he a priest of something?'

"(Laugh) No. Brother Francis had a brother named Frank, who must have been older. Anyway, gossip had it that when Brother was born, his mother could not find the energy to name him, so he was always Frank's brother and eventually, just 'Brother'. But the story is about Brother's employment at the sawmill.

"It seems that Brother never wore shoes, ever. His feet were wide and calloused and were impervious to splinters or thorns, so having no boots did not affect his employment until one day, some bloke from 'Health and Safety' turned up at the mill and saw Brother rolling logs onto trolleys, feeding logs into the saw and then stacking and loading timber onto a truck.

"'What's this bloke doing working without work boots?' he demanded. 'He could lose a toe or worse!'

"'Nah,' laughs the boss. 'If Brother Francis's foot ever came in contact with a saw, it would be the saw I'd worry about.'

"But the law is the law, and Brother's employment was terminated. He did work with his brother Frank to harvest poles for pit props, which I think he did until he was old enough for the pension."

'What a character.'

"There were many characters around in those days, and I hope we are still breeding some, but I doubt it. Anyway, back to Arbor Day.

"Pam Bailey was a retired teacher and secretary of the school's P & C. She was keen on the idea, so I got busy and wrote the play and recorded the music on a tape recorder. I also invited George, other name forgotten, unfortunately, to give a talk. George had a nursery and was leading the business of cloning to remove viruses from seed potatoes.

"He brought with him what he called a pro-sequoia tree and

explained that it was the forebear of the California giant sequoia of today and that there are more advanced specimens in the park beside Gosford Railway Station, so we had a tree planting. I remember George pointing to a large grey gum and saying that a tree like that removed a thousand litres of water per day from the soil, and by that, he stressed the importance of trees in maintaining the water table."

'So, you put on the play with a cast of eight, kinder to year four?'

"No. Sally got busy through a play group she had started and rounded up half a dozen kids between four and five to be nymphs and fairies. The play got a lot of attention, then the teacher did take early retirement and a new, but temporary young, enthusiastic teacher arrived.

"We did another play at the end of the year, and then in the new year, because of Sally's recruitment drive and a new enthusiasm at the school, we had ten or so new enrolments and the school was safe.

"In the following year, we had our new permanent teacher, Paul Maish, who I reckon was the Barnaby Joyce of teaching, minus Barnaby's less-endearing qualities. Paul was a rough diamond in some ways, a Vietnam vet, with a wonderful understanding of how kids think. All the kids worked hard for Paul, so the school became a vibrant hub of education.

"Paul was interested in the musical plays and encouraged me to write more. He also arranged for me to buy a four-track cassette recorder through the school, which allowed me to multi-track backings, using the guitar and bass plus a drum machine for percussion.

"This is the source of backing for *B.C.*, a tongue-in-cheek Nativity play that is set in the 'El Posh' Hotel in Bethlehem, whose proprietors take advantage of the inflow of people returning for the census to make a killing. The play ends with the traditional Christian Nativity and some carols.

"Then I got the idea of recording the kids' voices on the multi-track so the volume of all singers on stage could be balanced with the backing. The recording sessions were great fun, and the finished product was close to professional standard.

"But I was limited by my instruments until I saw what some teachers were doing with Mac computers and the Notator program using sound modules, so I invested in an Atari Mega, a keyboard, Notator, and a printer. Later, I added a hard drive; 750 Megabytes for $750. (Laugh) Now I buy USB sticks for about $1 per gigabyte!

"So, for the next few years, we produced a couple of plays per year, that included the whole school, some written specifically for the infants, but most not.

"Later, I realised that having all the kids doing the senior plays was one of the reasons the plays had such a wonderful effect."

'How was that?'

"By that time, the school was paying me for a day a week to teach programs that included music and drama, plus other areas that Paul thought needed a boost."

'What were they?'

"(laugh) I reckon if the Health and Safety bloke had come to one of my 'hands-on-science' lessons he would have closed that down too. Most of the science we did was outdoors, using situations and materials lying around, like the huge log of nearly a ton in the school yard.

"I challenged the kids to work out what it weighed. We sat on the log and thought for a while, then one of the kids suggested that we could lift each end with a lever and weigh the ends separately, then add the two weights.

"For me, that meant we needed to explore levers, so we used some bricks to establish that the distance from fulcrum to load multiplied by the load was equal to the effort times the distance to the fulcrum. We then repeated the process for the other end and came up with the weight.

"We went to the small park near the school and investigated pendulums using the swings. A couple of kids had stopwatches to record the 'period'. We put a small child on a swing, gave her a push and measured the time to complete ten oscillations. I then asked how we could make the period longer or shorter. Suggestions included pushing harder, which to their amazement made no difference, so they tried a heavier person and that made no difference, so it was suggested we shorten the chains, and we found that did decrease the period.

"One of the students wanted to know how much we needed to shorten the pendulum to halve the period, so we ran a length of fishing line through a screw-eye to the lintel of a doorway, with a lead sinker on the end. We found that by shortening the line we could decrease the period, but the question was 'How much shorter did it need to be to decrease the period to half?'

"First, we tried half the length, but the period was still more than half, so we just continued shortening it until we achieved half the period and decided it had something to do with Pi and left it at that."

'Seems the kids had a lot of fun doing the experiments?'

"Yes, but I frightened myself with the conservation-of-energy experiment. (laugh) You remember those round discs in parks with rails radiating from the centre, called carousels?"

'Yes. But I haven't seen one for ages.'

"Right. Maybe my experiment got back to the powers that be, because we did create a bit of excitement and (laugh) excitement is no longer allowed. I had a few smaller kids sit at the edge with the vertical rail between their legs, then a bigger child standing at the outer end of each of the rails, hanging out into space and a few other big kids to run around and push to make it spin. When I blew the whistle, the plan was for the big kids hanging off the edge of the disc to pull themselves into the centre. It frightened me, how it accelerated until it was really whizzing around. The little kids at the edges were screaming, so I blew the whistle for the big kids to let themselves move to the edge again. Other kids wanted to have a turn at being the movable mass, but I said we had the results we wanted and needed to get back to the classroom to write it up. Phew!

"I also taught the kids to touch type one year, and we had all the kids and some parents playing guitars one year. We had a lot of fun."

'Can I get you back to the plays? It seemed you were able to use the school to workshop them.'

"Yes, I did. But most of the plays went on pretty much as written. I didn't give myself a lot of time. I took the plays from concept to stage in about six weeks, so it was pretty intense."

'Did you get to measure the influence the plays had on the kids?'

"After the first couple of plays, Paul said there was a significant jump in reading ages, particularly in the younger children, after each play. That got me thinking about why that should be. It was pretty obvious in the end, so I wrote a paper on it."

'What happened to that?'

"Well, nothing. I never did get to finish a degree, so that precluded me from being taken seriously in the age of credentialism. But I do know why it works."

'Can you explain it to me?'

"Yes, simply put, it's about vocabulary. If a child comes across a written word that has its oral equivalent in memory, the written word is connected to the mental picture and understanding happens. If there is no equivalent word in memory, the written word is meaningless.

"I didn't dumb down the language in the plays, so all the kids in the play (and in a small school that was all of them), even the kindies, hear 'adult' language.

"Then, because they then act it out and say the phrases many times in a meaningful context, their vocabulary jumps very quickly. It's a macro approach. We speak in phrases, not individual words. The phrases they use in the play become theirs, first to recognise, then to understand, then to use in other contexts. It's like learning a foreign language.

"My Jess spent a year in Belgium, where everyone spoke French. She came home fluent in French and a Frenchman we knew declared that she was 'Parisienne'.

"Acting in plays is like that. The student is immersed in the language of the play and takes it in organically, as do babies learning their mother tongue. Why drama is not the centre of literacy programs, I will never know."

'Do you still have those plays, and the music?'

"Most of them, I do. (laugh) I sent about a hundred USB sticks to small schools all over the country with the plays and music, plus the rationale and some directions for use as a gift.

"I have one thank-you note from a teacher in Tasmania and a Christmas card from one in country New South Wales. I guess most teachers are busy and don't want to be burdened with something they probably dread, like putting on a play."

'(laughs) Yes, I remember my school plays and I never got a major role. Most of the time, I sat around watching the show-offs.'

"(laugh) I remember that well, from my own school days. But I developed a method by which every kid gets to play a major role in every play, and all are gainfully employed all the time, but I won't go into that here, except to say that Brian Cambourne, who had been a professor of literacy at Wollongong University, looked at what I was doing and was very impressed. But again, lack of a degree precluded any further examination of what I regard as my most important contribution to education. It might die with me, but somewhere, sometime, someone will study it for a PhD and that would be amazing."

'What happened to the kids who were exposed to your plays?'

"They excelled. Of the first set of four who had been performing in my plays from kindergarten to year six, Caroline Toovey was dux of Wyong High and was headhunted by Price Waterhouse, who paid for her degree in accounting. Kathy Maish has two masters' degrees at my last count, and among other things, teaches at Macquarie. I lost track of Chantelle Webster, but she was a very accomplished ballet dancer, so maybe that's the path she followed and the fourth was my Matt, who topped his year in chemistry, was second in physics and did well in three-unit maths. He did start uni but joined the Police Force. While he was in year 12, he edited the school's poetry magazine."

'Did you continue doing the plays after your kids finished at the school?'

"I did for a year or two, but then Paul moved into private school education and teachers who came to the school after him were not as supportive, so I stopped doing it."

'So, that was the end of your play writing?'

"Not totally. Recently I wrote two short plays in our local Indigenous language, Dhurga, and a full-length play telling a juicy story that I found in the diaries of my maternal grandmother, Eusebia, that reveals a great love, then its destruction through pressure from the Exclusive Brethren.

"But back then, I redid the music of some existing plays with my new equipment, then tried commercialising the plays and the system, offering them for hire firstly, then for sale as kits, including the tape and libretto plus a teachers' book of instructions and hints."

'How did that go?'

My partner Dianne and I are hopeful that we can make a business from the play hire. We doubt that anyone has caught up with our tape system and because it is all done by me, except for some of the singing, ongoing costs are minimal.

I had bought the computer, keyboard, printer and programs, an outlay of about $8,000. When Dianne becomes involved, then years later, she puts in $18,000, which she says is the total of her property settlement with ex-husband Chris, and we buy a commercial photocopier, a couple more gismos to enhance the sound recording, and start producing kits.

I am surprised that after over twenty years of marriage, with both having good incomes, that is all she comes away with. I guess they spent it as they went.

We get mailing lists from the state departments and send out five thousand letters to schools across Australia, then orders begin to trickle in.

After only a few weeks, we start getting many of them back with terse little notes saying they were not suitable for one reason or another, then one comes back from Gympie with a similar note. But whoever copied it left one of the photocopied pages complete with the image of the binding tucked inside the libretto and we realised that we had a problem.

I visit a local school that has asked me to call in with a few plays. The principal brings out a cardboard box to show me the plays he already has and there are two pirated plays of mine. I point out that they were stolen, but he isn't concerned. 'Everybody does it,' he says.

"We send letters with advertising to schools all over Australia, and we think we are doing okay. Then we have a flood of returns for refunds, but we know at least some were copying them and sending them back. The postage costs were starting to hurt."

'How did you know they were just not what they wanted?'

"Good question. One school had obviously copied the libretto and presumably the tape and carelessly sent back one of the photocopied pages tucked inside a libretto, and one school I know had two pirated copies."

'How disappointing.'

"Yes, but there were also hundreds of lovely letters and cards from schools who loved the plays. One school bought one copy of every play for their library, so there were honest people out there.

"But the ideal was shattered for me. We had spent all our seed money, much of that from Dianne, so I called a halt and closed up shop. Dianne was upset that I drew the line, and maybe she was right.

"But now that tape players with double decks could copy tapes and photocopiers were so good, material was too easy to steal. Later, more attention began to be paid to copyright, so maybe if we had persevered, we could have made it work."

'If anyone wanted a play now, could they get one?'

"(laugh) Of course, at least until I drop off the perch. I have a file of almost all of the plays and music, digitised by my friend John Bartlett, with backing tracks and singing tracks, all there ready to go on www.staffordray.com from where you can follow the links.

"The effect of plays on literacy is amazing, but the teaching method I developed is vital for ensuring the improvement of all students, not just the gifted.

"I have tried to get the material and lesson plans some attention but am dismayed that teachers still do not understand how potent drama is in the building of literacy."

'Can you give me a potted version of the rationale?'

I listen in dismay to the recurring discussion of 'whole of language' versus 'sounding out words' as mutually exclusive methods to teach literacy, and in particular, reading.

My experience tells me that they are complementary. Children learn most of their language by living in a society that speaks that language, with words and meanings absorbed organically. At school, they study individual sounds and blends that are the building blocks of words. But again, if the word is not recognised in memory, that word is still meaningless until it and all its meanings are present in memory.

My observation of the process identifies vocabulary as the principal limiting factor.

"In the classroom, macro, or organic learning of language through drama offers a super-efficient way to increase vocabulary with repeated use of new words in context in a high-motivation environment.

"Viewed in phrases, sets of words are said, read, and acted out in context so that any new words are understood then practised many times until they become part of every student's usable vocabulary. The other factor is energy. Motivated kids learn quickly, and they love showing off in plays.

"But this is best done concurrently with students being trained in sounding out words, so he or she understands the building blocks of words, the sounds of letters and blends.

"Kids invest a lot of energy in plays and that is the secret of retention. I say that plays are the magic bullet.

"If you ask any person what they remember about their school days, most will tell you about their part in a school play."

'(laughs) Yes, I remember my school plays and could probably quote my lines if I tried. So, how's the old school going now?'

"Mmm. At the peak, we had forty-two kids, two teachers and a part-time ancillary. We put that down to the results we were getting generally, but mostly it was about the plays. We found that there are other benefits to a universal drama program.

"We had one kid, Barry, who had been expelled from two other schools for serious antisocial behaviour. At our school, he became a star actor. In fact, he was scary when he acted, he was that good. He could act out his anger in a play and be applauded for it, then be the model student for the rest of the time. His transformation was amazing to witness.

"The whole school tone was happy and cooperative. We had no behavioural problems."

'And now?'

"I almost want to cry when I drive past the old school, not that I often do. The last teacher there seemed to have little interest in teaching and seemed more interested in politics. He had no time for the plays, so I stopped and in no time, the school closed.

"The teacher's house was sold first, then the school itself. My departure also coincided with another downturn in my hearing, so I didn't try too hard to convince him of the value of what I was doing."

'Did you abandon any other ventures that you now suspect you could have persevered with?'

We have been growing lettuce for a year and although we are turning out a top product, the return is not enough to make it worthwhile, so Sally and I borrow Bob's car and drive to Toowoomba. It has been arranged by my agronomist to see celery growing in action, so we arrive and are kindly shown the process from seed propagation to harvest.

Our coastal river loam farm is so different from Toowoomba's volcanic soils that I start with one bed to try it. We have a hot house, so we get the seedlings up to plant-out stage and Benny puts them in. We set up irrigation and they grow well alongside the lettuce.

I think they are at least as good as Toowoomba celery and am planning to harvest them, thinking about packing cases and cooling them in the cool room, when I discover they have a disease that makes them, in my mind, unmarketable.

"Early on, I grew many different vegetables, but that was a scattergun approach that did not endear me to produce agents. They needed constant and reliable supply. I started studying Horticulture at Orange Ag College by correspondence because I felt a need for marketing expertise.

"As a kid I had grown beans and sent them to market only to make a loss after agents' fees and cartage were deducted, so I knew there needed to be more planning and control. I interviewed two agents to get advice on the best crops for the Newcastle market and was advised to grow lettuce and given an average price as a guide.

"I bought new cases at a $1.20 each, then plants at $40 per thousand, paid some friends to help plant them out, set up irrigation, bought a high-clearance tractor, developed special tools to cultivate close to the plants, and we were away.

"They grew well with no diseases, so we didn't need to spray. We planted them in sequence so we could pick a thousand cases a week.

"By summer, we needed a cool room, so we bought one and I set it up with forced-fan cooling.

"Nobody said that a thousand cases a week was more than the market could bear, until the returns started coming in at one to two dollars a case less than we expected. All expenses had been paid, but there was no income for us. We had worked the whole year for nothing. Actually, my lovely neighbour, Neville Kirkwood, often turned up in the paddock with a knife and helped us pick and pack, so if he had not been there, we would have lost actual money."

'How awful.'

"(laugh) Yes, but it gets worse. We had decided to cut back on the size of plantings and offer less to the market. That also cut back on labour costs, but prices didn't improve enough. Then, the first flood hit and wiped out the entire crop. We expected floods to come occasionally, but in that year, we had four major floods and decided we needed to go for a crop that could withstand flooding.

"While at Orange Ag College, I was talking to a lecturer about that, and he arranged for us to visit Gerry Bennett in Cowra, who grew asparagus on river flats where flooding was a constant. Gerry was very generous and showed us his operation.

"He used horses to collect picked asparagus. I met the horses, Clydesdales, that he had trained to not need drivers to pull sleds, stopping at the right places and only requiring guidance when the sleds were full and needed to be taken to the packing shed.

"I planted a trial bed of asparagus, but as you know, asparagus takes several years to reach a stage where it produces commercial quantities, so I needed something else to fill that time and garden space. I chose small savoy cabbages, not much bigger than the average lettuce, very sweet and quick to grow.

"When our first planting reached maturity, we sent them off to market in lettuce cases. My new agent forwarded most of them to Sydney Market and they caught the eye of an exporter who repacked them for Singapore. Our return was almost $10 per case. That was an amazing price, so I went to Sydney to talk to the exporter so I could pack them as he needed for export. He thought that was a good idea and would result in even better returns."

'That sounds like an ideal direction to take.'

"Yes, in retrospect, it was. But after a few months I found that borers had infested the next batch of mature heads, so I ploughed them in, like I did with the celery that tasted great and was perfect except for target spot on the leaves. I needed my produce to be perfect for me to feel immune from criticism. To me, any defect rendered the vegetables unmarketable in my name."

'So, I'm guessing you didn't seek advice?'

Dismay feels a bit like shame. I look at the celery and it is perfect except for target spot, a fungus that is easily prevented. I think back to the first cabbages I grew and remember rejecting any with the slightest sign of fungus in the base that could have been removed in the trimming. Early-Curly cabbages with borers, a preventative spray could fix that, but I can't go to the agronomist and look foolish, so I abandon them and look for a new direction.

"No. In my older age, I'm happy to seek advice on anything and see no shame in it. But when it really mattered, I was not able to. Everything I grew needed to be so good that nobody could criticise it and anything less caused me to feel inadequate, a failure, so I ploughed them in and concentrated on the asparagus and the plays, apart from a couple of inventions."

'Have you wondered since why you were so quick to abandon projects that, it seems to me from your telling of it, were salvageable at least and potentially good business?'

"Yes, and what I wouldn't give to be able to turn back time. If I had fixed the celery fungus or the cabbage borer problem, who knows where that would have led and, dare I say it, maybe Sally might have made different choices."

'Don't punish yourself. You can't know that.'

"Maybe, but she did say a few things that indicated that she was dissatisfied with my management of the property, not that she offered concrete advice."

'Would you have taken it?'

"I don't know. I suspect not. That might have meant admitting fault and that was to be avoided, although I did respect her opinion on most things. We never really discussed the everyday decisions, and I suspect she would rather I made them alone."

'So you wore the blame?'

"No, that's a bit harsh. I think she saw the man's role as the leader and fortune maker. I was a flawed leader and never a fortune maker, although had I taken a different path after Wollombi, a fortune was there to be created, but not in farming."

'Did your thinking go beyond farming back then?'

"No, and that is important in understanding what happened. I was panicked by the deafness and the only pathway I could see after teaching and music was what I knew something of, and that was farming, not that I had ever experienced a really successful farm. Our small acreages and Coromandel were hardly outstanding exemplars of success."

'So, you think you have overcome that shame, slash, inhibition?'

"(laugh) No, not totally, but I have employed an editor for my latest novel and am delighted to receive suggestions."

'Are there many… suggestions?'

"No, but I would welcome more and have been happy to be edited since I joined the Eurobodalla Writers many years ago where I found my tribe and they were wonderfully supportive."

'Do you still belong? Do you still see them?'

"No, unfortunately, I have not felt up to it with my medical situation as it is, but I do see the occasional one and they invite me to their outings sometimes. I go when I can."

'Okay. It seems that your father's refusal to support your endeavours unless he could use them to showcase himself did not kill off your creativity. Despite his 'What do you think you are doing?' put-downs, you still invented, designed and made things. I remember your scooter sidecar and the tree house with a lift, and all the others. You mentioned improving designs at your first job at... where was it?'

"Coote and Jorgensen."

'Right, and you continued to do that throughout your life. Did you always invent better ways out of necessity?'

"Yes. At Wollombi, and I'm now going back to the mid-seventies, I needed to replace all the boundary fences on the hundred acres before I could stock it. The old posts had rotted off at the ground and were lying like dead soldiers along the boundary lines. There were plenty of ironbark trees on the property with the right diameter, so there was no shortage of new posts. However, I was accumulating tons of old posts, with over sixty years of drying that made them ideal firewood.

"But to cut them up into suitably sized blocks using a chainsaw was to invite disaster. I found myself holding them with a foot and cutting right beside my foot with a saw that, if it slipped, could cut right through flesh before it could be stopped.

"Even I could see how dangerous that was, so I invented a device to hold them, which I called a Blokka. When I moved to Dooralong, I refined the design and eventually got around to patenting it and then found a local fabrication company to make me a few prototypes to show around. Andrew, the engineer, saw the potential and asked to be considered as the manufacturer if it got into production.

"I took the first one, plus a few more, to a country show and sold them, so Andrew made several hundred that I continued to demonstrate at country shows and also at chainsaw shops.

"Then I realised that, spart from offering safety while cutting rough timber like old fence posts, the Blokka was far and away the best device to hold any piece of timber that needed to be ripped or sawn longitudinally. The way it was held by Blokka meant that there was no limit on length, but at that stage, the shape of the jaws was ideal for any shaped log, but not suitable to support all sizes of sawn timber. To make it even more versatile, we redesigned the jaws, and Andrew came up with a welded frame that was more versatile and attractive to look at.

"So, along with Tom Olyslagers, Andrew's salesman, I approached Bunnings in Melbourne. "We met Peter Sandercock and demonstrated Blokka to him. He decided to stock it at Bunnings with an initial order of over a thousand at $150, wholesale. Manufacturing cost was $130 per unit, so I had a margin of $20 for me and my costs.

"I then set up a bar code and an automatic reordering system, sent off the first order and waited for the reorders to roll in. Nothing happened, so I went into a Bunnings store and asked to 'see a Blokka'.

"I received a blank stare and was referred to a manager who, after consulting his computer, said they had arrived in the loading dock, and they were waiting for the supplier to move them onto the shop floor."

'What was that about?'

I call up head office and tell them that I'm only one person and cannot possibly get around all the 110 Bunnings stores spread between Cairns and Hobart to move the Blokkas from the loading bay to the shop floor. I'm told then that I need to advertise it. I remind them that they are withholding a percentage of my returns for advertising, and I thought that was all I needed to do.

He says that is only to pay for an entry in the catalogue, so I get some mates together and we make an ad showing Blokka doing its stuff.

I pay $24,000 for a series of airings on TV at times that handymen might be watching.

Then I get a call from Bunnings in WA, asking when they will be receiving their Blokkas, because customers are asking for them. We have 300 in readiness for repeat orders, so I offer them to him at $150 plus freight. He says the advertising is offering them at the same price for every Bunnings in Australia, so it must be retailed at that price, and I need to cover the freight.

"I was not aware, but became aware, that it seems all Bunnings does is maintain the building, pay its staff, who are really tour guides, and collect the money. The wholesaler, that's me, delivers the goods right to the shop floor and maintains the display. We also pay for promotion. That was not explained to me, so I guess Peter presumed that I was already aware of the business model."

'So, what happened in the end?'

We have set up at Walcha show and my mate, Steve Snedden, selling chainsaw accessories, is next to me. I sell one or two over the two days and spend most of my time chainsawing – cutting a round log into 4X2 planks, then ripping those into palings. Sometimes I fashion a miniature table and chairs from a round log and sometimes I just sit on a log supported by a Blokka to show how stable it is.

I leave my roped-off area to talk to Steve and see a bloke step over the rope with a tape measure and proceed to write down Blokka's dimensions.

I tell him to piss off, but then realise that he has taught me a valuable lesson. Any farmer with an oxy torch and a welder can knock up a similar device from scrap metal that is lying around on most farms, gathering rust. Of course, the time taken is rarely considered by such people, so my market was probably not the bush, but hobby farmers and suburbanites with wood stoves or heaters; the ones who might shop at Bunnings but maybe gather logs from the side of the road.

"I had high hopes for the Blokka at Bunnings, but I was not able to fulfil all the roles from manufacture to shop floor that were required of me, so I pulled the plug. The price was already at the top end of what I thought the market could bear. Then I got a call from the company that supplies Bunnings in WA. He wanted to know if I was interested in Blokka being manufactured in their Australian-owned factory in China.

"Of course I was, so I authorised them to send a sample to China. Their sample came back, identical to our product but could be landed in East Coast ports for $50 each."

'I bet that made a difference!'

"Well, no. Bunnings was interested in the new version, but only if we bought back at wholesale all unsold stock, then resold them back for $50. We are looking at hundreds of thousands of dollars here, so I was spooked and refused the deal. As it turned out, I came out of it neutral in dollars, but of course, my time and effort returned nothing, except that I have one of each model of the Blokka, the last one being made in China."

'Did Bunnings chase you after that?'

"No, I got a nice letter from the general manager saying they were sorry that my experience with Bunnings was less satisfactory than expected, and I heard no more. But I did see some Blokkas for sale at a fire-sale price of $50, so I guess Bunnings lost on the deal, and I did feel sorry for Peter who probably copped some flak over his decision to buy them.

"The bottom line is, unless you're a wholesaler selling multiple lines made cheaply in China, and therefore can support a team of salespeople to service your product in Bunnings stores, Bunnings is not for you, and I guess the same goes for all the other big hardware chains.

"I think Bunnings is a wonderful store for the buyer and I shop there often."

'Once bitten, twice shy. So, did you invent any other devices for the farm?'

"Andrew's main business was manufacturing and installing screw piles for building foundations that were on unstable ground. I had an idea for a steel fence post with a similar principle. I drew it up, and Andrew made a few prototypes of different lengths. He also made an adapter that allowed us to use a portable post-hole digger as the power source to drive them in, and we tested it, first in the laneway behind the factory, which was lightly sealed with tar and gravel underneath. The 'post-hole' disappeared into that hard soil in seconds, then one of Andrew's tradesmen inserted a standard-length industrial post and tried to move it sideways. The post-hole stayed in place, but the post bent."

'Success!'

"Better than we imagined, so we tried it in other soils and found we could screw in the 'instant post-hole' and insert a post in less than thirty seconds. We tried it with a team of three, two to operate the modified post-hole digger and one to first hold the 'post-hole' in place, then insert the posts. We also tried it in wet ground and found that it was just as effective.

"Andrew said he could make them in bulk for $8 each for the standard length, a little more for longer ones we used in wet or sandy ground, so I took out a patent for Australia. Just then, there were floods in Queensland that had destroyed hundreds of kilometres of fencing and farmers were battling to keep stock under control.

"Here was the ideal situation where the instant post-hole could be used to lay kilometres of new fencing in a day so that they could quickly regain control of their stock. I rang an agency there and told him about our 'instant post-hole'. He asked if I had a prototype, so I posted it up."

'Well, I'm waiting for the successful ending.'

I'm sitting in Andrew's office. There has been no reaction from Queensland for the instant post-hole, and we are discussing the Bunnings failure and wondering if we can go on with Blokka. I have travelled to hundreds of chainsaw shops and demonstrated Blokka at numerous shows, but they are not selling well enough to support the effort, so I decide to call it quits on both products but tell him he can have the patents and take it further if he wishes.

Andrew is upset and talks about suing me, and I'm sorry about that, but he was paid for every unit he made, and I had cleared all his stock. I'm now sixty-seven, and tired of battling.

"There is no successful ending for either of those inventions, the only ones I ever patented. But I did have success with a set of farm devices that I used that saved me heaps and allowed me to let Benny go."

'Who is Benny?'

I am without a farm hand to watch and act if needed while we visit Julia in Townsville, so I call the Labour Exchange in Wyong. They have a young man available who is interested and send him out. Benny Spee has done his best to look presentable, wearing a pale blue tuxedo, black pants and a white shirt that all clearly came from Vinnies.

His old falcon is gleaming with every bit of chrome glistening with fresh polish. I walk out to the gate to meet him. He climbs out and despite his youth, he is bent like an older man and his face says 'Beaten'.

He shakes hands and then waits for me to say he is not suitable. I look again at the car and ask him to show me the motor. His eyes light up and his back straightens. Under the bonnet, the motor is shining, clean and red. The rocker box cover is chrome-plated and spotless.

Then I notice the extractors. 'Extractors!' I say, and he goes on to describe what he has done to the engine. I take a glance into the cabin, and it is just as immaculate. I'm impressed and invite him in for a cuppa.

"Benny was sent by what is now Centrelink, to look after the farm while we visited Julia on that fateful trip to Townsville where Sally took off to Darwin. I had been let down by a neighbour who had first agreed to cover for me, then couldn't stay for the whole three weeks, so Benny was it.

"He did not present well, but his car did, and I was hooked. If he could take that level of care with his car, then my farm machinery was in good hands.

"Benny was born in Holland, had a speech impediment, was small for his age and admitted to being bullied at school. He lived with, and cared for, his alcoholic mother, so there was little money.

"On that first day, I got him talking about his car first, and then his history. He had no experience on farms, but I had a couple of weeks to check him out. He stayed for two years and showed he had a great work ethic and could be left alone to complete tasks.

"I sometimes came home to find he had finished all his allotted jobs and was sweeping out the shed or washing the tractors. He was a great worker and even had a wry sense of humour that I guess very few people saw."

'Why did you let him go?'

"Basically, I made a couple of devices that increased my productivity so much I didn't need him."

'So, what became of Benny?'

I ask to see the manager of Flemmings in Wyong and tell him about Benny. He asks me if Benny knows anything about refrigeration, so I tell him we have a cool room that Benny uses, and that he is a natural with machinery. He starts Benny right away to manage his cool rooms and freezers. I see him when I am in the shop occasionally and he is sporting an impressive beard. I laugh when I see it and ask him if Management approves. He smiles and tells me they threaten to fire him if he keeps the beard, so he shaves it off and starts a new one. Then he tells me he is engaged and invites me to the wedding.

"I approached a local supermarket and put in a good word, and they hired him. He stayed there for many years that I know of. I was at his wedding, where the aunts brought the food, a mate played records and Benny supplied the beer.

"All up it would have cost a hundred dollars for the hall hire and that's it. But it was one of the most joyous weddings I have ever attended and the start of a successful marriage.

"She was smart with money, and it was no time before they had a home. It was small, one bedroom, but they added more rooms as children arrived and by the time I left to go sailing ten years later, they were thriving.

"But whenever I saw Benny at the store, he would call out to me through various stages of beard growth: 'Can I have my old job back, Boss?'"

'So, what was the invention that replaced Benny?'

"There were two. The first allowed me to plant 10,000 seeds per day into growing trays."

'How did that work?'

"The growing trays had seventy-three compartments, so I made a hollow frame the size of the growing trays, with seventy-three tiny holes on the bottom surface. Attached to the frame was a vacuum cleaner that I could turn off and on and under that was a sheet of plastic foam, into which I had burnt, using the rounded end of a coach bolt, corresponding dimples. Seeds went into the dimples and the frame sat on the foam. With the vacuum cleaner on, I gave the frame a tap to make the seeds jump and then lifted the frame with one seed held to each hole by suction. Then I placed the frame over the growing tray filled with seed mix and cut off the suction, so one seed fell into each compartment."

'Neat.'

"Yes, then I had a tub of water where I placed the tray to allow the mixture to saturate while I processed the next tray, then stacked the seeded trays in the hothouse for three days. On the fourth day, I spread out the trays on benches to grow. Next day, most seeds had sprouted.

"They were watered every few days and usually by four weeks were ready for transplanting. As I said, that made seed raising cheap and efficient, saving me most of what I had been spending on seedlings. But we were still planting out by hand and that was not only slow, but backbreaking work.

"Seedling transplanters were available but needed a team of people plus a tractor driver to operate. That was no good to me, so I made a one-man self-propelled planter."

'Did you patent that?'

"(laugh) This was a few years before Blokka or the instant post-hole and it was at a time when I was propagating all my seedlings for lettuce and cabbages. I even tried tomatoes, and one year, I cornered the market in cucumbers. I didn't have enough in the ground to make real money, but it did teach me something about business.

"I had a section of land that had, at some time in the past, been an orange orchard. I planted several crops there that came to maturity and then died mysteriously.

"I did call in the agronomist..."

'And you felt okay about asking for help because you were sure you were not at fault?'

"(laugh) You know, I have never thought of that, but yes, probably. He said the ground had been poisoned with a herbicide called Hyvar X, which is very effective in citrus orchards but deadly to almost any other plant, and it persists indefinitely.

"The cure recommended was to grow successive crops of oats and before maturity, plough the oats in. So, when the third crop of oats was tall and green, I planted cucumbers into the oats in that section, then after a day or so, sprayed the oats with glyphosate. The oats started to wilt in a few days, then I saw dark green vines climbing out of the drooping oats. By the time the oats were dry and flat on the ground, the cucumbers had spread over the carpet of oat hay. Then rain fell and kept falling.

"My cucumbers developed, then I picked the first dozen boxes and received $16 per case. That was about four times the usual price. For most farmers, cucumbers on the ground had rotted because of the rain, while mine thrived. Then I got a call from a greengrocer in Broadmeadow near Newcastle who would pay me $16 cash per case for ten cases. I said I would deliver them on my way to Newcastle next evening and asked him to have the cash ready because I would be in a hurry. He agreed.

"I arrived outside his shop as arranged and started unloading the cucumbers under the watchful eye of his mother. There was no sign that she had the cash, so I stopped halfway and asked her to get the $160 as agreed.

"She said she knew nothing about that and that he would send it, so I started reloading them into the ute. She wanted to know what I was doing, and I said that wasn't the deal and I might as well take them to the market where I would get the same price with guaranteed payment, so she disappeared for a moment, then handed me the cash.

"I thanked her, and next time he rang, I wasn't interested in side deals."

'So, how did the planter work?'

"It looked like a Heath-Robinson machine. (laugh) I took an old Atco mower engine, a motorcycle gear box, some belts and pulleys, and set all that at the rear to drive two motorcycle wheels. That was the propulsion end. At the other end, mounted on a chassis I made from lightweight square tubing, were two more motorcycle wheels on the ground, then another axle attached to trailing arms on which were removable bicycle wheels. I had sets of interchangeable wheels with protuberances welded at various intervals, so when it rolled over the ground, a pattern of indentations was left in the beds into which I could push the seedlings."

'Did you ride on this contraption?'

"(laugh) Oh yes. There was a hessian sack stretched across a frame, adjustable so my bum was just above the plants. That was the seat. The frame projected forward to sit on the indentation-wheels axle, so my weight was enough to make just the right sized indentations. But the seat was wide enough for two, and Nan loved helping, riding on Benny."

'So, you called it Benny?'

"(laugh) Yes, I could plant more in a day with the machine than Benny could plant in a week and Benny was never lazy."

'Where is this marvel now?'

"Unfortunately, we don't have even a photo of Benny. Once I had planted the whole property out with asparagus, Benny sat in the shed and rusted until I cut him up with the oxy torch and sent him off to the scrap yard.

"Ashley Unger, the Wyong High School Ag teacher, brought a group of kids out one day and they videoed it working. One of the kids was brave enough to be uncool and ride with me to try it. They might have the video, but I was never one for taking photos, unfortunately."

'So that was the last of your inventions?'

"No, there were two more worth mentioning. With both of them, I built a prototype on the farm, then tried to get someone interested in manufacturing them, but to no avail.

"One was a pair of tin snips that could cut any shaped metal, like guttering, without distorting the job. There are devices now that will do that, but this was a simple in-the-hand snips that anyone could use anywhere. The other invention grew from the instant post-hole idea. I made some for myself to take camping, and they are amazing."

'Okay, I'm still listening.'

"I hope you're being paid to listen to me rave on."

'Oh yes, and I think it's good for you to tell me about the things that worked.'

"Yes, well, I made some stainless-steel tent pegs that had a half helix made by splitting a stainless-steel washer then welding that to one end of a twenty-five-centimetre bolt, head removed, one end flattened like a screwdriver, then another washer welded side on, a centimetre from the other end.

"With a cordless drill, the peg is screwed into the ground and the tent guy rope attached to the washer on its side. It was quick to get in and almost impossible to pull out. To get it out, the drill was reattached and reversed direction. None ever gave way, even in heavy wind. I still have mine and as far as I know they are unique."

She looks at the time, then shakes her head.

'That went quick. You mentioned a Dianne. Can we talk about that relationship next time?'

I nod, pick up my sunnies and leave. I'm not keen to talk about that, but I am here to sort out the demons and some certainly came through her.

Session 16

I come through the open doorway and see a coffee and a Monte Carlo biscuit. She smiles and indicates them with her head.

'I saw the look on your face when you left. You might need a little sustenance.'

I split a biscuit in half, take a napkin, leave the rest on the plate and sit.

"I know we've talked about how my transactional approach to relationships has, in the end, led to resentment and worse. Well, this one is a doozy."

'How did you meet her?'

She is sitting at the front table with a teenager who must be her daughter, clearly wanting my attention. In the break, I get a Coke and ask if I can sit with them. She is a big woman, with big hair, big face, big smile and a big body, but I feel an attraction. She has a deep voice and a cultured accent, and we talk. The girl mostly smiles. At the end of the gig, we cross the road for a roast potato dinner and talk some more. I'm drawn to her warmth.

She is driving a red MX-5, so I presume she isn't short of a dollar. I watch out for her at the next gig. She is there, so we spend all the breaks chatting, and she invites me to visit her in Charlestown. I tell her I have herpes, and she invites me anyway.

Her house is empty. We have a drink, then sex. Afterwards, she tells me that she is a masseuse but is unable to work because of tendon strain from overuse of her arms. She is trying to live on $240 per week benefits, while also supporting her 16-year-old daughter who is studying massage in Sydney.

Over the two years playing at the Kent, she is the third woman I meet there and go out with. The first is a just-retired school principal, attractive and interesting. The other is still teaching and is a deputy principal, intelligent, attractive and available. I walk away. There is something missing. But with this one, it is here, and it is strong.

"I met her at my Sunday afternoon gig at the Kent Hotel, and we got talking. That led to us having dinner, and I went back to her house at Charlestown."

'Was that at the first meeting?'

"I don't think so, more likely the second, because I told her I carried the herpes virus when she was in her car ready to go home, so it was probably the second or third time that I followed her home, and we had sex. We then talked, and she revealed some of her situation."

'She had a problem?'

"She had multiple problems. She couldn't work because of an injury that would take years to overcome. Her car was leased, so that was a regular monthly cost."

'Did she tell you the car was leased?'

"Not right away. She told me it was leased sometime later when she could no longer find the money. But for a few months, she kept it, and we had one holiday at Charlotte Pass when we drove down in the Mazda."

'Could you afford that?'

"(laugh) If I had to pay, no. But she had the massage business at the Chalet. She was close to the manager's wife, so if there was a spare room she could stay there, free, for three or four days, which we did a few times."

'So, if she had the massage business at the Chalet, why wasn't she working there?'

"I guess she did at the beginning, but she also had a business in the Hunter wineries, where she had worked mainly, so she sent girls to Charlotte Pass for the ski season, and they mailed back half their earnings in cash."

'Half? Wasn't that a bit excessive?'

"I thought so, but that was the deal, and the only girl I met down there seemed happy to do it for the cash, plus plenty of time to ski.

"Maybe she had free board too. I know it cost us very little to be there, but it eventually came to an end a few years later after we stayed there for almost a week when there was no accommodation available, so we camped in the staff common room. We should not have gone there, or came home, but she thought it was a temporary glitch that would be fixed. But it wasn't, and resulted in the manager giving her a mouthful, ending her right to run the business there.

"I heard some of it. He was appalled that she collected half the money but did none of the work. By this time, she had regained some strength in her wrists and had started doing the occasional massage at the resort at the head of the Dooralong Valley near the farm.

"I took the ute down and brought back her equipment, then, with Matt away, I added an outside entrance into Matt's room and set it up for her to work there."

'Okay, so I gather that was some time after she moved in. How did Matt cope with her taking his mother's place?'

"I was a bit worried that Matt might object, so I arranged for them to meet casually. He played baseball with his mate Paul, who was an outstanding pitcher. I was rostered to ferry a couple of the team to games some Saturdays, but when I wasn't, I went anyway because I enjoyed watching the game.

"So, on a day I was not rostered on, I took Dianne to a game to meet him. We were sitting in the small pavilion when Matt finished the game and came over. I introduced her as a friend and Matt was polite, but later, said he didn't like her."

'Did that change?'

I have set up a target on a tree and stand back to watch Matt shoot his newly acquired Brno .22 at about thirty metres. His first shot is at the edge of the bullseye, so I point to it and then stand back. He shoots again. I look and can't see a new hole and tell him he must have missed. He asks me to look more closely, and I am dumbfounded to see that he has put the second bullet through the same hole, enlarging it only a little on one side.

This is seriously good shooting, so we continue at longer distances and his marksmanship is extraordinary.

He buys shooting magazines to read the articles so when he is introduced to Dianne's brother, Bob Penfold, a big game hunter, he knows exactly who he is. In his home, Bob has a trophy room with animal heads on the walls, a full-sized stuffed bear and all sorts of shooting paraphernalia.

He is so excited, and Bob is pleased to have such a knowledgeable young person there to show off his collection.

"Matt's views on Dianne did change. I don't know whether Dianne set it up, but the conversation got around to shooting and her brother Bob, a big game hunter. I can't remember how we came to have Matt with us when we visited Bob, but Matt knew a lot about him, and when he was shown Bob's trophy room, he was rapt and from then on seemed to accept Dianne.

"Then she and her daughter, who we called Bunny, moved in. Bunny and Matt got along well, so it was working."

'You mentioned earlier that Matt was away. Where was Matt?'

"(Laugh) At Bob Penfold's house, Matt asked him if he took students for work experience in big game hunting. Bob said he didn't but would make an exception for Matt, so we applied to the school for Matt to do that."

'I bet that was a first.'

"(laugh) Yes indeed. But the school agreed after I took out special insurance and signed a waiver of some sort. We put him on a plane to Darwin and he was gone for six weeks or so. When he finished year twelve, Bob hired him as a guide, so he spent the next three dry seasons working with Bob up north as a big game hunting guide. In the off season, he picked and packed asparagus for me and worked at Woollies as a checkout-chick."

'So, he gave it up after three seasons?'

I get a phone call from Matt. He will arrive at Maitland Airport and gives me the time, so I meet the plane, really a two-seater with Matt curled up behind the pilot in the luggage area. He looks tired and depressed. We get home and he tells me that he is disappointed at the lack of shooting skill of most of the hunters and appalled at the suffering the animals endure when not killed instantly.

He tells me stories of men, mostly from Spain and the US, he says, who can't shoot and will just hit an animal in the body anywhere, leaving Matt to finish the poor creature off.

"I saw an article in a hunting magazine about Matt. The story goes that he was guiding a client and had been stalking a herd of camels. The man lifted his rifle and shot into the body of a camel, which took off, bellowing in pain. Matt grabbed the rifle, ran to a small tree and with the rifle steadied, shot the galloping camel through the head at over three hundred metres.

"The reporter thought that was remarkable, but I knew it was everyday stuff for Matt.

"I had, to my everlasting regret, taken Matt duck shooting, me with a pump-action 12-gauge and Matt with a .401. A flock of ducks passed overhead, and he brought down five with four shots. I didn't shoot, and I don't believe Matt shot ducks after that, but the camel episode finished it for Matt.

"He started looking for a job as a park ranger, protecting animals rather than hunting them. No job came up, so he took himself off to Albury and university there, where, before long and before he was anywhere near graduating, he was recruited into the Police Force."

'Did he become a weapons specialist with the cops?'

It's his first day at the pistol range and Matt is given a Glock semi-automatic and seven rounds. He laughs as he recalls the instructor walking along the line of recruits marking their scores. He is counting the number of hits in the target area and saying the scores out of seven. He goes along the line, 'Three, five, two' and so on, until he sees Matt's target.

"No, but he told me what the instructor said when he saw Matt's score with the pistol. He just leaned in and whispered: 'Smartarse!'

"He told me he joined because he wanted to help people."

'So, where did Matt live when he came home?'

"I acquired a medium-sized caravan and installed that in the shed.

He seemed to like that, giving him more room and autonomy.

"By then, I had met Dianne's three boys. They were all big and handsome and seemed to take to me immediately, so I found myself surrounded by a boisterous mob of young people and was committed to the relationship."

'Did you meet the ex-husband?'

Christmas is approaching and I hear Bunny talking about her dad being alone for Christmas, so I tell her to invite him to our place. I had met him, and he seemed okay. As all four of his children would be celebrating at the farm with their mother, it would be mean to exclude him, so he comes.

"Yes, he came to the farm for the first Christmas, and we visited each other's homes a few times, where we played Five-Hundred and had dinner. It seemed pretty relaxed, but I was uncomfortable with what I saw as his inappropriate sexual talk and off jokes in front of, not only his kids, who were adults, but his grandson, who was only two or three.

"I thought he had a warped sense of humour, but I must say, the kids were pretty open about their sex lives too, but not to his extremes. What they said was okay, but what he said, and so constantly, was always a source of discomfort for me."

'How was Dianne in that way?'

Dianne is always willing, so our sex life becomes a non-issue and for the first time, I relax into it, and it is just fun. Then she starts suggesting that she might push her finger up my bum (some men like it). I'm not keen on anyone touching me there and discourage her, so she drops it. But the thought stays with me.

We are in bed on the yacht, and she is on top, as she prefers, and she has already had an orgasm. I lift her until my penis is out then move her forward until it is at her anus, and I wait. She asks me to be gentle, so I leave it to her, and she lowers herself gently until I am in up to the start of the shaft. I feel excitingly naughty and come quickly.

"She was always keen for sex, sometimes suggesting something a little kinky, but I was happy to have conventional sex as I saw it, until in the last few months I tried anal sex with her a couple of times."

'Why do you think that was? Why the change?'

"I don't know. It just occurred to me to do it. I had never tried it and wondered how good it was, and I was excited by the naughtiness of it, I guess."

'Did she like it?'

"I thought she would, considering what she had suggested sometimes. Looking back, she seemed willing, and she could have refused."

'Did you ask her if it was okay?'

"Yes, and she said just to 'be gentle', which I was, but I really thought it was a bit gross and stopped doing it after a couple of times. I have had no inclination to do it with any other partner, before or since."

'Now, that is interesting.'

"Maybe, but I have always been sensitive to anything to do with my anus. Thank goodness they knock you out to do a colonoscopy!"

'Do you remember any very early experience when someone did something to your anus?'

They are always saying I am too thin. I feel well, I run everywhere, I have abundant energy and am strong for my weight, but their comments leave me discontented with my body shape. It makes me wonder about myself. They try worming me – a three-day fast, then take some purging muck, then they go through my faeces.

There are no worms, so Dad decides I need an enema and brings out a yellow enamelled container with a long rubber hose ending at a rubber device that looks a bit like a dog's dick. I bend over, and Dad pushes the thing in and turns on a tap. I feel the warm sudsy water gurgling in my guts. It keeps going until I am bloated, and then he pulls it out and I run for the dunny.

"I had quite a few enemas as a kid, and that was not pleasant."

'Who did them? A doctor?'

"No, Dad gave them to me. He used to say I was too thin and must have worms, so I was wormed and had enemas."

'Did they work?'

"(laugh) No, and eventually he gave up and accepted that I was destined to be a skinny person, which I was until I reached my mid-twenties, when I filled out a bit."

'So, he eventually accepted that you were just built that way?'

'His chest is too low.'

Trying not to show emotion, but there is a smugness there too. Your son isn't perfect. That will hurt you. Maybe if I dive into the dam and don't come up, he will be sorry.

But the hurt comes back like a judgement from God.

Holding the rifle to my head. Will I pull the trigger? It would be easy, but what about Judgement Day?

'You will burn and burn in Hell forever. You'll never be the man your father is!'

He won't be sorry.

"Mmm, I don't think so. The comments continued."

'Okay. I do want to pursue that further, but today I want to get back to what happened with Dianne. You found this person who needs your help, so we are again in a classical co-dependent situation. You have offered your house, taken in her daughter and even altered the house so she could work again, and you are keeping her in the sense of paying her costs. Did she share her unemployment benefit with you?'

"She told me that when she changed her address, they stopped her benefits. That was a bit of a shock to me too, because, although I was going okay, there wasn't much to spare after expenses.

"She kept whatever money she made doing massages, which didn't start until a few years after she arrived, but eventually she had a steady stream of clients, who all paid cash. There was her settlement money, as I said, but I covered all expenses, including the phone bills, which were significant at about $400 per month, and remember this was in the late 90s.

"We needed a fax line for the business and when I was out playing music, which I was able to continue to some degree, despite my hearing loss, she spent a lot of time on the phone to Newcastle.

"Back then, Newcastle calls were 'trunk line' calls and expensive. The bill came with itemised calls, so I was able to point out that over half the phone bills were her calls to Newcastle.

"She wasn't prepared to cut back on them, understandably, because most were to family, but she never offered to pay any of the bill."

'Did you ever give her cash for herself?'

"Early on, before she was earning again, she once said that she appreciated that I was keeping her, but that she had no money for herself. It was during an asparagus harvest, so I gave her the cheque that came in that day for just over a thousand dollars.

"At one stage, she cooked up a scheme to open a café in the village hall in partnership with Beth, a neighbour. I rang the council and asked if we could put on afternoon teas and the like in the hall and whoever was on the phone said if it had a kitchen, it was there to be used, so we got to work.

"She organised to have the kitchen floor recovered in vinyl to commercial kitchen standard. A client of hers did that, and if there was payment, she paid it.

"I bought a second-hand glass-fronted refrigerator and made about thirty timber trays that she used to serve 'ploughman's lunches'.

"Soon the Saturday lunchtimes and Sunday mornings were buzzing with customers, and she had two women working with her. I did the washing up.

"Beth didn't agree with the direction of the operation and wanted her money back, with an itemised account of over $4,000, which I paid."

'Were you receiving any of the income?'

"(Laugh) No, I was doing it to let her build up her bank account again and that was happening."

'But surely she should have paid the $4,000?'

"Yes, but I felt that somehow it was my responsibility and had no idea how much money she had. She didn't offer, and I didn't feel entitled to ask her if she had the money, so I paid it anyway

'So, how did that end up?'

It is Saturday lunchtime and there are twenty or so people eating in the hall. We have been operating for almost a year and nobody had objected, then a ginger-headed man in shorts walks to the centre of the room and bellows: 'What's going on here?'

He was the council health inspector and was out for a drive with his family and chanced upon Dianne's operation.

"One day, by chance the council building inspector came in to see what all the activity was about and blew his top. He demanded it be closed down immediately, which happened. People walked off with their lunches in their boxes, and that was that.

"We sold the equipment at a 'garage sale' but left the fridge there to be used by the community. I got some money back, but not much."

'Did she come up with any other idea for you to finance?'

"Yes, she did a three-day course in Adelaide in lymphatic drainage, which was a special type of massage, and that led to some good outcomes and an ongoing source of income for her."

'Did you pay for that?'

"Er, yes. But it was well worth it. I saw what she achieved, particularly with women who had had partial mastectomies and suffered lymphedema-induced swollen breasts. I remember one woman coming to her who had one breast so enlarged that the surgeon offered her breast reduction surgery.

"Luckily, she was referred to Dianne, who had her breast down to normal size after a few sessions, and after a few months, as far as I know, it stayed that way."

'So, she was good at it?'

"Yes, she was. I once helped her handle a man who had elephantiasis. She spent maybe three hours on him and at the end, his limbs were still swollen but were almost normal.

"From the breast work, she developed techniques that could lift saggy breasts, and some women came for that. She even made a 'before and after' video of a young woman, and I must say, the results were amazing.

"She said she was invigorating the muscles that supported the breast. Whatever was causing it, she was getting results and declared that she wanted to write a book about it."

"My Atari was a great computer, perfect for music composition and recording, but its files were not transferrable to any other system, so I bought a PC and MS Word for her and set it up in the massage room."

'How did she go with that?'

"I saw her sitting there staring at the screen for a long time, then realised that she was probably functionally illiterate. So, I started putting her ideas into my words.

"I also did research and found that her type of breast work was rare, but there were a few other practitioners around the world doing it. I wrote to them and got back information that I was able to incorporate into her book, so the book grew.

"Alan Hayes, a neighbour and friend of mine who had published several books, got involved and was very interested. He said the book was not long enough and added a section on diet. "That's when she made the video.

"Another friend organised a professional video photographer and by showing 'before and after' shots, she had proof that the techniques worked.

"Alan had the book printed, I don't know how many, but perhaps a thousand, then lined up media, and we were ready to go. A week or so out from appearing on a TV program, Dianne decided – after being so enthusiastic about publicity for her method, then organising and directing the video – that her treatment of her clients was too private to be exposed to the media and pulled out."

'Wow! So, what happened then?'

"Alan and his publishing partner, a solicitor, talked about suing her but in the end didn't. That was about the same time we moved onto the yacht."

'That seems like a story in itself, so let's come back to that later. Were there any other ways you helped her regain her financial independence?'

"Just before Sally and I completed our property settlement, I came across a newspaper story that claimed, if a road cuts through a property, the owner is entitled to a separate title for each section.

"There was a road that divided my property into two, so I wrote to the council for advice. Their reply was that I couldn't do that because the road had gone through after 1915, when the law changed to disallow that right for future road easements.

"I went to Maitland and looked up maps of my property made before 1915 and found that the road was there already, so I had the block surveyed, applied for a separate title and got it."

'What did that mean for you?'

"That meant that I could sell that block of about five acres and that would allow me to buy Sally out and keep the farm. I was in the process of finalising this when the settlement fell due, so I didn't have the money to pay her at that time.

"I mentioned it to my friend Jack Grimsley at a gig, and much to my amazement, he pulled out a chequebook and said: 'How much do you need?'

"He wrote me a cheque for fifty thousand."

'Now, that's a real friend!'

"Indeed. So, I wrote him a receipt, which included a promise to pay him five per cent until it was paid back, which took another six months. But the block sold, and I paid Jack."

'You were going to tell me another way you helped her bottom line.'

"Yes, well after the dust had settled, I had about eighty thousand to invest in something, so we looked for a house to buy."

'For eighty thousand?'

"(laugh) We borrowed twenty and bought what must have been the worst house in Tuggerawong. It was on a large corner block, across the road from a little bay in Tuggerah Lake, so I intended to rent it out and wait. It was really a future knock-down and rebuild proposition, but it needed urgent work to remedy a termite infestation, as did a reasonably new shed that had been used to house greyhounds."

'Didn't you get a building inspection?'

"No, I thought I knew enough about building to do that myself, and we had no spare cash, so I took the risk. Anyway, I knew it needed new ant-caps on the brick piers and while replacing them, I found termite highways into the frame and started checking. One whole wall of the kitchen and one of the shed walls were full of termite nests, held together by cladding and paint and had to be rebuilt. A termite exterminator did the rest, so we got rid of them eventually. But I spent a couple of months fixing things before we could rent it out. Outside the back door, there were piers that had once supported a veranda, so I rebuilt that with tallowwood flooring I had resurrected from a demolished boatshed, and when I had finished, it looked inviting."

'Did you keep it long?'

"My sister-in-law Julie rented it. Then she had a robbery when she lost her jewellery. To get in, they wrecked a window and its fly screen. That wasn't what prompted us to sell, but it was part of it. The main reason we sold was to buy the live-aboard yacht."

'That is a huge change of direction. What led you to do that?'

We are sailing the Hobie 14 on Myall Lakes and find ourselves a long way from the launching ramp when the wind dies to a soft breath. It takes hours to get back, and it is dark and cold as we load it onto the trailer. We agree that a yacht with beds, and maybe a motor, would have been ideal.

"Do you remember when AMP issued shares to its policyholders?"

'Yes, I do, but I didn't have a policy with them. You did?'

"Yes, and I found myself with about fifteen thousand dollars' worth of shares. I kept them for a few months, watched their price rise, and sold when they were $19.

"They went up to $21, but then they dropped and kept dropping. In any case, I finished up with about sixteen thousand and as it was 'free money', I bought a used trailer-sailer for that price, plus I traded in the catamaran.

"It was a Benito, a New Zealand design that was twenty-four-feet long with a half-ton lead keel and a swinging centreboard, so it was heavy but very stable.

"Inside, it had a spirit stove and a sink, and bench seats along each side of a cabin with a fold-down table, making an almost double bed one side. There were two tunnels under the cockpit seats that were extra beds, so it could sleep four. In the sail locker was a spinnaker that had no rigging, so I added pulleys, a halyard, a couple of cleats and a spinnaker pole, and we had a nice sail set."

'Where did you take it?'

I read in a newspaper of the Milang to Goolwa boat race on Lake Alexandrina, in South Australia run by the Goolwa Yacht Club. It is held annually and open to any watercraft. That gets me thinking about Lake Alexandrina and the Murray River, and I hatch a plan to sail down the Murray and over Lake Alexandrina to Goolwa.

The Yacht Club is interested and directs me to Ron and Elizabeth Baker, who produce a book of maps of the Murray, which they revise every year, showing the course, lock information and navigation tips down to where dangerous snags lurk. My friends Viv and Rae Davenport also have a trailer-sailer, and want to come, so we leave the Dooralong Valley in late October 1999, two boats on two trailers.

We camp in the boats at caravan parks, and we arrive two days later in Renmark, which Ron's map advises is the furthest up the

Murray where we can rig the masts without needing to drop them for low bridges.

The plan is to launch the yachts at Renmark, then drive to Goolwa, to leave the cars and trailers with Ron and Elizabeth. We catch a bus back to Renmark, and we are on our way to the mouth of the Murray, five hundred and fifty kilometres of river away.

On the bus back to Renmark, we find James and Judy, neighbours from near Dooralong, who are visiting relatives in SA, so we invite them to join us for a few days, which they do, and they are great fun.

"We had days on Lake Macquarie and sometimes a couple of weeks with the yacht on Myall Lakes, where we also took a tent and camping gear for the kids, so Dianne and I slept on the yacht, the kids in the tent and we ate, all crowded into the yacht cabin."

'Was that just Matt and Jess?'

"Before Dianne, and before I bought the yacht, we had many holidays at Legge's Camp on the Broadwater with Matt and Jess, when Sally was still with us, although she usually only came to visit for a day or so, then went home."

'Was she really going home?'

"Mmm. Never thought about that, and it didn't worry me at the time.

"We were joined by our friends and neighbours, the Casamento family, who had a tent.

"You remember, I talked about Greg?"

'Yes, of course, the man you could talk to.'

"Right. I brought along the catamaran and that was great fun, and Matt fished, his favourite occupation at the time.

"We had a tent and a slide-on camper, which slept four, so we were comfortable and that became our school holiday go-to destination for a few years, really until Sally left. Then Jess went to Bowral, but Matt still came until he was off to the Northern Territory with Bob Penfold.

"At Myall Lakes with the trailer-sailer, my sister Dianne came once, and I remember a holiday with Julia's two kids and Carlia, David's younger daughter. That almost ended in tragedy."

'What happened?'

We have been playing cards in the boat until after eight and the grandkids are sleepy, so we herd them into the tent, then Carlia wants to go to the toilet. I take a torch, but it is bright moonlight, so we leave the torch off and follow the white sandy track through low scrub. Carlia asks if there are 'any snakes here'. I say there could be and switch on the torch to reveal one step ahead on the path, a death adder. We stop and watch it disappear into the grassy verge.

"Carlia and I almost stepped on a death adder near the camp at night. We were far from civilisation, and I am not sure there is a road into the camp site because we always came by boat. In any case, I doubt we could have got medical help in time. But the best holiday I ever had in my life was when Dianne and I sailed down the Murray."

'You sailed down the Murray. (laughs) Can you sail on the Murray?'

"It was suggested that maybe we were the first. But apart from the experience of the Murray itself, again serendipity stepped in, and we had many adventures that I doubt could have been planned. The timing was just right."

'Would you like to tell me the highlights?'

"The first was coming up to a slow-moving houseboat that was shadowing a man in a canoe, who was himself shadowing a man swimming. Viv and Rae's boat was faster, so they were out of sight.

We asked the canoeist what they were doing, and it turned out that they were prison officers, relay swimming from Mannum to Murray Bridge to raise money for charity. "Dianne and I had been swimming regularly and were in good shape, so we tied the yacht to the rail on the houseboat and swam with them for an hour or so until we felt the cold and swam back to the yacht. That night they came into Murray Bridge and tied up in a line with many other houseboats, and we had drinks with them.

"We had secured our yachts to bollards at the side of a park near the Bunyip."

'The Bunyip?'

"(laugh) Yes, the Bunyip. In the park is a shed covering a well, out of which, upon the insertion of a twenty-cent coin, a 'bunyip' emerges from the water to emit a satisfying roar, then submerges, waiting for the next twenty cents.

"We had arrived in the middle of a pageant, with stalls, bands on trucks and all sorts of entertainment. We were sitting having a hot dog when we noticed two men in uniform hanging about the yachts. We realised that they were not happy we were parked there, but we just watched, and they eventually went.

"Later, we realised why they would rather we weren't there. We had front-row seats to watch water skiing displays, then after dark, fireworks.

"Just as the fireworks were about to start, we were surrounded by kids who asked could they sit on the boats to watch the displays, so they did. If we had known what was to happen later, maybe we could have done a deal, because well into the early hours, kids were constantly activating the Bunyip, and our sleep was less than peaceful.

"One of the swimming team insisted that we look up a mate of theirs who lived in Wellington East, a canal development off the Murray.

"When we arrived at their wharf, there were balloons to welcome us, and they invited us to dinner and insisted we sleep in the house. Viv and Rae tied up to their wharf too but stayed on their boat.

"Next day the husband joined Viv and Rae on their yacht for the run to Goolwa and what a day that was.

"We pushed all day into a stiff south-westerly. Their yacht was much faster than ours, so they soon left us behind. For the whole day, I fought the tiller, and Dianne fed me because I never had a free hand, and we needed to hurry to be there by dark."

'Is the lake that big?'

"It is huge. We sailed over eighty kilometres that day, mostly into the wind and tacking, so it was long and hard, but at the end, we were met by an enthusiastic crowd of sailors from the yacht club. My right hand had just about frozen into the shape of the tiller, but a laughing bloke slipped a cold schooner into it, and we were made to feel very welcome.

"Then they gave us the keys to the clubhouse so we could use the showers.

"We took Ron and Elizabeth Baker out to dinner at the Corio Hotel to express our gratitude and the next morning Viv and Rae headed home. (laugh) I remember ordering kangaroo after being assured that my previous experience of it being tougher than a soldier's boot was due to the cooking, so I ate it, and it was tender and delicious."

'So that was the end of your adventure?'

We are a few days into the trip when I am reminded it is my birthday, and the others have planned to shout me a lunch at the Overland Corner pub. We tie up to a shaky jetty and walk the half kilometre to the pub to find an imposing limestone building on the Goyder Highway that was once a stopover point for coaches travelling between Melbourne and

Adelaide. In the stone blocks are millions of seashells. I order a steak, and it is huge. It hangs over the edge of a large oval plate. I say to the waiter: "I can't eat all that!"

'I bet you do,' she replies, and she is right. I ask her to compliment the chef on the best steak I have ever eaten, and she tells me that Murray Tickle, the man who grew the Murray Grey steers where the steaks came from, would be in that evening and I could congratulate him myself.

So, we have an afternoon nap on the boats and come back to find Murray and his new wife having dinner. We introduce ourselves and he invites us to join him and pours each of us a generous glass of red. We learn that he grew the grapes and also made the wine.

We talk about what we do when not sailing on the river and discover that he prints wine labels for many of the world's wine makers. He is on his honeymoon on a refitted 1870 paddle wheeler, which explains the old boat tied up near us on the river. He then invites us for a ride in a genuine riverboat, which we all accept, of course, and we are soon romping along at about ten knots upstream, sitting on fake wool bales, sipping champers, and watching wildlife on the bank illuminated by powerful ark lights.

Suddenly, one of the paddle wheels reverses, driven by a Caterpillar engine, and we spin about to charge downstream and arrive back at his mooring sometime in the early hours.

"Not quite, but in the second week of our safari, my birthday arrived as we came to Overland Corner and what a day that turned out to be! They shouted me a wonderful lunch at the historic Overland Hotel, then in the evening, one of the patrons, there for dinner on his honeymoon, took us for a couple of hours' ride in his Caterpillar-powered paddle-wheeler.

"Next morning, because we had lost a day of travel, we started out at daybreak. We cast off and let the current carry us past our generous host's boat so as not to wake the honeymooners on their first morning."

'So, you went home from Goolwa?'

Ron's map stops at Goolwa, but the river continues on to the sea, so we go through the lock and enter the shallow stretch to the mouth. We wade much of the time, guiding the yacht through the shallows until we are almost at the mouth where we motor into the breakers coming over the bar, then turn and head into the Coorong, passing Hindmarsh Island to our left. We anchor for the night. I wake to find the keel bumping the bottom, so I wade to the anchor and carry it to deeper water where I am up to my neck, then clamber back aboard. It is only then that I imagine sharks circling waiting for an encore. We continue next day but are soon bumping unseen outcrops of ancient coral and decide to abort.

'No, we continued to the mouth and then up the Coorong, an amazing stretch of water that parallels the coast for a hundred and fifty kilometres toward Melbourne but is only a kilometre wide most of the way. After half a day of sailing up the Coorong, we were in danger of damaging the boat on coral outcrops, so when we saw a lock that would take us back to the lake, we used it.

Before we did, we tied up and walked over the sandhills to the sea, where we saw the frame of an old wreck protruding through the sand.

"Then we went through the only remaining hand-operated lock left in the system that lifted us through the Tauwitchere barrage and back into the lake. That was interesting and fun and took about an hour before we were once again under sail.

"Then ahead of us, we saw a yacht race and decided to join in. We were at the back, so when they turned into Lake Albert, we dropped out and tied up to a jetty at the junction of the two lakes, where we spent the night after being visited by some Aboriginal kids who were interested in what we were doing. Next day, we sailed back to Goolwa, loaded the boat onto the trailer and started home, exhausted, happy and very much satisfied with the adventure."

'So, you had a lot of fun with Dianne?'

"Yes, we did, but that started to unravel, I think when I bought *Heavy Metal*."

'Why did you do that?'

We are having such a good time on the Murray that we begin talking about living on a yacht. I am now sixty-seven and eligible for the age pension but living on a farm limits the benefit. The farm is being threatened with resumption to accommodate an ash dam for a proposed power station in Dickson Road, so I have no motivation to replace the old asparagus plants, now well past their prime.

As Gerry Bennett in Cowra said: 'They should have a short life, but a merry one'.

The house needs a new kitchen and bathroom work before it is fit for rental, so we sell the Tuggerawong house and Dianne keeps half the proceeds, using part of that to renovate the farm kitchen and bathroom.

"After the Murray adventure, we thought life on the water was, in some ways more social, and certainly simpler than on the farm, which was becoming difficult. We sold the investment house and Dianne used much of her share to renovate the kitchen and bathrooms. Her son, Brett, did the work and she spent about $35,000. I was keeping my half intact, ready to buy a yacht.

"When the house was ready for rent, we found a tenant and moved into Dianne's mother's house while we looked for the right boat."

'Was that difficult?'

"Yes. We looked at yachts all over the eastern seaboard, including Tasmania. I think the best value was one we saw in the Tamar near Launceston, but it had a double keel, and at that time, it wasn't what we were looking for. Later, Dianne was against the one I really wanted to buy."

'Why was that?'

We are led to the water by the son of the dead boatbuilder. It is in brackish water at Milperra in the Georges River. Inside, the instruments are new and down below, a new Caterpillar motor and all new transmission and shaft. The mast is on a tabernacle, so it can be lowered to fit under low bridges and that also makes any adjustments to rigging simple. It has a draft of under six feet, so it can go places that are not so deep. The price is a steal at $30,000. That is about half the value of the equipment, so the hull is free, and I want to buy it.

I can finish the interior and would cover the exterior with epoxy as I had seen done.

But it is concrete, and Dianne wants steel. So, we keep searching, ending up in Bowen looking at an unkempt steel ketch that has been sitting in the harbour, unmoving, for many years. For some reason, known only to him, the owner will not open it for us to see the interior, or start the motor, so we look in through the windows and see it has big spaces and plenty of headroom, one of the factors that has turned us off other yachts of similar size. Looking over the side, we see that there are almost metre long tentacles of seaweed growing on the hull.

He wants $180,000 and I offer him $120,000. He is insulted, so I say I will pay $150,000 if I can see it out of the water and know the hull is sound.

"The one I wanted was professionally made of concrete, but unfinished. All the bits I couldn't do myself were in and new and it had a few features I really liked, like a two-ton crane that could lift a small car onto the rear deck and a folding mast that allowed it to pass under low bridges, but she was adamant, and we eventually bought a steel yacht in Bowen from the man who built it."

'Why was she so against the concrete boat? Seems like a good idea to spend less money and have new equipment.'

"Look, if you had asked me that at the time, I might have said she was afraid it was not safe, and I still think that to a point. But there might have been another motive that made more sense nine months later, when she left. If I had bought the concrete boat, I could have worked on it, paying for materials out of money I earned and would not have had to sell the farm."

'So, this steel yacht from Bowen needed a lot of work and expense to bring it up to standard?'

"Yes. I gathered the owner had gone broke because it had not been out of the water for years. I got it for $150,000 eventually, then spent another twenty or so having the hull sandblasted from the waterline down, all the anodes replaced, and a dodger added. It originally had only a basic compass, so we also had a depth sounder and GPS navigation fitted, plus a new solar panel.

"We should have had the rigging replaced then, because a stay parted not far into our voyage home, and we couldn't use the sails. We had replaced almost everything else, so I should have spent the money, but I was trying to avoid selling the farm.

"(laugh) When we took delivery, the boat had been stripped of everything loose. The vendor was so cranky that he even took the mooring lines so the agent had to find some, or it would have drifted off."

'Is it usual to sell a boat as a walk-in, walk-out proposition?'

"Always. What is on the boat when it is inspected stays on the boat. But he took all the kitchen stuff, bedding, ropes, everything that was not strictly of the boat, like sails. So, before we could go anywhere, we had to buy a complete set of bedding for the trip home in July."

'Was it just the two of you?'

"No. I had never been ocean sailing, so although I had heaps of experience in dinghies, dating back to my first little sailboat, I knew nothing about navigation or taking a big boat into a port, or where on the coast were the ports we would need to visit to refuel, etc., so we had two experienced sailors along who came for the fun of it, and they were invaluable."

'Were there any close shaves?'

"Yes. On the second night out, we dropped anchor behind Middle Percy Island, knowing there was a strong wind warning for later that night, but we were well sheltered and thought we were safe until someone got up and realised that we were being blown backwards at considerable speed, with the anchor doing nothing.

"It took a few minutes to get our bearings, wind the anchor in, and get the ship heading in the right direction. We pushed into gale-force winds all night, with seas breaking over the bow. One of the sailors, Gus, remarked how well she held her speed.

"We were able to maintain seven knots until in the morning we came to Great Keppel Island and dropped anchor in still conditions for a well-earned sleep. We stayed there until the next day, but before we dropped the anchor again, I inspected it and found that the hinge was frozen so the flute couldn't swing to dig in.

"Why we didn't test it by pulling back to be sure it was set, I don't remember, or more likely it did set but the wind change pulled it out and it couldn't re-set. In any case, it was useless."

'What could be done about that?'

Gus decides we should go behind K'gari through the Great Sandy Straits so we can find a quiet anchorage for the next night. Coming through Hervey Bay, we see whales breaching and flapping ahead, then one comes straight at us. We all stand along the rail to watch as it comes within a metre, then rolls over to eyeball us as if to say 'hello' before peeling off and continuing north. We stop for the night at Garry's Anchorage, a narrow waterway between a small island and K'gari, where we put out all the chain in the hope that the weight will be enough to hold it there. It does, and after breakfast, we head into Tin Can Bay to find a welder.

"We left Gus in charge on the drifting yacht with Dianne, then I, with Gus's mate, John, took the anchor in the dinghy and went ashore, where I spoke to a man I will never forget. I can't remember his name, but he was a non-stop sayings machine."

'(laughs) Can you remember any of them?'

"(laugh) Yes. He said he was as 'busy as a long-tailed cat in a room full of rockin' chairs', which is pretty self-explanatory. There was another that I am still scratching my head over, but it made me laugh at the time.

"We were in his ute, that he called his 'horse and sulky' and were coming back after he had taken 'the hot wand and the big hammer' to the anchor, successfully freeing up the flute, when a young man came toward us on a motorcycle at speed.

"He remarked that he knew 'the feller' and he 'didn't have enough brains to shove up a fruit-fly's arse with a straining post!' He had dozens of them, and he let us have them as he worked. It took about an hour, and then he asked for twenty dollars, so I gave him fifty."

'Money well spent, I'd say.'

"Indeed. So, we stopped at a few more anchorages with no more dramas and arrived in Newcastle harbour on the 1st of August 2002 to tie up at my newly purchased berth in the new Newcastle Marina, where we farewelled Gus and John. The voyage took exactly two weeks."

'And you had rigging to replace. Before you go into that, let's stop and continue another time. I want to know what happened to make her leave.'

My face must have shown my feelings because she pats me on the back as I walk out.

Session 17

She has a new jacket, at least new to me, and I'm reminded of the change of seasons and how many weeks we have been meeting. She is reading her notes as I enter and sit. The coffee is there, plus a blueberry muffin this time. I'm more tense than I have been, pick up the coffee, but leave the muffin. She turns to me and smiles.

'I want you to go back a bit and tell me what happened after you arrived in Newcastle with the yacht.'

The whole complex is new, and the marina building not fully tenanted. We meet other long-term boaties, and I am included in the crew of Woodstock, *a yacht for Sunday races that end with a nosh-up on Marco's dive boat,* Centurion, *catered for by Lynne.*
Centurion *seems to never be quite ready to head north but does go eventually just after I did. I am assigned to crew for Greg, a one-eyed prawn trawlerman and meet his live-aboard wife, Katy, who is part of an all-female crew for the Sunday races.*

Dianne's book has been printed but seems destined to go nowhere.

Then, Dianne gets the idea of a massage service at the marina, and she takes up the lease of 130 square metres facing the water. Chris, Dianne's ex, builds the internal walls for three cubicles and a foyer, where Dianne puts a large natural slab desk and a couple of lounge chairs and a coffee table. She buys a safe, that I bolt to the floor under a table, and she is in business.

I don't have much to do with the massage part, but I bring in the PC and install an accounting program, e-Record, so a few times a week I enter her income and outgoings into the program.

"Soon after we settle in, Dianne takes out a lease of a unit in the marina building and sets up a massage service. The plan, at least the plan I am told of, is to set the business up and then hand it to Dianne's daughter, Linda. We will then cruise in the yacht, coming back when required for Linda to have a holiday for instance, but keep a financial interest in the business to create income for Dianne.

"Internal work on the space is organised with Chris, her ex, and I take on the accounting, using the PC I bought for her to write the book. My time is taken up mainly in re-rigging the yacht and other maintenance and there is plenty to do."

'What is happening with Blokka at this time?'

"By this time, Blokka is just about dead, except for the glimmer of interest in manufacture in China. We are at the marina when the Chinese copy arrives, so I am very busy. As I said before, Bunnings, understandably, is not interested unless I buy back all the old stock and by this time, I am beginning to think that maybe the age of the chainsaw has passed, and the market might be shrinking. I still take it to country shows but am not selling any, so I declare that Blokka is no more and put it down to experience.

"The 'instant post-hole' has likewise not attracted interest, nor the 'no-distortion tin snips'.

"Before I started the Blokka project, I didn't use an accountant, but now the business was more complex, I felt I needed one and went to Dianne's. I was impressed and happy with him until the end when it turned out he was complicit in the plan to relieve me of half my assets."

'Let's come back to that. I'm interested in the time on the marina. Give me a sense of day-to-day life there for you.'

We are up early, a drink of water, then, rain hail or shine, Dianne, Linda and I go to Newcastle ocean baths at about six-thirty and swim for forty-five minutes, have a hot shower there and are back to the boat for breakfast. The women go to the salon, and I do the housework then walk a few kilometres, picking up rubbish along the foreshores of Crosby Basin.

"We swim every morning, and they go to the salon. I usually walk a few kilometres, then work on the boat. This becomes a routine. I still have a couple of gigs a week, and that keeps a few extra dollars coming in for me. I enjoy playing and the camaraderie of my musician mates.

"Then, we lose the tenant at the farm and there is still the mortgage to pay. I have used all the remaining money from the mortgage for the rigging, so the loss of the tenant means I can't pay the mortgage and decide to sell the farm, pay down the mortgage and invest the rest in real estate for my retirement income."

'So, Dianne was okay with that plan?'

"Yes. She didn't say much but seemed supportive of the decision to sell. The property sold quickly to a young couple and after paying off the loan, I had about $450,000."

'Did she say anything then about what she thought she might be owed?'

We deposit the cheque, fifty thousand into the joint account ready for costs I know are coming and four hundred thousand in an interest-bearing deposit to sit while I look for investment properties. I note, but don't ask about, Dianne's excitement as I allot the proceeds to the two accounts, interpreting her manner as being pleased for me being free of debt and worry. I have retired.

"She said nothing, but thinking back, she seemed excited when I deposited the money and now think she expected me to put half of it into her account. Soon after, she said that a loan of $20,000 from her stepfather, toward setting up the salon, was causing tension in the family, so I paid him from the joint account.

"Then we had the first burglary. They came in through the false ceiling and cleaned out the cash box. The safe was untouched and the tablecloth that hid it seemed to have not been moved. Other furniture had been pushed around, and I realised that they had found the safe but didn't have the tools to open it.

"I was sure they would be back. At the time, I knew there was $3,000 in the safe. I could imagine the thieves finding the safe and carefully rearranging the cloth to make it look like they had missed it, moving other furniture around to indicate a thorough search. I advised Dianne to take the cash onto the boat and hide it there. She insisted it was safe because it was 'in a safe'.

"Then, sure enough, a few nights later, they came again and cut the safe open with an angle grinder. They were never caught."

'Where had the cash come from?'

"I thought it was takings but had no way of knowing because she never talked about what she earned to me. I knew there must have been cash, but she only ever gave me EFTPOS receipts to enter into the accounting program. I did ask a couple of times if she should show some cash because the tax department has some idea of the mix of cash and card for a whole range of businesses."

'So, you think it was cash from earnings?'

"It could have been, but after she had gone, I noted that she had withdrawn two amounts from the joint account, one of $5,000 and one of $8,000 without telling me, and I am no longer sure of the timing."

'All right, so, tell me what happened when she left.'

The plan is to cruise the Whitsundays and elsewhere around the coast, where she will offer massages in our spacious saloon on board. That, plus my pension if I still qualify, and any other income I bring in through music plus rent from properties I am still planning to buy, will be enough to support us and maintain the yacht.

Then the business opportunity at the marina comes up, and we decide to set Linda up there and return from time to time to give Linda a break.

We lose our tenant, so I sell the farm. Then I hear from Eden that a motel is for sale for $500,000. It is cheap because it is rundown and needs refurbishing. But it comes with a manager's house and in any case, the land value is at least equal the asking price.

I say that it might be a good investment for me to go into with Brett, Dianne's eldest, who is married with two children and struggling a bit.

I think Brett could live in the house and do the units up, unit by unit, until it's ready for us to sell at a profit. Like the massage business at the marina, where we could return to give Linda a break, we could take the boat to Eden and give Brett a break when he needed it, so we all go down for a look and say we will buy it.

Then it is withdrawn from sale, so I start looking for houses for investment to augment my pension, and the plan is still alive.

I have sacrificed my farm to finance a lifestyle she says she wants. But she seems to be making other plans. I have retired, and except for the occasional music gig, I'm committed to Dianne, the salon, and the plan to go cruising.

Then, out of the blue, Dianne demands half my assets, or she will leave. There is no mention of all those years of me paying off her debts, paying her bills, and supporting her in every way I can, even gifting her half a house.

"It seemed to come from nowhere. She just demanded half my assets, or she would leave. I was gobsmacked. I thought we were on track to go cruising as soon as Linda was comfortable in the business. When I realised that she had set me up and that she was determined to take half my life's savings and with it my retirement plan, I said, "Well, fuck off then," and went off for my walk.

"When I came back, she had gone. Next day I was on the boat when a sheriff arrived to serve me papers. My assets had been frozen, and there were documents demanding half my assets. It was clear to me then that she had set it all up in advance, and I felt betrayed."

'Wow! So, what did you do?'

"The first thing I did was ring our accountant to ask him if he knew what she was up to and what law she might be relying on. He said that after ten years of cohabitation, she was entitled to half my assets and admitted that he had helped her 'set me up'.

"I felt gutted that she would do that and went to see her to try to have the situation mediated right away with a lawyer and maybe her son, Brett along as someone we both trusted. She was angry that I wanted to have Brett involved."

'Why did you want Brett involved?'

"I had lent Brett money, written letters for him and been like a second dad. So, I thought he would be a good influence on her in any negotiations. She was having none of it, so I had to engage a solicitor. I also gave her my mobile phone."

'Why was that?'

"It just seemed the right thing to do, because all the promotion for the business, including the sign outside, had my mobile number on it. (laugh) That came back to bite me big time a few months later."

'Were you trying to appease her?'

"I guess so, and I still thought we could settle the issue of the property for something less than half, because she had a money-making business, and I had retired. I didn't want a legal fight over it. I just thought mediation was a sensible thing to do. But she was determined to use her solicitor and make my life as miserable as possible.

"When I gave her the phone, I got a new one with a new number and rang most of my friends and music mates to alert them. But my old mate, Milton Saunders, inadvertently opened up a line of complaint that got me into court."

'Do tell.'

"The first I heard of it, I was being given an AVO by a police officer who also asked me to surrender my guns."

'Did you have guns?'

"On the farm, I had a .22 rifle, a 12-gauge pump-action shotgun and a .410 pump action. I also had an ancient .410 single barrel shotgun that had been the 'snake gun' that was always in the house when I was growing up. But I had given the old gun to Matt and traded all the other guns to another farmer as part payment for a tractor.

"At that point we had decided to live on a boat, and I had no need for firearms. Dianne was there when I took the guns and brought back the tractor, so she knew. Apparently, she told the police that she was frightened of me because I had guns.

"At the time, I was playing every Sunday evening at the Kent Hotel, and she almost always sat at a front table and stared at me. I have no idea what she wanted to achieve, except try to intimidate me, but it was uncomfortable, and I avoided her there, so we never spoke.

She also claimed that I had caused my friend Milton to harass her by calling her 'at all hours of the night'."

'Did he call her at all?'

"Yes, he did. Twice. The first time was just after Christmas about eight months after she went. It happened like this: Milton had been given a new phone for Christmas and asked his grandson to transfer the numbers from his old phone to the new, so he did. But Milton had not removed my old number, so that was included.

"Soon after that, he wanted to speak to me about a gig, but inadvertently rang my old number. Dianne was very curt with him, just saying that 'Ford,' that's me, 'doesn't live here anymore' and hung up. Then a few days later, Milt being Milt, still did not remove my number and did it again. That was the sum total of the harassment.

"But she also rang around my friends with stories that included I was having an affair with Katy, the wife of my mate Greg, the prawn man."

'Were you?'

"No. After I met Sally, I never had the urge to stray from any of my relationships, but when I was at sea, one of the things I missed was a library. That is a common complaint made by cruising sailors. But in most ports, there is a shop that swaps books usually for ten or twenty cents per book. There was one in Newcastle near the marina, so I used it, as did Katy.

"When I learned that Katy also got books at the shop, we started swapping our books. Greg was always there, and often delivered them both ways. That was the extent of our relationship. Dianne really went out of her way to poison my friendships and, as the saying goes, 'Lies are halfway around the world before truth gets its shoes on'. Many good and long-term friends dropped me, and that hurt.

"Of course, some, like the Casamento family called her out on it."

'So, what happened in court?'

Milton is there to explain the phone business and I am there with Nan, who is appalled at the whole situation and has brought with her a character reference from Sally that attests to my basic honesty, and how I negotiate fairly. Dianne arrives, crying, escorted by a female police officer, who, I guess is there for her protection.

Milton is taken aside by a court officer and interviewed in another room. He drops back to say that his story has been taken, and he leaves. The matter comes up, and I am instructed to not go within a hundred metres of Dianne and not contact her.

"It's all surreal. She has police protection, is in tears, the picture of fear and distress. The judge doesn't bring up the phone matter, so I guess he got the message about that, but I am instructed to not go within a hundred metres of her, so I say, 'I can't do that' and of course His Honour asks why, and I say, 'I have a regular music engagement where she comes and sits at the front table, not four metres away, and stares at me just about every Sunday. Do I have to leave or does she?'

"He stares at her. She says nothing, and he says: 'That's ridiculous.' He then turns to me and says: 'But you will agree not to approach her for twelve months?'

"I say, 'I have never approached her or tried to contact her since I first tried to initiate conciliation, and I have no intention of ever speaking with her again, Your Honour.'

"He just smiles, the gavel drops, and we leave. On the way out, one of the cops told me that they never did believe any of what she said about me, but I still had the AVO in place."

'So that was the end of that?'

I get a phone call from the Tax Department who ask me to attend Dianne's salon and explain the financial computer records. I had been sending, electronically, monthly returns but apparently, she has not used the computer since she left the boat. I find the program and show the two men from the department what I had entered. They ask about cash, so all I can say is that I was not privy to anything to do with the massage business and only entered the figures she gave me. That's all they want from me, and I leave.

"Not totally. I was called in to show the tax man what I had entered into her computer as financial records. I had the chance to dump her in it when they asked about cash, but I told them I had no idea how much, if any, cash she took because I just entered into the program the information she gave me."

'If you had mentioned cash, you might have been implicated.'

"Yes, I guess so. She was quite secretive about her finances. For all our time together, she basically kept her income, and I paid the outgoings."

'But the AVO and all that would have left questions remaining at some level, I guess.'

"Yes, and I suspected it might have been part of the strategy being played by her lawyer. In any case, I had to resort to getting legal representation. I picked one out of the phone book but wasn't happy with the first one I hired because she didn't seem to understand how much I had invested in money and effort into Dianne's rehabilitation and current success. So, through Jess, Rodney recommended Hura, a Newcastle solicitor, so I went to him. Big mistake."

'Why's that?'

He is middle-aged, grey everything – grey suit, grey hair, grey skin – but he comes highly recommended, so I lay out the situation. He wants evidence of bank transactions and an account of the relationship in terms of money spent on her behalf, so I spend weeks putting together a dossier, which he reads and hits me with a bill for a lot of dollars.

This repeats many times over almost two years until I have spent almost eighty thousand dollars. Finally, we have a court date, and I meet with Hura and his barrister, who convince me that I will, in the end, be ordered to give her half my assets, so I should agree to do that and save court costs, which they say will probably come down in her favour.

I am gobsmacked that in the end we are exactly where we were two years ago, but it has cost me a small fortune in crap legal advice.

"I got a solicitor who, I say, milked me of eighty thousand dollars over two years, to get to the same place we were in the beginning. All that time my assets were frozen, but I had too many assets to qualify for the pension, so at sixty-eight I had to go back to work to live. There was no adjustment for the money I had already paid out, like the twenty thousand to her stepfather, the money she had taken from the joint account, all the hand-outs and payments made on her behalf over the years and half the Tuggerawong house."

'That seems like malpractice to me. Did you try to take it further?'

"Yes, I realised that he had kept me dependent on him until the time came when it had to be resolved. I realised what he had done, and sought the advice of a solicitor in Gosford, who gave me advice free of charge.

"He agreed that I could sue him for malpractice and probably win. But he warned that if I went down that road, I 'would be up against the Law Society, who would support their member,' and did I want to 'spend the next ten years in and out of court?'

"I took his advice and dropped it, but my plans for retirement were no more. Property prices had risen over thirty per cent over those two years.

"I was now living on a yacht, part of my share of the settlement, that would require maintenance and was a diminishing asset. But I guess I was so beaten by then that I didn't want to make any decisions. I then decided to have a cruise or two before I sold it, if I could sell it. I had nowhere else to live."

'At least you were done with her and could get on with your life.'

"Yes, but this was different. Vera got three-quarters of my assets, including a house and business in Sydney. Sally got half the assets, but in both those cases, although they came to me with nothing and left with houses plus other assets, I had time to rebuild my fortunes and did. But by the time Dianne swooped, my working life was over.

"That and the delay to settlement while property prices scooted up, left me with less than I needed to buy a house for myself. If I had sold the yacht then, I might have had enough to buy a unit, but I was too battered to see that as an option."

'At the beginning, did you consider a pre-nup agreement?'

"(laugh) At some level, I knew they existed, but her persona exuded trust, and if I am honest, I never had the self-confidence to feel empowered to protect my assets from any partner."

'So, you basically sold out your financial security for sex?'

"Looks like a pattern, doesn't it?"

'Yes, but for it to cost you, it needed to have a woman willing to exploit it, and it seems to me that all your wives, but mainly Sally and Dianne, did that to a greater or lesser extent.

'In any case, your feelings of not being worthy of sex for its own sake were set up for you in childhood. Your father's fear of the judgement by God and how that was manifested in his treatment of his children, mainly you and Eleanor, with his bizarre attitudes to anything sexual, and maybe more importantly, the idea of original sin and the rod that your father took from the Brethren created in you an extremely confusing set of rules to take into the real world.

'Your exposure to Wanking Wesley and other ideas through Ron, that no child of that age could be expected to process into heathy attitudes toward sex, might have done less damage if your parents had fostered more trust and you could have received guidance. (laughs) I think I am now stating the bleeding obvious. Your journey has brought you to where you are now. By the way, do you have a pre-nup with Jo?'

"(laugh) Yes, but she initiated it. Don't get me wrong, if the boot had been on the other foot and my wives or lovers had more assets, I would not have wanted to get back more than what I had brought to the relationship."

'I doubt you would. But that is not about to be tested, is it?'

"(laugh) No. But there are everyday little adjustments that are made in our sharing of expenses and so on, that demonstrate her generosity. As I said, I am blessed."

'Yes, you are. Now back to the narrative. Did you still own the lease of the marina berth?'

I decide to sell the remaining equity in the lease of the marina berth that I paid for when we first decided to buy a yacht. It cost me fifty thousand for a twenty-year lease, so it was still worth quite a lot. I called George Keegan who was managing the finances and told him to sell my equity in the marina berth.

"Yes. I had no intention of coming back to Newcastle with her there, so I put the marina berth up for sale. The manager rang me to tell me that Dianne had seen the notice for sale and was furious, demanding a share of the proceeds.

"The property settlement had been finalised. She had no claim to anything in my name, so I at least salvaged that. By that time, I was in Eden nursing Mum."

'Tell me about that.'

Robyn makes it clear that that she is not interested in ocean cruising. The trip from the Whitsundays back to Newcastle is without serious incident, and Robyn makes the most of it, but I understand that she is frightened at sea, and I must admit, sometimes, so am I.

The berth is free when we get back, so I tie up there and Robyn goes home, thankfully taking Bear, my lovely old Belgian Shepherd dog with her. We are still friends, but I think we agree that we can't live together, and that is a shame.

Then I get a call from my sister Jen, that Mum has had a severe stroke and is not expected to live. Bill picks me up and we drive to Merimbula and see that she is badly affected. She can't speak, swallow, or move her right-side limbs.

Without teeth, she looks like a corpse, but she opens her eyes and stares at me, then, with her one good hand, she points to my beard. I have let it grow for the eight months we have been sailing, so it is a good match for Ned Kelly's.

I think she doesn't recognise me, so I find a barber and have it shaved off. When I return, I realise she did recognise me and was amused that I had it removed.

After a few days, Mum is taking water intravenously. Then they insert a PEG tube so she can have water and be fed at home and the decision is made for her to go to Jen's house in Eden.

"In October 2006, Mum suffered a severe stroke and was in Merimbula Hospital. I came down with Bill to see what needed to be done. After a couple of weeks, she was to be discharged into Jen's care. I wasn't tied to anyone or anywhere, so I went back with Bill and with my sailing mate Ray, brought the boat down to Eden and tied up with the trawlers, where I stayed until January 2008."

'Did your mum die in Eden?'

"(laugh) No. Jen's daughter Eleanor had gone to New Zealand to look at properties where she planned to raise horses. Jen went to visit, leaving me and George to look after Mum. Then George was summoned to join Jen in New Zealand, and I was left alone with Mum, who we had to release into professional care.

"By this time, Mum was able to swallow and walk with help but was still unable to speak, except for a couple of slurred words. Then she announced that she was emigrating to New Zealand."

'You're kidding!'

"(laugh) No, but before I get to that, I must tell you what happened when we thought she had died."

'Did she have an advanced care directive?'

I am playing maybe the fourth or fifth game of Scrabble, and Mum seems okay. Then she suddenly seems to stiffen, then sweat, then lose consciousness. I run around the table and catch her as she falls sideways, easing her to the floor. I call Jen and we carry her into the bedroom and lay her on the bed. She has instructed us that she is not to be revived, so we don't call an ambulance. We are torn between wanting to revive her and honouring her wishes. This is really hard, and I can see Jen weakening. But I have sat with her when she has bemoaned the fact that she can't be let die, so I suggest we go to town for a coffee, and we do.

I then get us Danish pastries and we eat them, then have another coffee. After an hour and a half, we decide it is safe to go back.

"I don't think there was a document. But Mum has told me that she was sick of being sick and wanted to die. She asked that she not be revived if she has a relapse, and we agreed. But then, when she did pass out, our first instinct was to call the ambulance, so, I took Jen to a café, and we stayed there having coffee and Danish pastries.

"We went back, and, despite all that coffee, Jen put on the kettle for a pot of tea. Jen had a whistling kettle, so it boiled and shrieked. Then, as Jen lifted the kettle off the flame, we heard Mum's little bell ringing, her signal that she wanted a cup of tea!

"Anyway, Jen rang me from Dunedin asking me to put George on the first flight out of Merimbula, and he was gone. After a week, Jen announced that she was buying a house in Dunedin and would not be coming back. I couldn't handle Mum on my own, so I got her into Imlay House in Pambula.

"I had a little motor scooter, so I visited Mum every day to play scrabble and chat through the 'qwerty' board I made for her. After a few days, I could see that she was very unhappy there, and it was easy to see why.

"Mum, though unable to speak, was intellectually untouched and was her normal intelligent self. However, despite an exhaustive report from the carer team who visited her in Eden, and through the TRAC program, the staff spoke to her as if she had advanced dementia.

"She was not incontinent, but they often ignored her bell, so she was forced to wet herself."

'Aged Care'

She sits and she stares
at the door to her world
from which she came,
to this allotted space.

Beautiful mind, cruelly spared.
Taunted though empty days
and long, long, grieving nights,
by mem'ry of lost relevance.

Craving assurance;
a human embrace,
while latex plastic hands
touch only from necessity.

This little time, a miser's gift.
Last chance to ease her passing,
with what will not be given;
The final validation of her existence.

I complained to the manager, whom I knew from a writers' group. She apologised and promised that she would try to help, but they were short-staffed, so it seemed nothing changed. Mum was still not happy, so as I said, she decided to go to New Zealand."

'Why was that, do you think?'

"I think she wanted to be near Jen. If I remember correctly, Jen's daughter, Eleanor came over and took Mum to Dunedin, where she was accepted into Ross Home and she appeared to be as happy as she could be, sending me photos of outings and activities."

'So, she died there?'

I had toured New Zealand with Rod McKuen in 1973. Back then I didn't need a passport, so when I get the message that Mum has pneumonia and is asking for me, I try to book a flight. I am asked for my passport number and don't have one.

I pay for an expedited application and wait. The passport becomes available on the 10th of November, my birthday, so I book a direct flight, but later that day I get the message that Mum has died. If I had been a bit more savvy, I would have contacted my federal member and got him to intervene, but I didn't think of it.

Bill and Ros are on the same flight, so we arrive together and are in time for a memorial service held at Ross Home, and I am impressed by the compassion of the staff, who clearly loved Mum.

"Yes, she died on my birthday, but I couldn't get there in time and missed saying goodbye. "That was painful, but I was grateful that the staff at Ross Home had been so good to Mum and was pleased to meet them at her memorial."

Marjorie

In my childhood,
my difficult childhood,
she was there for me.

In her decline,
her long, cruel decline,
I was there for her.

But her love
was greater than mine.
She died to set me free.

 'She was quite a woman.'
 "Yes, she was."
 'So, after Dianne, you had other relationships?'
 "Yes, the next one that lasted a while was with Helen."
 'Okay, let's start there next time.'

I pick up my sunnies, and as I leave, I smile, visualising Helen at the market, where she is in her element.

Session 18

I am on time, and she is already sitting, coffee in hand with one for me on the table between us. I say hello and sit. She is smiling.

'Tell me about Helen.'

I look to the ceiling and let out a long breath. In Eden, nursing Mum, I am lonely. I pay a subscription to RSVP and contact a woman who lives in Merimbula. She visits me on the yacht, then invites me to her house. We have a lovely Thai dinner in the 'Haunted House', a restaurant, then back to her place where we chat, and I go to bed in a spare room.

Her bedroom door is open, but I don't feel inclined to go in.

Next morning we have breakfast, and I am ready to go, when she says she is worried that the neighbours might get the wrong idea. I think this is strange, considering that she invited me to stay, so I don't follow it up.

Then there is Elizabeth, who is travelling north from Hobart via the Princes Highway and calls in. We find that we share many political and other values and enjoy a couple of days together. On the night before she leaves, she says: 'You're not going to let me leave without a fuck, are you?'

I oblige to the best of my ability, which is not all that able, but she invites me to visit her at home, so I do. Mum has gone by then, so I spend a few very pleasant days in Hobart hanging out with her, where I meet Bob Brown at a meeting of the Greens.

I chat with Bob and express my dismay at the lack of political will on Climate Change. He tells me, 'You always feel better if you become active'. I'm sure he is right, but by then, I have been active for thirty years.

I'm back in Eden when Gus, who was the skipper of my yacht when we took delivery, turns up and asks me if I could crew for him and his girlfriend over to Hobart. I jump at that, so off we go.

We tie up in Triabunna. Elizabeth meets me there and drives me back to her house.

"Before I met Helen, and while Mum was still in Eden, I followed up one more contact through RSVP. She was in Tasmania, so I flew to Hobart to stay for a few days. Only a few weeks later, I helped crew a yacht to Tassie and visited her again. This time, she said she needed to sell, but the roof was leaking and that was a problem. So, I took apart some of the roof, replacing a rafter, some battens and sealed the leak."

'Here you go again!'

"(laugh) Maybe. But I soon made the judgement that her lifestyle and my income were incompatible, so we decided to remain friends but go our separate ways. In the meantime, while I was there, I made a bad decision that cost me dearly."

'Was this about the time of the GFC?'

We visit Queenstown and Zeehan, where real estate seems very cheap and demand for accommodation from miners strong. I can see the GFC coming and cash in all my shares, bar one lot of gold mining stock that has already dropped to one-fifth of the price I paid. It is not a lot of money, so I keep them and look for real estate.

Rent to outlay is very attractive in Zeehan, so I borrow a hundred thousand and buy two two-bedroom furnished units in Zeehan for $260,000. They are both tenanted, so I go home expecting rent to flow. But, a month later, one tenant had not paid a cent.

There is no response to phone calls, and as I don't have an agent, I fly down to find the place abandoned and trashed.

I spend a few weeks patching walls, fixing windows, fitting a new washbasin in the bathroom and then refurnishing it. It also needs a new dividing fence, so I write to the owner of the adjoining property and plan another trip down in a few months.

"Yes. I liquidated most of my shares in time and invested in two units in Zeehan. (laugh) What I didn't foresee was the downturn in mining activity in Tasmania, so found myself with only one tenant, who stayed for only a few more months, then I had no tenants and a mortgage to service.

"I also had a lot of maintenance to do. One fence had fallen over. The next-door neighbour, who I discovered was the previous owner of my units, refused to help, so I rebuilt the fence, then repainted all the interiors and the place was in good shape again. Then I engaged Doug Murchie, the only agent in Zeehan to manage the properties for me and hoped for new tenants.

"But they stayed basically empty, then partially rented, until I sold them ten years later for half the price I paid."

'That's unfortunate. So, did your fortunes change after you met Helen?'

Helen visits me in Eden and stays on the boat with me for a few days. We spend time with Mum and Jen and find we have a lot in common. It is comfortable to be with someone nearer my age who has grown up under similar circumstances, and the sex works.

I remember that first night on the boat when she is concerned that I might know her real age.

"Helen always wanted to be in business. Her early efforts were rewarded and her guest house on Dangar Island was successful. For a time, she was also CEO of Netball Australia and then the Hockeyroos, and I believe that sort of fundraising and promotion job was her forte. She was always aware of her age but carried it well."

'You know, when I first visited you in Eden and you gave me coffee in that mug?'

"The Too-sexy-to-be-70 mug, you mean?"

'Yes, that one. I was shocked that you might've known I was really seventy when I had told you I was sixty-six.'

"(laugh) Your dating app photo was sixty-six. I didn't care then, and I don't care now."

'After her first visit, did you decide to follow her to Sydney?'

I get the yacht ready for the trip. My wharf neighbour has a hookah, a type of air supply for shallow diving that connects an air compressor to a regulator by a long tube, so there is no need for air tanks. I spend a few days under the water, scraping the hull and prop to free it of weed and shell. In the debris floating around me are clouds of tiny crustaceans that inhabited the weed.

I feel a sensation of being watched and turn to see a huge stingray two metres behind me. As I stare, it slowly turns and flies away, to return regularly to observe.

The boat is ready, and I am joined by Brian and Alida Dixon and Ray, *my old faithful sailor mate, and we head north, stopping first at Bermagui, then Batemans Bay where we tie up to the town wharf and plug in for power. I have finished the first draft of CULL, my first novel, but have no printer. Brian buys me a printer at Harvey Norman, then he and Alida leave for home. I have secured a mooring at Brooklyn on the Hawkesbury and can ride the motor scooter to Helen's place at Castle Hill, where I meet her daughter Lisajane and granddaughter Alicia.*

"Not right away. I came up to Sydney by bus and train and spent a few days with her at Castle Hill, where she and her daughter were renting while attempting to get an online business going, I think in jewellery. A few weeks later, we brought the yacht up to moor in the Hawkesbury at Brooklyn, where I stayed for a few months until Helen decided to move back to her house at Mudjimba on the Sunshine Coast and start a business there.

"She did not discuss business matters with me, but I now think the rent at Castle Hill was too much.

"Ray and I sailed *Heavy Metal* to Mooloolaba where I found a berth on the Fishermen's Wharf at $550 per month plus power, which was never charged because my solar plus batteries were enough."

'(laughs) How long did it take for you to find a way to help?'

"Not long. I found that all the light fittings and window winders in her house were seriously corroded, so I replaced them all."

'(laughs) You couldn't help yourself.'

"Right. But then Helen decided that the screen room needed a spa, so she bought one. To fit that into the screen room without disturbing the foundations required one whole wall to be moved a hundred mils and a floor built to carry it.

"Then she decided that the room needed an outside door to facilitate entry from the beach to avoid carrying sand through the front door.

For all of August she was in Sydney, so while she was away, I put in the doors, built a timber walkway with lights and a rope 'handrail'. Then I put up an outdoor shower and a timber seat.

"She and Lisajane had rented space at the Noosa Market and a kitchen with cool rooms. She bought a commercial oven and baked all sorts of pastries and cakes.

"I had bought Elizabeth's old station wagon and brought it up from Tasmania, but she needed a refrigerator van to carry all that food from the kitchen to the market. I found her one in Adelaide, took her grandson, who needed hours up on his 'L' plates, and we brought it back over two days. He drove most of the way while I did crosswords.

"I used the station wagon to carry the marquee and benches. We did that until it was clear to Helen that she needed to sell the Mudjimba house to clear her debts."

'How were you feeling then?'

I haven't been brooding on it, but I'd say I feel depressed, but it could be other issues, like what I'm doing now, or rather, how I see what I'm doing now seems less joyful.

I'm no longer sure I want to be here doing what I'm doing now, helping Helen.

Waiting for Helen to sell up and retire is what I'm doing. Then we have some decisions to make about what we do next, maybe that's it. Maybe it's just the uncertainty, the need to wait for things to happen.

Then she hits me with the basket, and I am no longer feeling like I want to be there 'no matter what'.

"I was hanging in there waiting for the house to sell. It must have been hard for her, having had quite a bit of property, to be looking at bankruptcy. Then she hit me with a basket."

'She hit you? Why was that? Then what happened?'

"She basically threw a tantrum. Breaking things and yelling, crying. I just wanted to go."

'But you didn't.'

"Well, I did. I went as far as the car, then came back and waited for her to calm down."

'What made you come back? Why didn't you keep going and not come back?'

"I felt she needed support right then, so I couldn't go and leave her on her own."

'Why did you feel responsible for her... then... or at all?'

"I don't know. It's always been like that. Always."

'Okay, so she calmed down and then what?'

"She cleaned up some of the mess... there was broken glass under her bed that she missed. (laugh) but it was gone a week later when I looked."

'So, you didn't tell her then? Because it was her responsibility?'

"I wanted to sweep it up myself. In a way, it seemed mean not to, but I drew a line then and decided not to pick up after her any more on principle."

'(laughs) And you stuck to it?'

"(laugh) No, not all the time, but I did wonder what it would be like when she moved onto the boat, where I have to be responsible for everything... I can't leave lids off bottles and not stow stuff properly on the boat."

'No, I guess not. So, were you having second thoughts about the relationship?'

"No, I wouldn't say that. I no longer had warm fuzzies whenever I saw her, and I was not as interested in sex as I was... It changed after that incident.

"Meanwhile, the real estate market had dropped and was dropping, so in the end, she gave the keys to the bank and walked away with her personal stuff and a car. It was very hard for her."

'When she left the house, where did she go?'

"She moved onto the yacht for a while, and we sailed it to Cowan Creek where I spent some time at anchor in Yeomans Creek while I fixed up Helen's launch."

'What was wrong with Helen's launch?'

"A lot of the inside timbers had rotted from being locked up in the damp and sun, so I replaced them. The seats needed recovering and other odds and ends, like there was no bilge pump and the alternator didn't work, so I fixed all that so she could sell it."

'Did she stay with you there?'

"Sometimes. Most of the time she stayed with Tim, her son, at Cottage Point, and that was when David was killed."

'What did you do then?'

"Legally, I couldn't leave the yacht unattended for long, and I had Helen's launch tied alongside, so I just kept on working on it."

'How did you feel?'

Every day I have breakfast and get to work. It is fiddly work, shaping the timbers to fit inside the cabin. A boatbuilder would have dismantled the cabin and started again, but I don't have the place to do that or the time. It helps keeps my mind off David.
Police have the perpetrator in custody, and he has been refused bail. The trial is a long way in the future, so I plod on, filling the time. I am feeling trapped here with no plan and no money.

"Numb. In my imagination, I re-created many times when I could have done more for David and imagined many scenarios where he recovered his addiction and was happy. I was never convinced that I could not have done more than I did.

"Maybe I should not have been there on my own, but the work on Helen's boat kept me occupied and challenged for a few weeks, and it was illegal to leave anchored vessels unattended. Then Helen was offered a berth in a marina where she had kept her launch for years. They offered her a week free of charge, so we took the yacht there while we considered what to do.

"In Mooloolaba, I had been running a very tight budget, with the mortgage in Tasmania and paying for the berth leaving me about $30 per week to live on. Some of the time I ate at Helen's, but I managed to stretch what was left.

"I was aware of Helen's buying habits, so I thought I needed to talk to her about budgeting."

'Did she have problems with money management?'

"Helen was fine while there was plenty of money, but it was my attempt to try to impose a budget that brought to a head what was always going to be a problem. She came back with groceries and showed me the receipt, and silly me pointed out where she had spent unnecessarily. I picked a bad time to do that because she was at the stove cooking rice.

"She picked up the pot and threw it. I don't think she actually threw it at me, or I would have been seriously injured, but it hit the base of the table and sprayed rice all over the floor, leaving a sizable dent in the saucepan. Then she walked out."

'Was that the end of it?'

"(laugh) Well, sort of. She came back when I wasn't there and collected her stuff and took away the front cabin mattress that we had made to fit the space."

'Why would she do that?'

"When Dianne left, she took a circular blanket that Mum had

crocheted for me, which I thought was mean, and I thought the same about the mattress. It was pretty useless off the boat, and it was a bit of a deal to make one.

"She also wanted her two lounge chairs back."

'Where were they?'

"Helen really wanted her two lounge chairs on the boat, but the only way to get them in was to remove a window, which was glued and bolted in place, so I did that and then took the window out again to give them back."

'But you didn't get the mattress?'

"(laugh) No. I didn't ask for it. I made a new one after I got to Batemans Bay."

'So, that was the end of your relationship with Helen?'

"No, there was still a lot of affection, and we have kept in touch. She has just read my latest novel and sent back suggestions, and I have agreed to read hers and do the same for her.

'Mmm... Okay. So, what did you do with the boat? Could you stay at the marina?'

"No. It was far too expensive for me, so I found a mooring in Booker Bay near Gosford for $800 a month and I could just afford that, so I sailed there solo and stayed for a few months while I started to deal with Wally's estate."

'Who's Wally?'

"Wally deserves a book of his own. He was my eldest cousin, Mum's sister Ella's only child, and quite a character. His estate was a nightmare, with a contested will, but in the end, all his assets went to the Bible Society who had given him a 'Passport to Heaven' for his ongoing financial support and in the end, his fortune."

'Where did you go from Booker Bay?'

I am ill with flu, and my sister Dianne comes to look after me. It is inconvenient on the mooring, with all excursions on land starting with a dinghy ride, but while she is here, she signs me up to a dating app. I get a couple of hits and meet a nice woman who comes out to the boat for lunch. She is pleasant and attractive, but I can tell the boat puts her off, and I never hear from her again, then I have one in Campbelltown, so I meet her for coffee on the way to see Jess at Mt Kembla, where she wants me to build her a roof over her deck.

There is no spark there, so we have coffee and a nice chat, then I am on my way.

"I was there for a few months and met a couple of women on a dating app with no interest in a follow-up, and that was when I made contact with Jo, who we have already talked about. What I haven't told you about was our trip south."

'Was Jo a sailor?'

"(laugh) No. Jo had never sailed, and I was a bit surprised when she decided to come on the voyage to Batemans. Before we left, Matt had agreed to come as crew, and he was experienced. But then the day before we were due to leave, Matt pulled out and it was just us or cancel. My lease was due for renewal next day, so we went without him."

'I'm trying to imagine two people aged seventy plus sailing a big yacht.'

"I was seventy-seven, but just before we left Mooloolaba, I had spent the best part of a day at the top of the mast replacing the masthead lights. I was pretty fit then.

"Anyway, I gave Jo a crash course in use of the radio and how to steer the boat by hand, and we were off.

"The trip down was idyllic. By then I knew the anchorages and we had a pleasant trip over four days until the very last bit when we were hit by a sudden storm, with high wind and seas whipping up, but Jo took the helm and did exactly what she had been shown while I took the sails down, so we were never in danger."

'(laughs) I wonder what she would say about that?'

"(laugh) Yes, she might have a different take on it, but knowing Jo, I am sure she would have said something then if she had felt the need. We sheltered behind Snapper Island then came into the bay on the high tide, tied up to the town wharf and in a way, I was home."

'Did you keep the boat?'

"When I went to live with Jo, we didn't have a romantic relationship. I was there as her carer, and I was happy with that. I had wounds to lick, and she needed someone to monitor her, particularly at night in case she had a hypo and went into a coma.

"Over the years, I have had to intervene several times, but now she has technology to do that, so I don't need to be so vigilant.

"There were a few times over that first year, I had my doubts, so I kept the boat in case I needed to leave. It all settled down, so I sold the boat and paid off the mortgage in Tasmania.

"Then I sold the units, so I was out of debt with enough in the bank to buy a car. I have been here eleven years now, and we are used to each other and there is a lot of trust and affection there too, so I am very happy to be with her."

'Do you still feel as if God is watching?'

"(laugh) No. But I have also become comfortable with those who do, which is a surprise to me."

'Not to me. To be really free of it, this is where you needed to be, and you are there now. How long did it take?'

"Over eighty years, and I sometimes wonder, uselessly of course, what my life might have been without the Brethren upbringing and the corrosion of confidence in my capabilities, my judgement and my body image. All the gaslighting that is part of the modus operandi of the Brethren, delivered by my father and his family, kept me almost schizophrenic in the sense that I lived at two levels.

"Then I think of all the wonderful and sometimes unusual people, experiences and situations that made, well, me and I'm just thankful I survived it all and have all these amazing memories."

'Have you ever thought of the parallels between your father's seeming approval of you only when you were helping him or doing something for him – like the ninety barrowloads and bringing in money with the tractor – and your need to help your women?'

"Now that is a good question. You know it wasn't only 'my women' as you call them. I think it probably applied to most of my relationships to some degree. It might even have led me into teaching when there were probably more suitable callings there like engineering."

'So, you see the connection.'

"Yes. Despite the beltings and the gaslighting and all the Brethren damage I was still left with a space where I could feel successful but that was mainly when I was helping and fixing. Things. Over all those years and all those relationships, I never realised that I was buying approval, trying to create obligation so they would like and appreciate me. It's obvious now."

'In the light of that realisation, how do you feel about Vera and, say, Dianne now?'

"I am saddened that I was not able to help Vera. She was more of a victim than I was but back then, I was not able to get past my sex needs. If I had understood her demons, and had more wisdom, perhaps her life might have been better.

"Dianne? Helen heard the story of Dianne and said to me that the longer I continued to refresh those memories, the longer they would cause me grief. I took her advice and shut up about it until I talked to you. She was right, so I am now in a really good place."

'Yes, I think you are. I must say, your story is a bit out there, but you lived long enough to come to terms with all life threw at you, so well done!'

She stands to extend her hand to be shaken, and I take it. Then she moves closer, and I hug her warmly before I pick up my sunnies and leave for the last time.

Also by the Author

Cull

A white knuckle ride of a political thriller is too real for comfort. Harry Fromm, career diplomat, takes us into the murky world of realpolitik, where a deal is done to 'manage population reduction' by nuking three billion people. A thousand warheads are minutes from target and Harry, the only person who can stop them, is in jail.

Originally conceived as a play set in The White House, this political thriller sees Harry Fromm face a dreadful dilemma: solve two of the biggest problems facing humanity, by betraying humanity.

Harry Fromm's life's work as an ambassador has been dedicated to finding peaceful solutions to political conflict. Finding himself party to an international conspiracy to solve the twin problems of overpopulation and climate change by destroying half the world's population, he is pursued by the CIA across the US and into Canada.

When Harry loses the confidence of the conspirators, they decide he must be killed. His wife Felicity and his daughter Sam are also threatened, but are whisked into hiding by his Russian friend Yuri.

When Harry and Yuri are arrested by Canadian Police, the violent deaths, of more than three billion people seems inevitable.

ISBN: 978-0987607706

Australian Gulag: A Love Story

Tom McKinnon, is SAS Specialist Sniper, a veteran of Afghanistan. But extreme violence and collateral damage have worn him down, so that by the time he returns to his native Broome, he cannot settle and takes his Post-traumatic Stress Disorder to a shack on a secluded Kimberley beach. There, he spends his days diving for oysters.

With his dog as his only companion and minimal contact with the outside world, he finds peace of sorts. But following a storm, his dog discovers a young woman on his beach, more dead than alive, forcing him to be up close and personal with another human being.

The Wet Season keeps him marooned as he nurses her back to health and for three months she challenges his prejudices, insisting on helping with his diving work. He is forced to recognise her competence as she becomes his uninvited partner.

Then, as the months tick past, she comes to love this aloof but gentle man and he grudgingly admits and then admires her attributes. Eventually, she comes to his bed, instinctively understanding his hurt and his need.

Still he refuses to admit his own growing feelings and it is not until she has gone (having finally handed her over to the authorities) that he realises he loves her and will do all he can to get her back. By then, however, she has disappeared into the labyrinth of detention centres: first Villawood then Nauru and Manus Island.

As a woman alone, she is fair game to some, and a threat to others. Through the occasional act of kindness, she is able to leave messages and a trail for Tom that brings him close enough for her to know he cares. But doors that might have opened remain closed, even as his actions take him up to then beyond the limit of the law.

Australian Gulag is a story of our times. It takes us where people should never have to go and shows us that when we get behind the barbed wire, there is still love and compassion, even in the unlikeliest hearts and places.

ISBN: 978-1925403350

Are We Planet B?

Julia Porteous leads a team of young Australian scientists taking samples from Antarctic ice, investigating ancient climate change.

In an ice core taken from the five-million-year level, they find modern human remains under a polycarbonate dome.

Her boss, Stan Nightingale, is reluctant to give the findings credibility, but nevertheless, funds the building of a lift to access the dome and the human remains.

Inside he dome, Julia becomes infected by a bacteria that appears to share DNA with one brought back by a NASA Mars probe.

Jim Somerville, Stan's American colleague's attempt to compare the bacteria samples draws the attention of Hiram Caxton, rogue CIA Director, who has Sommerville arrested and tortured.

Caxton learns enough to have the dig sabotaged to protect the re-election prospects of his fundamental Christian president, who needs the votes of those who believe in Adam and Eve and a ten-thousand-year-old universe.

Agents sent by Caxton disable the lift, trapping the Australian team under the ice, where they will die unless rescued quickly. But it is winter in Antarctica where nothing moves except the wind.

ISBN: 978-1-7638888-1-4

Rhyme and Reason

Rhyme and Reason is a collection of short stories, limericks and poems. Many are funny, some are tragic and some are fiction, Some comment on politics and current events, but most are snippets of lives of real people that are either amusing or interesting.

In the tiny hamlets of Wollombi and Dooralong, in rural New South Wales, where the author farmed for a time, lived old people, whose stories are from an era when story-telling was the entertainment, now almost totally replaced by commercial TV, streaming, and mega shows in huge auditoria.

These characters had the space and freedom to be eccentric and unique, in an era that we will not see again, more's the pity. The author was privileged to be there, to listen, then later, reproduce some of their stories for posterity – an honour indeed.

ISBN: 978-1-7638888-2-1

www.ingramcontent.com/pod-product-compliance
Lightning Source LLC
Chambersburg PA
CBHW060349080526
44583CB00012B/230